No Limits to Their Sway

No Limits to Their Sway

Cartagena's Privateers
and the Masterless Caribbean
in the Age *of* Revolutions

Edgardo Pérez Morales

VANDERBILT UNIVERSITY PRESS | NASHVILLE

© 2018 by Vanderbilt University Press
Nashville, Tennessee 37235
All rights reserved
First printing 2018

This book is printed on acid-free paper.

Library of Congress Cataloging-in-Publication Data

LC control number 2017006647
LC classification number F2161 .P464 2018
Dewey classification number 972.9/04
LC record available at lccn.loc.gov/2017006647

ISBN 978-0-8265-2191-0 (hardcover)
ISBN 978-0-8265-2192-7 (paperback)
ISBN 978-0-8265-2193-4 (ebook)

For Julius S. Scott,
Pioneer Historian of the Masterless Caribbean

O'er the glad waters of the dark blue sea,
Our thoughts as boundless, and our souls as free,
Far as the breeze can bear, the billows foam,
Survey our empire, and behold our home!
These are our realms, no limits to their sway—
Our flag the scepter all who meet obey.
—Lord Byron, *The Corsair*

Contents

	Key Figures	xi
	Introduction	1
1	Slavery, Seamanship, Freedom	15
2	Heralds of Liberty and Disobedience	28
3	Cartagena de Indias and the Age of Revolutions	40
4	The American Connection	56
5	Detachment from the Land and Irreverence at Sea	75
6	Under the Walls of Havana	93
7	Haiti: The Beacon Republic	109
8	"Horrors of Carthagena"	119
9	Robbery, Mutiny, Fire	133
	Epilogue: From Amelia Island to the Republic of Colombia	145
	Acknowledgments	159
	Abbreviations	163
	Primary Sources: Cartagena-Flagged Privateers, 1812–1816	165
	Notes	171
	Index	229

Key Figures

Juan de Dios Amador: Cartagena merchant; Spanish American independence partisan; supporter of federalism; member of Cartagena's revolutionary government; later exiled to Jamaica.

Louis-Michel Aury: French sailor and privateer; sympathizer of the French Revolution; Spanish American independence partisan; commodore of the State of Cartagena; captain of the *Bellona*; later scorned by Simón Bolívar.

Simón Bolívar: Caracas patrician; Spanish American independence partisan; exiled to Cartagena, Jamaica, and Haiti; supporter of centralism; later supreme leader of Colombia's liberation army.

Manuel Palacio Fajardo: Caracas lawyer; envoy of Cartagena's revolutionary government to the United States, with instructions to recruit privateers.

Pedro Gual: Caracas lawyer; envoy of Venezuela's revolutionary government to the United States; recruited Louis-Michel Aury on behalf of Cartagena; later member of the revolutionary government of Amelia Island and Colombia's secretary of foreign affairs.

Ignacio the Younger: Haitian sailor; likely born a slave in Port-au-Prince; man of color; lived through the Haitian Revolution; *Bellona* crewman; accused of piracy by Spanish authorities; sentenced to unpaid labor in Havana.

Pablo Morillo y Morillo: Spanish general; veteran of the Napoleonic Wars; architect of the destruction of Cartagena's revolutionary government and the Spanish reoccupation of Tierra Firme.

Alexandre Pétion: President of the Republic of Haiti; man of color;

antislavery leader; strong supporter of anti-Spanish privateers and partisans.

José Ignacio de Pombo: Cartagena patrician; Spanish American independence opponent; strongly prejudiced against people of African descent; hesitant about preserving slavery in Spanish America.

Pedro Romero: Cartagena blacksmith; man of color; leader of Cartagena's artisans; Spanish American independence partisan; member of Cartagena's revolutionary government; later exiled to Haiti.

José María García de Toledo: Cartagena patrician; Spanish American independence opponent; leader of Cartagena's conservative elite; reluctant member of Cartagena's revolutionary government; later executed by Morillo's forces.

The schooner *Bellona*: Cartagena-flagged privateer; probably built in Cuba; outfitted and commanded by Louis-Michel Aury; manned by "all types of sailors, such as Spaniards, Frenchmen, Englishmen, Americans, and [Haitians] . . . most of them of color."[1]

Introduction

ON SEPTEMBER 6, 1808, French mariner Louis-Michel Aury wrote home with delicate news. He had proudly left Paris five years before as a sailor in the French navy, bound for the Caribbean. Now twenty years old, Aury told his loved ones he had switched to working as a privateer. Although his change of job implied no immediate change of allegiance—he was still sailing under French colors—working as privateer meant he could accept job offers from other countries too. Over the following years, Aury would indeed take commissions from other polities, depending on the shifting political fortunes of old monarchies and emerging states. Anticipating a poor reaction to the news because of the negative reputation of privateers, Aury attempted to reassure his relatives that Caribbean privateers waged war in a "loyal" fashion, just like regular sailors aboard navy ships. Aury's honor and standing, and by extension his family's, would not be compromised, he said. In short, he was writing home to say he had not become a pirate.[1]

Aury is an ideal figure to journey with through the worlds of privateering during the Age of Revolutions, across the Caribbean and the Gulf of Mexico and along the US East Coast. As we shall see, however, many privateers hailed from backgrounds quite different from Aury's, and their likely motives for taking to the sea were wide-ranging. Aury's life and the itineraries of his associates and adversaries, as evidenced by written records in Spanish, English, and French, mirror the rise and fall of revolutionary privateering, especially from the vantage point of Cartagena de Indias (in modern-day Colombia). A crucial yet little-known locus of early anti-Spanish sentiment and revolution in northern South America, Cartagena propelled

Aury to fame, making him one of the earliest privateers to join the struggle for Spanish American independence.

The line separating privateers from pirates was a decidedly blurry one, even though Aury suggested in his 1808 letter that it was not. Some background on privateering is thus necessary. The term *privateer* designated an armed vessel owned, outfitted, and operated by private individuals with formal authorization (in the form of a letter of marque) from a monarch or a sovereign government to attack and capture enemy merchant ships during war. But the victims often accused privateers of outright piracy, refusing to acknowledge the legitimacy of privateering authorizations and casting doubt on the legality of privateers' actions. A *privateer*—the word also referred to the captain or any member of the crew—was at sea what a guerrilla fighter was on land. Often portrayed as maritime mercenaries with no real loyalty and very little discipline, privateers were crucial to winning wars but did not have the status of regular navy personnel.[2]

Unlike regular members of the French, Spanish, or British navies, privateering sailors could hope to take a share of the booty following successful attacks on merchant ships. Privateersmen called the ships they took *prizes* and their earnings *prize money*. As long as prizes were deemed lawful spoils of war by a maritime court of the commissioning country, they could yield very handsome profits. The lion's share of the prize money, however, was divided up between the government, outfitters (investors), and officers. With warfare and privateering flourishing at the turn of the century, the ambitious Aury must have thought he had chosen just the right moment to go into this lucrative business. He aspired to become an outfitter himself, to grow rich, and to build a name as a republican revolutionary. Aury came closest to achieving his goals operating out of revolutionary Cartagena.[3]

During the Age of Revolutions—roughly from 1776 to 1830—the intertwining American, French, Haitian, and Spanish American revolutions swept across Europe and the Americas. From the very beginning, privateering, which had long existed, was a crucial

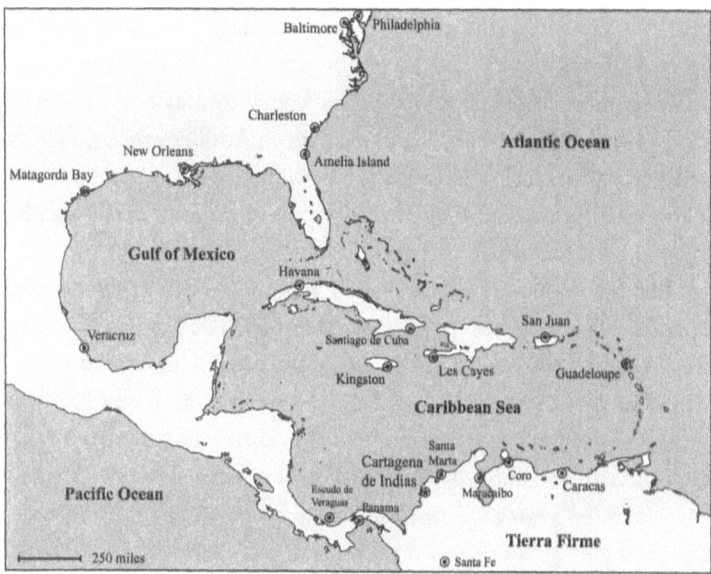

Figure 1. Cartagena de Indias and Tierra Firme in the Americas. By Eric Schewe.

tactic of war in these conflicts and employed by polities on both sides of the Atlantic. Whether people were loyalists or revolutionaries, and European, African, or American, they engaged in privateering for a variety of reasons, ranging from chances to undermine one's enemies to opportunities for profit and glory. Aury, like many other privateers we will encounter, had to calibrate his personal goals and his own changing political ideologies against the dynamics of shifting international conflicts.[4]

Privateering peaked during the international wars following the French Revolution. In 1793, revolutionary France declared war on Great Britain and the Netherlands. Other nations joined the conflict, and the fighting soon spread to the waters of the Caribbean, where European powers tried their best to defend their colonies and attack those of their enemies. Although the British navy had inflicted serious losses on regular French forces by the summer of

1794, the French continued the fight by turning to irregular warfare. From their island of Guadeloupe, they sent dozens of privateers to cruise against British shipping. They began to attack US ships in 1796. When Aury first arrived in the French Antilles in 1803, French privateering in Caribbean waters had already become legendary—a maritime business involving people from very different backgrounds, often at odds with each other.[5]

Aboard French privateers sailed not only French natives like Aury, but also scores of Africans and people of African descent from the French Caribbean. Hundreds of thousands of slaves had populated French colonies such as Saint-Domingue and Guadeloupe. They had risen against their masters and European colonists beginning in 1791. In mid-1793, they had achieved the abolition of slavery—for a few years in Guadeloupe, and forever in Saint-Domingue. But the fighting continued until in 1804 Saint-Domingue declared its independence from France, becoming the new nation of Haiti. Collectively known today as the Haitian Revolution, these events were bound up with the ongoing conflict among European powers. Haiti's liberators actively participated on the maritime front of the conflict. Many former slaves were experienced seafarers long before the tumultuous 1790s, and engaged in regular naval warfare and privateering alike. Some even became officers.[6]

Aury, who would never rejoin the French navy, thus found himself working alongside a variety of people. While many hoped to escape from the harsh legacies of slavery, others aspired to achieve fortune, political power, or revolutionary change. By 1810, Aury had made enough money to purchase his own vessel. He traveled to New Orleans, hoping to become an outfitter by investing in and leading a privateering operation on behalf of France. He had the sailing experience and probably some ideas on how best to recruit Afro-Caribbean sailors. Nevertheless, the enterprise proved difficult.[7]

Privateering under French colors out of US ports remained too complex an operation for a modest seafarer striking out on his own. As the United States maintained a policy of neutrality in the international conflict, ships outfitted as privateers in US ports were liable to confiscation. A federal marshal seized Aury's ship and most of his money. Aury tried to outfit again in Savannah and Charleston to no avail in 1811. Further complicating things, enlisting sailors in American ports could get outfitters in trouble not only with the government but also with people unsympathetic to the French cause. In Savannah, Aury lost two ships when a group of rioting federalists, upset at the presence of French seamen in port, set both craft on fire. Disappointed by his fate in the United States, he needed a new theater of operations—perhaps a target different from British merchant ships and a sponsor other than the French government.[8]

Not far from the United States—just a couple of weeks south by sea—an unexpected opportunity for privateering would arise, on the shores and in the hinterlands of northern South America, then known as the Spanish Main or Tierra Firme. Divided into the viceroyalty of the New Kingdom of Granada (which included modern-day Colombia, Panama, and Ecuador), with its capital city of Santa Fe (modern-day Bogotá), and the captaincy general of Venezuela, with its capital city of Caracas, Tierra Firme had been undergoing revolutionary troubles of its own since 1809, following Napoleon Bonaparte's 1808 invasion of Spain. In November 1811, as Aury defended himself from angry rioters in Savannah, patricians in the city of Cartagena defended themselves from an urban crowd—most of its members free people of color—demanding radical political change. The capital of a province roughly three times the size of Massachusetts, and the most important port town in Tierra Firme, Cartagena declared its independence from Spain on November 11, 1811.

INDEPENDENT CARTAGENA WAS short-lived, surviving only from 1811 to the end of 1815. Revolution, however, transformed Cartagenan society in dramatic ways. Revolutionary Cartagena, in turn, played a leading role among neighboring Tierra Firme provinces. Many of those provinces joined Cartagena in a federal polity named the

United Provinces of New Granada, successfully rejecting Spanish authority from 1812 to 1815. With its growing maritime connections, increasingly radical anti-Spanish leaders, and vibrant cosmopolitan dynamics, Cartagena was at the center of early struggles for South American independence.[9]

Historians have studied the importance of independent Cartagena within regional politics, the tensions between the city and its rural hinterland, the participation of free people of color in politics, and the self-assertion and political complexity of local leadership.[10] However, there remains a significant dimension of independent Cartagena that we know little about: its development into a privateering republic, a polity that welcomed foreign outfitters, officers, and sailors by the hundreds, authorizing them to attack Spanish shipping on its behalf for a share of the prize money. Between 1812 and 1815, foreign seamen cruised the Caribbean under the flag of the newly formed State of Cartagena de Indias.[11] Mexican, Argentine, and Uruguayan revolutionaries would follow Cartagena's example, making privateering a trademark of other movements for independence from Spain.[12]

The majority of sailors who privateered for Cartagena were men of African ancestry. Most of them hailed from newly independent Haiti, but some had been born when that country was still the French colony of Saint-Domingue. Some were former slaves themselves, and almost all of them had slave forefathers. These seafarers worked alongside veterans of the French revolutionary wars, Spanish American revolutionaries, and other seagoing individuals from Atlantic port towns like Baltimore, Philadelphia, New Orleans, Kingston, Cádiz, and Bordeaux.[13] Commanded by outfitters and captains mainly of French, French Caribbean, and US origin, Cartagena's privateers captured and destroyed Spanish property, at times engaging in combat with the Spanish navy.

Aury was among the many seafarers who participated in these events. With his experience in the trade, Aury was a perfect candidate for privateering under Cartagena colors, and in the spring of

1813, Pedro Gual recruited him for the new government. Aury seized the opportunity and, with multinational crews, he was soon cruising aboard Cartagena-flagged privateers, most notably on the remarkable *Bellona*. The *Bellona* and her crew went on to become Cartagena's most famous privateers.[14]

The *Bellona* (*Belona* and *Velona* in Spanish sources), an armed schooner aptly named after the ancient Roman goddess of war, was at once an inanimate object and a living entity. The name *Bellona* refers to the planks, masts, and sails that together formed the ship, and at the same time to the crewmen who made her move by harnessing the power of the wind with canvas, wood, and rope. The ship and the men were equally important, as neither could exist without the other.[15] First outfitted as a Cartagenan privateer in April 1814, the *Bellona* may have been built in Cuba and first operated in the French Caribbean in late 1805.[16] Aury was both the captain of the ship and an investor in the business. The majority of sailors on board were "of color," most of them from Haiti.[17] But aboard were also Europeans, Cartagenans, and men of "other nations."[18]

The *Bellona* was an emblem of the Atlantic world in the Age of Revolutions—a floating work site and an instrument of war that was multinational and multiethnic in character. Consider the schooner's itineraries across the Caribbean and the experiences of the top officer and some of the sailors on board. By 1814, Aury, born in Paris to a middle-class family around 1788, had already seen much of the Antilles, as well as a good portion of the US seaboard and the Gulf of Mexico.[19] Hilario and Ignacio, two Haitian sailors who worked on the *Bellona*, spoke French or Kreyòl and knew some Spanish. Both were born in what was then the French slave colony of Saint-Domingue, but at two different moments in its history.

Born around 1768, in Port-au-Prince, Ignacio came to the world at the height of slavery and French power in the colony. According to Spanish documents, Ignacio had no last name but referred to himself as "Ignacio *fils*," best rendered in English as "Ignacio the Younger." The lack of a formal surname strongly suggests that Ignacio was a former slave. Hilario was about twenty years old and had been born in Les Cayes, in the south of the colony. Hilario, who reported no last name, was also probably a former slave or the child of once-enslaved parents. He had been born during the Haitian Revolution (1791–1804).[20]

Before arriving in Cartagena in 1814, Ignacio, who was a married man and still lived in Port-au-Prince when not at sea, followed a path of transimperial, cross-cultural mobility that many former slaves from Saint-Domingue experienced during and after the Haitian Revolution. Out of Haiti (as well as other French islands like Guadeloupe and Martinique) came thousands of former slaves who became sailors, taking to the sea on the payroll of European powers or their agents. At Port-au-Prince, Ignacio first boarded a Dutch ship that took him to Jamaica, where he caught a British ship bound for Cartagena. He would not remain for long in Cartagena, however, as he soon departed again on the *Bellona*, under Captain Aury.[21]

The *Bellona* also illustrates the success of Cartagena's privateering policy. After her first cruise of 1814, the *Bellona* touched again at Cartagena in August. Her crewmen reported that they had captured seven ships, sunk twenty-three, and battled with two Spanish warships near Havana. Even if they were exaggerating, the cruise had been undeniably profitable. Among the ships sunk was the *Cupido*, which had sailed from Jamaica, bound for Havana with twenty thousand silver *pesos* belonging to the king of Spain. The specie was now to be distributed among the outfitters and the State of Cartagena. Aury's fortunes had changed. The sailors had probably been paid their wages in advance and may have obtained a share of the prize money too.[22]

ALONG WITH AURY, Ignacio and the *Bellona* are recurring figures throughout this book's narrative and help us better visualize this story. Chapters 1 and 2, beginning on the Caribbean islands long before Cartagena's independence, examine the intricate and often unexpected intersections between slavery, seamanship, freedom, and revolution. Most of the sailors manning privateer ships outfitted in revolutionary Cartagena were rooted in what historian Julius S. Scott evocatively called the "masterless Caribbean," an underground world of maroons (runaway slaves), deserters, and free people of color trying to elude masters and officials by keeping on the move. Some found sanctuary and a way of life as seamen on coastal boats and sailing ships, though they often had to jump ship again to escape physical punishment.[23] As slavery intensified and state control hardened across the 1700s, even a rough life at sea became an attractive alternative to life under the planter's whip or the bureaucrat's pen. Constantly moving from port to port, sailors could more easily flee from abusive bosses and find new jobs. Unlike plantation slaves, sailors worked under temporary contracts of three to five months at a time.[24]

Always catching wind of the latest developments, seagoing people and the working men and women of the waterfronts sustained informal but remarkably efficient networks of communication. Many were multilingual, some could read, and almost all carried news and rumor along their journeys, disseminating information that ranged from everyday matters to news of the Haitian Revolution and other epochal events. Bureaucrats and military chiefs tried in vain to stop their conversations. Accusations against people of color for spreading the spirit of revolution and slave emancipation, especially against those engaged in maritime work and with presumable ties to Haiti, became commonplace throughout the region, including in Cartagena.[25]

Chapters 3 and 4 delve into the Revolution of Cartagena, paying attention to the social and political changes brought about by independence and the establishment of the State of Cartagena. While Spanish authorities had kept at bay or hesitantly welcomed people from the French islands and other foreigners, revolutionary Cartagena opened its doors to anyone willing to recognize the legitimacy of the new State. Afro-Caribbean sailors, anti-Spanish agitators from Europe, Venezuela, and the inland provinces of Tierra Firme, merchants and adventurers from Jamaica and the United States, and exiles from the Antilles flocked to independent Cartagena, where they obtained shelter and even citizenship. Newly arrived Anglo-American and French privateers became instrumental to the State's privateering policy.

While seamen found Cartagena's open-door policy quite useful, they already granted only relative significance to borders and jurisdictions. For people used to a mobile way of life, the Bay of Cartagena was but another stop on their itineraries. Moving across colonies, nations, and empires as a matter of course, sailors saw the State of Cartagena as yet another polity for whom they could ply a trade that kept them only fleetingly—yet effectively—in touch with port towns in the Antilles, around the Gulf of Mexico, and on the shores of the United States and Europe. Indeed, Chapter 5 pauses to explore in some detail why and how sailors exercised various degrees of detachment from the land, feeling at odds with landbound people, abiding by their own rules, and clashing with authority figures. This chapter highlights privateers' irreverent attitudes and complicated forms of political identification, even as they brought the flag and the name of Cartagena out to sea—effectively helping the new State with the building of its sovereignty.[26]

Spanish Cuba and the Republic of Haiti played two very different roles in Cartagena's short life, as described in Chapters 6 and 7. Cuba took on an antagonistic role, whereas Haiti provided crucial aid to the State, with President Alexandre Pétion offering shelter to anti-colonial agitators and allowing Cartagenan privateering from Haitian port towns, most prominently from Les Cayes. This contrast is important for understanding the development of Cartagena's privateering policy, as well as the ways in which it reflected both Cartagena's internal politics and challenges and its external confrontation with Spain.

Later on, the authorities of the more stable, decidedly militaristic and centralist Republic of Colombia—the polity that emerged in Tierra Firme in 1819—disavowed the participation of seafarers of color in the early stages of the revolution, rejecting further collaboration with Haiti in hopes of recognition by more powerful countries. This tactic, underpinned by continuing discrimination against Afro-Caribbean people, explains in part why the story of independent Cartagena and its privateering forces has remained largely untold.[27] Chapters 8 and 9 and the Epilogue analyze the processes leading to this rejection, turning to the crushing effects of Spain's reoccupation of Tierra Firme, the internal divisions among revolutionary leaders, and the growing conflicts of interest between traditionally sea-oriented forces and people looking to build lasting bonds with the newly liberated continent.

Many privateers and revolutionary leaders felt pulled in two directions. Aury, who had by this point come to love Tierra Firme and identified with its early independent and republican governments (Cartagena and the United Provinces of New Granada), second-guessed his commitment to privateering. Although he continued to rely on privateering when he took his struggle against Spain to the Gulf of Mexico and the Florida Peninsula, in 1820 he tried to join Simón Bolívar's triumphant army of liberation in Colombia. But the "liberators" planned to rid themselves not just of Aury but of all the privateers and their connections to Haiti and the French Caribbean. Colombian leaders perceived privateers as liabilities, choosing to ignore their impressive ubiquity in the early revolutionary process and singling out sailors of color as particularly undesirable in the new republic.

CARTAGENA'S VIBRANT LINKS with foreign privateers furnish a compelling case for furthering our understanding of the revolutionary Atlantic world.[28] The history of the State of Cartagena, especially when looked at through the prism of its privateering agents and its cosmopolitan political leaders and policies, illuminates the "connected," "entangled," and therefore "interdependent" dynamics of processes unfolding in the Spanish-, French-, and English-speaking worlds. Those processes were not separable, nor are they simply comparable. They were crucial expressions of contact and tension, and followed both planned and unplanned trajectories.[29] The events in revolutionary Cartagena were inextricably bound up with other Atlantic dramas of the time, most importantly the American Revolution, the French Revolution, the Haitian Revolution, the Spanish Peninsular War, and the War of 1812.[30] Political revolution in Cartagena and Cartagena-sponsored privateering throw into sharp relief these interdependencies.

In spite of this electric atmosphere, evidence on Cartagenan privateering and the lives of common sailors like Ignacio the Younger is scant. Although the scribes of the State of Cartagena diligently produced and kept piles of maritime records, most have not survived (just one original letter of marque seems to have remained extant, for example). While some correspondence and logbooks written by privateersmen are available, an account of Cartagena's privateering policy can be achieved only by examining documents written by bureaucrats, journalists, and private individuals in or near places visited or affected by Cartagena's privateers.

As scholar Marcus Rediker has suggested, the common sailor challenges historians to "adopt his almost nomadic mobility and to follow him from port to port around the globe. His international existence beckons us to transcend the often artificial barriers of regional-national history."[31] What follows is thus based on sources kept in archives and libraries in Colombia, Cuba, France, Great Britain, Jamaica, Spain, and the United States. The evidence is varied and complex, and it includes eyewitness accounts, press reports, official gazettes, lists of sailors, memoirs, official and private correspondence, legislation, commercial documents, and even depositions from sailors themselves in civil and criminal proceedings. Although most of it was written by other agents—usually people unsympathetic to privateers—the available documents make it possible to track down individual ships like the *Bellona* and to piece together her crewmen's itineraries. They also yield information with which to paint a broader picture of the magnitude, impact, and geography of

Cartagena's privateering, while revealing the social origins of outfitters, officers, and common sailors. Moreover, careful reading of the evidence shows, from time to time, something of the sailors' sense of politics, forms of identification, and work culture.

A general understanding of anti-Spanish privateering during this period has begun to emerge from recent studies.[32] But Cartagenan privateering specifically remains little understood. *No Limits to Their Sway* unveils the details, scope, and relevance of Cartagenan privateering, testing three interdependent hypotheses. First, that Cartagena's precocious adoption of privateering is explained not just by its Caribbean location, but also by the political features of its revolution. Privateering from Cartagena, carried out by Afro-Caribbean and other foreign sailors, was a policy espoused by a radical government in collaboration with local leaders of African descent. Second, that Cartagena utilized privateering to defend its revolution and shore up its finances while articulating a vision of its privateering policy as a legitimate "act of sovereignty," effectuated by its attacks on Cuban Spanish shipping and simultaneous contacts with Haiti.[33] And, finally, that the State of Cartagena and its exercises of sovereignty (self-government, republicanism, privateering, and overseas contacts) demonstrate the historical relevance of "alternative communities" that were active before the larger national states crystallized. The State of Cartagena and the United Provinces of New Granada, as polities whose sovereignty their members took seriously and expected to be long-lasting, played crucial roles early in the revolutionary period, only to be dismissed by those who finally won the war against Spain.[34]

Spain of course did not recognize the sovereignty of the State of Cartagena, with its agents referring to Cartagenan privateers as "pirates." When and how someone ceased being a "privateer" and became a "pirate," however, depended on perception, balances of power, legal proceedings, and particular circumstances.[35] Sometimes Spanish officials spoke of "insurgent privateers," indicating that in their view, privateers from Spanish territories were operating in open rebellion against Spain.³⁶ This had serious consequences for seamen, especially common sailors of color caught aboard privateering ships. While Aury's status as an officer and his standing as a free white man from France afforded him better chances to slip from Spain's grasp, Ignacio and his crewmates, arrested in Panama, were tried for piracy and sentenced to death, though the punishment was commuted to eight years of work without pay in Havana's armory.³⁷ Life on board was not only rough and rowdy, but burdened with additional risk for those who had escaped from slavery or had enslaved ancestors.

Aury and the Afro-Caribbean sailors aboard Cartagenan privateers thus stood at the center of important tensions between slavery and freedom, revolution and counterrevolution, the old regime and new republics, hierarchy and disobedience, and the land and the sea. This book, which sheds light on those tensions and how they overlapped, pivots the history of Atlantic seafarers, usually told from a British or Anglo-American vantage point, toward Cartagena and its overseas connections. In doing so, it bypasses the "artificial barrier" often used by historians to separate the continent from the islands.³⁸ This, in turn, gives it the opportunity to recount the Revolution of Cartagena from a hemispheric perspective, rescuing in the process the participation of an international cast of privateers in the early struggles for Spanish American independence.

1

Slavery, Seamanship, Freedom

BY 1763, THE TWENTY-TWO-YEAR-OLD slave Olaudah Equiano had traveled to Montserrat, Barbados, Virginia, Canada, England, and France. It was not uncommon for people of African descent to be both slaves and sailors, like Equiano. They worked aboard ocean-bound ships and coastal boats, and on the docks and waterfronts around the Atlantic Ocean. People of color signed on or were forced to serve in the European navies. Equiano himself worked for the British Royal Navy. Other slaves and former slaves worked in the maritime trades as guards, stevedores, cooks, bartenders, innkeepers, laundresses, and seamstresses.[1]

People of color in the maritime trades, particularly those who worked as sailors in the Caribbean, inhabited an ambivalent world, very often straddling slavery and freedom. Masters, who profited from hiring out their slaves to work on ships, gave some leeway to their slave sailors, allowing them to keep a portion of the earnings, perhaps hoping to elicit loyalty. Many of the slaves hired out as sailors saved the money or invested it in petty trade, hoping to accumulate enough to buy their freedom. Equiano, for one, purchased his own freedom and became an ardent abolitionist leader, writing a memoir published in London in 1789.[2] This latter step made him exceptional, yet he had much in common with other sailors of color.

For some slaves, working as sailors opened the possibility of gaining a degree of autonomy. Affording opportunities for traveling, meeting new people, mastering new types of knowledge, and even earning some income, seagoing occupations represented an avenue for inching closer to freedom.[3] For others, pretending to be sailors—eventually becoming maritime workers in their own right—was an effective subterfuge for a rapid escape from captivity. Runaway slaves blended into the crowded waterfront communities. Therefore, people throughout the Caribbean, especially masters, recognized a "close symbolic connection between experience at sea and freedom."[4]

Colonial bureaucrats, sea captains, planters, slave drivers, and slave catchers realized that maritime employment could stimulate in slaves and former slaves defiant and self-assertive attitudes. Feeling on a more equal footing with respect to his captain, Equiano remembered, "I used plainly to tell him my mind." Even more risky was allowing slaves to transition from common sailors to skilled navigators. According to Equiano, many thought it "a very dangerous thing to let a negro know navigation."[5]

Nevertheless, economic growth increased the demand for sailors, making room for slaves desperately trying to escape brutal conditions on land. The spectacular expansion of plantation slavery and international trade across the 1700s necessitated a parallel growth in maritime shipping. Sailors were rarely hard-pressed to find jobs in port towns.[6] Moreover, maritime warfare proliferated in the second half of the century, especially during the 1790s, continuing into the first quarter of the nineteenth century. France, Great Britain, Spain, the United States, and emerging polities like the State of Cartagena required the services of regular and irregular seamen. It was the job of sailors to defend and expand jurisdictions, enforce laws and policies, and assert sovereignty in times of international conflict. Sailors often found themselves working not only on merchant ships, but also aboard navy vessels and privateers—ironically protecting nations to whom they had few or no ties, and sometimes defending "freedom," although they themselves were often slaves.

Even among individuals for whom it may have been the best option, transitioning from slavery to freedom through seamanship was a difficult process. Both for those who legally obtained freedom and those who simply absconded from their masters, working conditions remained akin to slavery. Sea captains could flog sailors, clap them in irons, and punish them further, even to the point of death. The risk of re-enslavement was also a constant: slave catchers and traders kidnapped unsuspecting sailors of color and spirited them away.

Yet, time and again, plantation slaves tried to better their lot or to run away by traveling to cities by the sea, where they could make their way onto the bilanders, sloops, feluccas, schooners, polacres, brigs, and frigates that plied the waters of the Caribbean.[7] Belittled, beaten, torn from their families and friends, and in many other ways tormented and humiliated, the hundreds of thousands of people in bondage who remained on land found little redress. Life before the mast, by contrast, allowed people to escape abusive bosses more easily. Sailors could switch jobs at the end of each voyage. Submitting to captains' authority only by contract, sailors were not permanently attached to any individual ship. As they changed ships and officers, seagoing individuals moved across colonial and imperial borders.

By the time the Haitian Revolution broke out in 1791, and long before Cartagena declared independence in 1811, a tradition of Afro-Caribbean seamanship and a robust maritime labor market had developed in tandem with plantation slavery, international trade, and imperial war. Among the vibrant seagoing communities, the lines between slave and free easily blurred, and mobility and cultural border-crossings became trademarks.[8] With the events in Haiti and other political upheavals in the region at the turn of the century, demand for mariners peaked as the struggle against slavery climaxed. Privateering expanded, and people of color became even more prevalent on ships. Seafarers of color thus gained the experience and created the networks that would make them and their offspring valuable assets to the State of Cartagena. There, a radical government would hire them and even offer them citizenship, setting aside suspicions raised by their connections with the revolutionary French-speaking world and their near-nomadic way of life.

SEAFARING DEMANDED RELATIVELY constant mobility. Almost by definition, most sailors became nomads and cultural border-crossers. As they sailed from port to port or coasted along insular and continental shores, even common sailors acquired a general understanding of the geography and politics of different places. In the Caribbean, political jurisdictions and cultural environments could change very rapidly. It took a day to sail from the south of Saint-Domingue to the east of Cuba, moving from French to Spanish territories. Seagoing individuals thus encountered different languages and cultures as a matter of course.[9]

Some maritime workers—be they sailors or waterfront laborers—spoke at least two or three languages. French, English, Spanish, Dutch, and hybridizations of these were common. Jean-Louis, a creole slave from the French island of Martinique and a "sailor by trade" who fled his master in Saint-Domingue in 1785, was described as someone who spoke "several languages."[10] Three decades later, the Haitian sailor Ignacio the Younger, who worked aboard the Cartagenan privateer *Bellona*, spoke French and some Spanish in front of officials in Panama. Better versed in Spanish, and a French speaker himself, the sailor Francisco Díaz translated for Ignacio.[11]

Sailing gave individuals other opportunities too. In his memoir, Equiano related that when his new master asked him what he could do, he answered that he "knew something of seamanship," was skilled at shaving and dressing hair, and could "refine wines," something he had "learned on shipboard." Equiano also mentioned that he could read and that he "understood arithmetic tolerably."[12] Some slaves who went to sea, especially those regularly working as seamen, could try their luck at multiple new endeavors such as these.

With the noticeable presence of hired slaves and free people of color aboard merchant and naval ships, slaves on plantations and in towns quickly realized that sailing could offer routes to freedom. Slaves with no prior maritime experience often ran away to waterfront communities with the intention of joining seagoing crews. These maritime maroons adopted seamanlike manners and attire to slip in and out of slavery or shake off bondage altogether. They learned the tricks of the trade, took note of the professional lingo and the ways in which seamen spoke, and even walked and moved like seasoned seafarers, thus embodying the masterless Caribbean. When the slave Tom King of Kingston ran away in November 1790, his owner announced in a local newspaper that King "having been at sea may attempt to pass for a Free Man."[13] Runaway slaves were difficult to tell apart from their free sailor colleagues, being similar in habits and complexion.[14]

The complicated ways in which slavery, seamanship, and freedom overlapped in the Caribbean appear vividly in the French colony of Saint-Domingue, which would later become Haiti. Saint-Domingue presented a dramatic spectacle of forced labor, suffering, and death. By 1789, there were around five hundred thousand slaves in the colony. They labored on sugarcane, coffee, cotton, and indigo plantations. Tens of thousands of captives arrived directly from Africa each year, with forty-eight thousand disembarking in 1790 alone. With the excuse that only the threat of physical punishment could prevent a slave uprising, masters and slave drivers sometimes tortured and even murdered slaves.[15] But even under the seemingly unbreakable power of the masters, tens of thousands of slaves managed to run away, sometimes temporarily, sometimes forever. Most fleeing slaves escaped to the woods and mountains, or they took refuge on plantations or in towns different from their own. Others took to the sea.

Many slaves relied on maritime subterfuges when running away. The *Affiches Américaines*, a newspaper published in the colony from 1766 to 1790, contains over ten thousand advertisements placed by masters seeking to recover their runaway slaves. Some had escaped by means of small boats and sailing ships.[16] Under the right circumstances, slaves who had been sailors could put their skills to good use when running away from their masters. In July 1767, the merchant firms of Gareschéé Brothers and Mesnier Brothers offered a bounty on a slave who had recently escaped. Described as a creole from Guadeloupe who "reads a little" and works as "cooper, mason, mattress maker & sailor," this slave had been a privateer during the Seven Years' War, the widespread international conflict that ended in 1763.[17]

Slaves outside of the maritime trades sometimes managed to enlist the help of free or enslaved seamen. In the parish of Petit-Trou, in southern Saint-Domingue, a man named Joseph, described as a mulatto in a runaway advertisement, fled in early 1783 with another man described as a creole black (both were coopers by trade) and a woman described as black and English (most likely born in Jamaica). They stole a canoe from the plantation on which they worked, located on Baradères Bay, just west of town, and rowed away with the help of four "black sailors" who worked for a coastal merchant named Pascal.[18]

ALTHOUGH IT IS difficult to tell whether they too escaped by water, other slave sailors appear in advertisements for runaways. The slave sailor George, a mulatto who spoke English and "a little French," according to the *Affiches Américaines*, escaped from the house of his master, one Monsieur de Laly. Noël, a "Creole from Curaçao" who was a "sailor and a bit of a cooper," also escaped his masters, as did Jean-Louis, a "Creole from Martinique, Sailor by trade." Born in Africa and described as a "Black sailor," the slave named Général ran away from the port city of Cap Français in 1785.[19] With a population of about nineteen thousand, Cap Français was the size of Boston at that time. Located in northern Saint-Domingue, the city was the colony's leading port. Dozens and sometimes hundreds of sailing ships could be seen on the bay. With so many people in town, and so many more coming in and out, it must have been difficult to ascertain with accuracy who was a runaway and who was a compliant slave going about her or his daily routine.

Both slavery and freedom were thus characterized by intense ambiguities. Life after slavery could be as harsh as life in bondage.

Former slaves rarely experienced complete liberty. Even for the few lucky ones who legally acquired their freedom, obtaining official documents as proof, life was often still tied to former masters, working conditions remained harsh, and the possibility of re-enslavement loomed large. This is exactly what Equiano experienced, for after purchasing his own freedom on July 11, 1766, he continued to endure the rigors of life at sea and the dangers of slave societies on land. In the British colony of Georgia, which he visited in trading voyages outfitted by his former master, he came close to being kidnapped by ruffians and re-enslaved on more than one occasion.[20]

Despite the risks, men and women continued to run away from slaveholders in French Saint-Domingue right up to the August 1791 slave uprising that inaugurated the Haitian Revolution. The masters, in turn, continued to offer bounties on "maroons" and to make other efforts to bring them back. Many runaways were located, thrown into jail, and then returned to their alleged owners. Liberty and bondage were not static states but continuously in flux. Some people slipped in and out of slavery, increasing or decreasing their autonomy with respect to others at different moments in their lives.

Maritime maroons were not only from the French islands. On the British colony of Jamaica, another plantation society, some slaves likewise worked as sailors, hired out by their masters, and some tried to escape their fate by joining crews or other maritime subterfuges. Sea captains sometimes accepted slaves on board as sailors, even if they did not have authorization from their masters. Some Jamaican maritime maroons worked on privateer ships. John Detruie, the captain of the Cartagenan privateer *Augustus*, was tried in Jamaica in October 1815 for "enticing," "inveigling," and "employing" a slave named Thomas, already advertised as a runaway by a master named J. P. Tardif. On board were six other alleged slaves: Bois Louis, John, Ely, Damas, John Marcus (known as Martine), and Peter (known as Pierre). Detruie was found guilty, had to pay a fine, and went to jail for six months.[21]

If Thomas and the rest of his colleagues were indeed slaves, they probably did not have to be enticed or inveigled by Detruie to work aboard the *Augustus*. Many slaves were drawn to the sea and, once off their home islands or away from the jurisdiction of their masters' polities, tried their best to pass as free folk. In Jamaica, local authorities often came across individuals going about as free people whom they suspected of being slaves. These men and women were then confined to prisons called "workhouses" or "houses of correction"—essentially jails for slaves, runaways, and people of color under no one's apparent authority.[22]

Thousands of people of color worked on deep-water vessels, on small coastal boats along the insular and continental shores, and on ships that traveled up and down the rivers that empty out into Atlantic waters. Skilled, knowledgeable, and vulnerable, they were reservoirs of human energy and intelligence of which naval, military, and political authorities were well aware. From 1791 to 1824, a period marked by the Haitian Revolution, the Napoleonic Wars, the War of 1812, and the Spanish American revolutions, slave sailors and former slaves-turned-sailors came to occupy center stage in the violent, unfolding drama—sometimes under pressure, sometimes of their own volition.

Beginning in the early 1790s, sailors of color, especially former slaves, joined the swelling ranks of French privateering forces. With the Atlantic world thrown into turmoil by the French and Haitian Revolutions, the Caribbean became a crucial theater of war. In the words of Julius S. Scott, "Never had the black presence on the sea been as central as it proved to be in this revolutionary war."[23] This generation of sailors of African descent built on the experiences of previous generations, inhabiting a preexisting maritime social world underpinned by culturally diverse and multinational crews.

SHIPBOARD WORKERS, ESPECIALLY on pirate and privateer ships, came from many different corners of the Atlantic world. The famous buccaneers and the feared Dutch sea rovers of the 1600s, for instance, included people from Europe, the Americas, and African societies.[24] While the pirates of the "golden age"—those who plied their trade in the early 1700s—hailed mainly from the English-speaking North Atlantic, there were Dutch, French, Danish, Portuguese, Belgian, Swedish, and Spanish sailors among them, as well as African sailors from Calabar, Ouidah, and Sierra Leone, and people who had escaped from slavery. They were referred to as "bandits of all nations" by authorities and by owners of the merchant ships they attacked.[25]

Even the vessels of European powers were staffed by multiethnic and multinational crews. It was difficult for countries to find enough native-born or naturalized sailors to man their warships, especially in times of conflict. This became a constant problem during the second half of the eighteenth century. As international warfare increased in scope and intensity, European and colonial maritime authorities had to accept the presence of foreigners on the lower decks in order to keep their ships afloat. People of African descent became especially common within the Dutch and British navies. Portuguese and Italian sailors abounded on Spanish men-of-war and merchantmen. By the end of the century, around 1,600 sailors from the island of Malta worked under Spanish flags. Irish seamen were also not uncommon on Spanish ships.[26]

Cartagena-flagged privateering vessels were similarly diverse, though Afro-Caribbean sailors seemed to have been the largest demographic aboard these ships. Consider the *Bellona*, outfitted and captained by Frenchman Louis-Michel Aury. The *Bellona* was manned, in the words of Ignacio, by "all types of sailors, such as Spaniards, Frenchmen, Englishmen, Americans, and many from the colony of the Guarico [Haiti] . . . most of them of color."[27] According to an 1815 Jamaican press report on her capture by the British brig *Carnation*, the *Bellona* had seventy-five men on board. Once in Kingston, most of them said they were Haitian natives.[28]

Sailors on merchant vessels, including slave ships, also hailed from different places.[29] Crews working on legal shipping and contraband trade spanned not just the Caribbean and the Americas, but the larger Atlantic. Evidence of this can be gathered from surviving "rolls"—records listing sailors, their places of origin, and shipboard occupations.[30] John Whelan, the captain of the *Governor Brook*, a merchant brig from Philadelphia, formally filed his ship's roll on February 5, 1798, with the Pennsylvania notary public Clement Biddle. Whelan and his first mate, Peter O'Brien, were Irishmen. From Malta came the sailor John Martin, while his colleague Peter Philips was originally from Germany. They were, however, naturalized US citizens. American by birth, the rest of the crew included John Fallena and John Gainer, from Pennsylvania; Mark Merrill, from Portland, New Hampshire; the cook, Abraham Cole, originally from Baltimore but a resident of Philadelphia; and finally, Gustavus Kean, a native of Philadelphia.[31]

This diversity was also common aboard ships trading in and out of Tierra Firme ports. Sailing from Jamaica to Cartagena in 1812, the *Rosa* had fourteen men on board, including the officers. According to official documents from the British Vice-Admiralty Court in Kingston, all the men were "of different countries," including Haiti, Jamaica, and Cartagena.[32] The *Blanche*, a ship of French construction and Spanish flag known by the nickname *General Monteverde*, offers another example. Her roll dated September 11, 1812, shows that while the captain hailed from the Spanish Mediterranean island of Majorca and one of the sailors was from Lisbon, the rest of the crew came from Santa Marta, Cartagena, Coro, Puerto Cabello, Curaçao, Honduras, Jamaica, Puerto Rico, and Florida.[33]

By the turn of the century, these multinational crews faced more challenges than ever. Between 1793 and 1801, the British Empire alone lost around twenty-four thousand men in the Caribbean.[34] With such heavy tolls, and regular naval tactics as well as privateering on the rise, there were jobs aplenty for seasoned and novice sailors alike. And with the slave uprising of Saint-Domingue and other rebellions in the Caribbean, the wars became conflicts over slavery itself, and military or shipboard service emerged even more clearly as a potential avenue to freedom, in spite of the greater risks.

PRIVATEER VESSELS MULTIPLIED throughout the Atlantic world during the Age of Revolutions. Privateering had existed for a long time, but it now became a tool used by both European powers and anti-colonial forces. The rebel colonists of the thirteen British North American possessions, French revolutionaries, British and Spanish royalists, and Spanish American patriots all turned to privateering. Beginning with the American Revolution and continuing well into the 1820s, this tactic of irregular warfare appeared frequently in the crucible of revolutions and counterrevolutions. Privateering had the potential to inflict damage on the enemy while economically benefiting the commissioning polity. It disrupted trade and generated income. Privateering was guerrilla warfare on the seas.[35]

Privateers usually relied on small or medium-sized sailing ships. In the Caribbean, privateersmen most often sailed schooners. Usually two-masted vessels, schooners were rigged with sails "suspended from gaffs reaching from the mast towards the stern; and stretched out below by booms, whose foremost ends are hooked to an iron, which clasps the mast so as to turn therein as upon an axis, when the after-ends are swung from one side of the vessel to the other."[36] Unlike ships of the line, schooners had good speed and maneuverability, due to their modest proportions and dynamic sails, making them ideal craft for fast operations.[37]

French agents took privateering to an effective and very profitable level, perhaps because they recruited hundreds of former slaves into their ranks. One of the most important centers of privateer activity during the turbulent 1790s was the French island of Guadeloupe, a plantation colony with about ninety thousand slaves.[38] Shaken by a slave insurrection beginning in April 1793, this island was taken by the British in 1794 and successfully recovered the same year by the French. Faced with immense pressure from slave-rebels both in Guadeloupe and Saint-Domingue, and threatened with British invasion, the French were forced to offer freedom to the slaves. French administrators first declared the abolition of slavery in Saint-Domingue in 1793. The National Convention in Paris later ratified this measure, which came into effect in Guadeloupe and all French colonies in 1794.[39]

French authorities had partly yielded to pressure to abolish slavery because they hoped that recruiting freed people as sailors and soldiers would increase their military and naval strength while keeping the newly freed men and women somewhat under their control. Effective privateering against the British could be accomplished only by turning to experienced seamen while opening the doors to fresh recruits. With the help of seafaring people of color, French revolutionaries waged a privateering war in order to defend their islands, undermine British power in the Americas, and steal as much as they could in the name of the republic.

Victor Hugues, governor of French Guadeloupe between 1794 and 1798, orchestrated French privateering in the New World. After declaring the freedom of all slaves, he presided over the recruitment of around 3,500 of these newly freed people as sailors. By the end of 1795, Hugues had authorized the outfitting of twenty-five privateer ships. By the end of his tenure, he had commissioned 121 privateers, which were subsequently responsible for capturing or destroying hundreds of enemy ships.[40] French privateering continued after the end of Hugues's regime. Between 1793 and 1801, at least fifteen of the privateer captains flying the French flag were men of color.[41] This frenzy of French-sponsored privateering spilled over into Spanish port towns, particularly in Cuba, and also affected the shores of Tierra Firme.

In the wake of the Haitian Revolution and the events in Guadeloupe, the near-hermetic seal kept on Spanish cities like Santiago de Cuba or Cartagena seriously began to give way. People fleeing warfare in the French islands sought shelter in Spanish territories. Others were illegally imported as slaves. Moreover, in the context of a new imperial alliance between Spain and France, many people came in legally, including privateering sailors. Nevertheless, these newcomers were regarded warily by Spanish speakers, especially by officials and slaveholders. Bringing news of warfare and the collapse of slavery in the French Antilles, those foreigners transmitted what many Spaniards saw as pernicious ideas of liberty and disobedience.

2

Heralds of Liberty and Disobedience

BOTH IN SPAIN and Tierra Firme, patricians and plebeians alike kept abreast of the unfolding events of the French Revolution, which began in 1789. With the outbreak of the Haitian Revolution in August 1791, the volatile political situation became especially alarming to authorities and slaveholders in the Caribbean. Many blamed the French Revolution for inspiring slave unrest in the colonies. Addressing the transformations underway in the French-speaking world became even more pressing in 1793, after King Louis XVI, cousin of the Spanish king, was guillotined in Paris. Spain declared war on France that year. Bureaucrats, planters, and newspapermen in the Spanish and British Caribbean demonized people associated with the French-speaking world, especially seagoing workers of color. In Tierra Firme in particular, the official gazette vehemently decried people and ideas linked to the French Revolution.[1]

Unsurprisingly, sailors—many of them slaves, runaways, or free people of color—helped spread news about France and its colonies to the Spanish-speaking world. Sailors generated, transmitted, and transformed information not only by word of mouth, but also by transporting and reading out loud newspapers and handwritten documents like private letters. For inhabitants of port towns, newly arrived ships and sailors represented the most common source of fresh news. However, it greatly concerned slaveholders, bureaucrats, and military authorities in places like Havana or Cartagena that these maritime heralds telling of anti-monarchical revolution in France and antislavery uprisings on the French islands were foreigners of color, many of them arriving directly from French jurisdictions. Nobody could guarantee that these outsiders were not themselves interested in fostering political unrest. Their presence alone, officials reasoned, could inspire locals to strike against slavery and the establishment.[2]

In spite of these fears, people from the French-speaking world became prevalent in Spanish territories at the turn of the century because of a change in international policy. Following the signing of a peace treaty between Spain and France in August 1796, which made these countries allies against Great Britain, French privateers were allowed to operate out of Cuba, mainly from Havana and the eastern port town of Santiago. French-flagged vessels also gained the privilege of sailing from French Caribbean islands such as Guadeloupe to the shores of Tierra Firme, where they could refit, resupply, and cast off in pursuit of British merchant ships operating in the area.[3] Still, people from the French islands were treated by Spanish officials and local elites with the utmost suspicion, even as their presence was tolerated as a necessary by-product of rapprochement with France.

Although no simple correlation existed between place of origin, language, status, and political inclinations, sympathizers of slavery and monarchy in Cuba and Tierra Firme had specific, if quite ambivalent, objections to outsiders. In Cuba, the growing class of sugarcane planters feared the spirit of revolution from the French islands. Putting profits before politics, planters nonetheless purchased enslaved people from the French Caribbean.[4] In Tierra Firme, local authorities and patricians likewise saw foreign people of color as carriers of a devastating contagion. Governor Anastasio Cejudo, for example, claimed to have discovered a plot by foreign slaves to kill him and all white people in Cartagena.[5] Authorities in Santa Fe insisted that all outsiders had to be expelled. Yet the changing dynamics of the conflict put Afro-Caribbean and French privateers in closer contact with Spanish subjects. A few years later, independent Cartagena would make a drastic change in policy, hiring as privateers the very type of people earlier accused of transmitting insurrectionist tendencies into Spanish territories.

ALTHOUGH THE PRESENCE of French seafarers in places under Spanish jurisdiction preceded the 1796 alliance between Spain and France, it increased thereafter, generating anxiety among Spanish administrators, merchants, and planters. In Cuba and other Spanish territories, local authorities looked upon foreigners with suspicion. As early as the 1500s, Spain restricted its possessions to trading exclusively with individuals and institutions from the Iberian Peninsula. Most Spanish officials assumed, correctly in many instances, that outsiders in their towns and provinces would seek to break this monopoly system by secretly introducing and selling foreign goods.

Antoine Labarrière, a Parisian who worked as captain of the schooner *Filibus Terre*, is a good example of a French privateer presumably involved in smuggling. Captain Labarrière had been in Havana for a few weeks when, in January 1796, another French captain came to town looking for him. Upon learning that a newly arrived Frenchman had inquired about Labarrière's whereabouts, local authorities ordered round-the-clock surveillance of the newcomer by five men (presumably soldiers).[6] The authorities' hunch was confirmed when Labarrière, who had no authorization to sail to any other Spanish port, left for Santiago de Cuba, on the other side of the island. Arrested and thrown into jail in Santiago, Labarrière claimed that he had not meant to leave Havana, but instead had accidentally drifted away after the rope securing his vessel to the dock broke.[7]

The supposedly "drifting" vessel was a British prize originally brought to Havana by Labarrière. The trouble began when the merchandise on board this captured ship mysteriously disappeared. The Spanish had reason to think that Labarrière had sold the goods illicitly. From his prison cell in Santiago, however, the Frenchman alleged in a written petition that the charges against him were based on false accusations. He claimed he had not touched the merchandise in question and had never broken Spanish commercial laws, which were very well known to him.[8]

Besides the traditional preoccupation with foreigners as potential smugglers, more recent developments in Cuba's economic outlook further stimulated animosity toward outsiders, specifically toward people of color from neighboring islands. Just a few years before the start of the Haitian Revolution, Cuba had begun building its own plantation society—importing more slaves, expanding its sugarcane estates, introducing new technology, exporting more sugar, and increasing trade with the outside world.[9] Francisco de Arango y Parreño, a highborn man of means from Havana, both represented and influenced an important sector of the Cuban slaveholding elite. In Madrid, he effectively advocated for fewer restrictions on the slave trade, which grew spectacularly at the turn of the century. Between 1790 and 1820, well over two hundred thousand captives were delivered to Cuba.[10]

As Cuban elites strove to replicate the French plantation regime, the 1791 slave uprising in Saint-Domingue posed the question of whether a similar event could occur on the Spanish island. Still in Madrid, Arango y Parreño hastily assured the government that Cuba would never face this kind of crisis. Cuba's planters—unlike their French counterparts—were allegedly loyal to the monarchy and treated their slaves very well.[11] But with people of color arriving directly from Saint-Domingue, often in obscure circumstances, Cuban planters, magistrates, and governors began to worry about serious challenges to the growing plantation system—that Cuban slaves would be contaminated with a spirit of unrest and insurrectionist sentiment, and that people from Saint-Domingue visiting or living in Cuba could potentially inspire or organize a slave uprising.[12]

The greed for vast profits from the slave trade and plantation agriculture trumped the planters' fears. The specter of revolutionary contagion did not stop investors in Cuba from purchasing captives who hailed from Saint-Domingue.[13] By 1804, when former slaves and their allies in Saint-Domingue defeated French forces and established the independent country of Haiti, thousands of refugees had left the former French territory for Cuba. By 1808, most refugees in Cuba were Africans and people of African descent. These individuals had been nominally free in the former French colony, but when they sailed across the Windward Passage to slaveholding Cuba, they found themselves at risk of captivity: Some were claimed as slaves by their former masters; others were simply kidnapped and sold as slaves. Even when they managed to hold onto their freedom, "French Negroes"—as bureaucrats and planters often called people of color from the French Caribbean—were watched closely by local authorities.[14]

At the same time, bureaucrats found it difficult to control the comings and goings of privateers and other seagoing personnel, many of them former slaves themselves. Active not only in the port towns but also just off shore in rural areas, some sailors were perceived as vectors of revolution. With each merchant vessel, slave ship, or privateer carrying people from Saint-Domingue/Haiti to Cuba, uneven and contradictory streams of information materialized, with potentially destabilizing effects. All during the 1790s and into the early nineteenth century, people brought news from the French/Haitian territories to the Spanish island. Even those who arrived as slaves encountered other captives and together "talked, interpreted and imagined what Haiti might portend."[15]

The increased sense of apprehension among officials was by no means exclusive to Cuba. Bureaucrats throughout the Caribbean believed that foreign slaves and former slaves might not merely passively transmit information (through oral reports, private correspondence, and newspapers), inadvertently inspiring unrest, but contemplate directly fostering uprisings and the overthrow of authorities.[16] Alarmed that British privateers were importing slaves from revolutionary Saint-Domingue, the Jamaica Assembly decreed in 1797 that those captives could stay on the island only for the duration of adjudication proceedings. Afterward, the captives had to be sold abroad.[17]

ACROSS TIERRA FIRME, including in Cartagena, local magistrates worried about people of color from the French Antilles, who sailed not only to Cuba but to all the Spanish territories of the Caribbean. Sailors, soldiers, and officers from the French world arrived in the Tierra Firme coastal provinces of Riohacha, Santa Marta, and Cartagena during the turbulent years following the start of the Haitian Revolution. Toward the end of 1796, for instance, a French privateer dropped off a group of "Frenchmen" in Riohacha. Local authorities immediately arrested the foreigners, sent them to Cartagena, and later deported them to Les Cayes, on the southern shores of Saint-Domingue.[18] The presence of these and other individuals—and sometimes mere rumors—put Spanish bureaucrats and military officers on alert about potential conspiracies.[19]

According to Spanish documents, an insurrection led by "Negros Franceses esclavos"—French Negro slaves—was foiled in Cartagena in early April 1799. The top-secret reports by Governor Anastasio Cejudo placed the blame on a core group of foreign slaves. These captives belonged to Spanish naval officers stationed in Cartagena, who had presumably purchased the slaves in the French Caribbean. In collaboration with local slaves and artillery sergeant Jorge Guzmán (a man of color), the insurrectionists had planned to kill the governor in broad daylight, on the city's promenade, following it with an attack on the forts and walls of the city, after which they would kill the "Whites," loot their property, and sack the royal treasury.[20] These were, however, typical accusations against slaves, usually made during times of political tension.

During the governor's investigation, the involvement of local colored militiamen such as Guzmán became apparent. Cejudo concluded that this alliance across the lines of slavery and freedom had ultimately sought to separate Cartagena from the Spanish government, bringing not just freedom to the enslaved but also political liberty to other nonwhites. As the governor put it, the suspects carried the "detestable maxims of liberty and disobedience."[21] Such notions did not exclusively allude to efforts, individual or collective, to undermine slavery. Spanish bureaucrats associated these words with people who participated in or sympathized with the interdependent French and Haitian Revolutions. The label "French Negroes" thus referred not just to foreigners who could presumably spark or inspire insurrection among slaves, but to those who could transmit the "godless" principles espoused by revolutionaries in France.[22]

Such multiethnic, cross-class movements—the bringing together of enslaved and free people to a common cause—seem to have been more imagined than real. The governor himself had been tipped off about the plot by a free man of color. When asked by a conspirator to join in the plan, Corporal Manuel Yturen, a volunteer of color, had played along, only to inform Cejudo at the first opportunity. The man who had allegedly approached Yturen was arrested and, based on his deposition, warrants were issued for other plotters. While several were thrown into jail, some managed to escape the walled city. Fleeing to the neighboring countryside, they set several estates on fire, the governor reported. However, Cejudo asserted, rural slaves remained under "submission and obedience."[23] There might have been some sort of political action in the making, but its details and actual goals remain hidden behind the governor's stereotyped accusations and political anxieties.

Cejudo continued to believe that any threat of conspiracy could have potential repercussions beyond Cartagena. It was not merely slaveholders and a few haciendas in the province of Cartagena at risk; the political stability of the entire viceroyalty was also at stake. If members of the local garrison, mostly residents of the interior of Tierra Firme, were to become enchanted with ideas of "liberty and disobedience," Spanish power in the region would falter, for it was the soldiers of the Cartagena garrison who had the responsibility of putting down any rebellions against monarchical authority. Although Spain had already sent almost four hundred professional soldiers from the Queen's Infantry Regiment to reinforce Cartagena, tropical disease had taken a heavy toll. Their numbers were down to 278. Cejudo requested a regiment of veterans from the peninsula to be sent as soon as possible.[24]

To the dismay of Spanish authorities, people from the French Antilles kept traveling to Tierra Firme. Given the alliance between Spain and France, French-flagged ships were allowed to sail directly into Spanish territories. In February 1803, a corvette from Guadeloupe arrived at the port of Chimare, in the province of Riohacha. The ship brought over two hundred "French negroes and mulattoes," all seeking shelter from the raging warfare on their home island, where French troops were soon to reestablish slavery.[25] Alarmed about their arrival, Viceroy Pedro de Mendinueta described them as "a class of people infected with the ideas of liberty, equality, and others that have been so pernicious and have caused many ravages and horrors on the unhappy French Islands." Fearful that these individuals might make their way into the interior of the viceroyalty, Mendinueta asked the governor to keep them under control, either by detaining them or deporting them back to Guadeloupe.[26] Little did the viceroy imagine that in a decade's time the most important Caribbean port town of the viceroyalty would be busy with Frenchmen and "French Negroes," and not in the context of an imperial alliance, but of a revolutionary government seeking Cartagena's complete independence from Spain.

MEANWHILE, BUREAUCRATS, SLAVEHOLDERS, and newspapermen continued to fear and decry people of color from the French Antilles. When they worked as privateers, they were demonized or ridiculed with epithets that employed not only metaphors of infection, with ideas of liberty and disobedience cast as the foremost threat to social order, but also older motifs about unruly and ungodly seamen. Haitian sailors and soldiers, and their country more generally, faced bitter opposition and defamation, perhaps because of their political achievements.²⁷ Although the French and their allies made great efforts to reestablish slavery and retake the former colony of Saint-Domingue, the former slaves emerged victorious in their liberation struggle. Haiti declared independence on January 1, 1804. The new independent country, however, quickly fractured into different polities. The Empire of Haiti lasted from 1804 to 1806, when the country split in two. The northern part first became the State of Haiti, transforming into the Kingdom of Haiti in 1811. The south emerged as the Republic of Haiti in 1806, which was governed by President Alexandre Pétion until 1820.

The ironic tone of a British press report from Jamaica reveals the gazetteers' scornful perception of the emerging new country. Reporting on the alleged confiscation of goods en route to Haiti for the coronation of the former slave Henry Christophe as King Henri I, a piece titled "The Emperor of Haity's Regalia" noted:

> All the *Regalia* of his Imperial Majesty Christophe I have been seized on board a vessel cleared out for Haity, as they were entered under the name of *wholstery*, in order to defraud the revenue of the duties that would have been payable on gold lace and jewelry, &c . . . . His Imperial Majesty will, no doubt, be indignant that an attempt should thus be made to defraud his Royal Brother Sovereign of his just duties. . . . Unless the Treasury, however, give an order for the release of the *regalia*, the Emperor's *coronation* must be postponed.²⁸

While the British government refused to extend diplomatic recognition to Haiti as an independent nation, British merchants and bureaucrats worked to establish trade with the new country.²⁹ Against the backdrop of this tension, the press report openly added insult to injury by equating the monarchs of Great Britain and Haiti as "brothers," mentioning fraud in relation to trade duties, and implying that the British held true power over the flow of goods to the former French colony. The delay in crowning the Haitian leader represented Great Britain's rejection of Haiti's functional sovereignty.

Jamaican newspapers, which circulated widely in the Caribbean, disparaged Haitian seamen as vigorously as they expressed disdain toward the new Haitian governments. The Kingdom of Haiti and the Republic of Haiti both turned to privateering as they waged war on each other, often coming across British forces at sea ready to take advantage of the conflict. In spite of the similarity between Haitian and British approaches to naval warfare, Jamaican gazetteers described Haiti's maritime exploits derisively. On February 3, 1812, the *Amethyste*, a Haitian frigate, engaged in combat with the British frigate *Southampton*. The *Amethyste*'s crew, commanded by a man named Gaspard, proved tenacious, killing over one hundred men in the action. Gaspard's men were dismissively referred to in the *Royal Gazette* as a "renegade set, consisting of Frenchmen, Americans, and all nations."[30]

These words echoed long-standing English expressions about enemy sailors and soldiers, including pirates. "Renegade" was often applied to an individual who held allegedly weak or insincere political and religious convictions. A renegade was a deserter, a traitor to country and religion, and an apostate. Borrowed from the Spanish *renegado*, the word was used by Spaniards to refer to fellow Iberian Christians who left their camps to join Muslim societies, renouncing their faith and adopting the religion and social habits of their supposed sworn enemies.[31] Gaspar, who died in the *Amethyste* engagement with the *Southampton*, had reportedly shared with his men an "avowed principle": that in the event they were "unsuccessful in battle with Christophe's cruises, rather than be made prisoners, they would set fire to their vessels." The account went on: "Such is the savage mode of warfare carried on by these ignorant people."[32]

Enemy privateers were similarly disparaged in British gazettes. Jamaican reports of privateers who hailed or supposedly hailed from Haiti were particularly full of stereotypes. The case of the *Edward* is telling. While the men on board this privateer ship claimed to be from France, an article in Kingston, based on the testimony of a sailor who had fallen prey to the *Edward*, said that "from the very defective manner in which they were fitted, being in want of almost every article of stores, it is supposed they are brigands of St. Domingo."[33] By calling the sailors "brigands" (treacherous thieves), clinging to the old name of Saint-Domingue, and assuming that everything emanating from Haiti was disorderly and defective, the Kingston gazetteers denied the legitimacy of Haitian independence, the legality of Haitian privateering, and the ability of former slaves to wage maritime warfare effectively.

During the War of 1812 between the United States and Great Britain, the British accused Haiti of harboring US privateers, whom they called "marauders," a word that became popular in the English language at this time as a term for soldiers who raided for booty.[34] The Jamaican press also reported on the actions of privateers sponsored by Cartagena over roughly the same period (1813–1815). Kingston gazetteers characterized the crew of the Cartagenan privateer *Kingston Packet* as a "band of desperados."[35] Borrowed from the Spanish language, the word *desperado* became popular in English after around 1750, referring to someone seen as "desperate, furious, without fear of danger or consequences."[36]

Negative descriptions of privateers became part of a larger set of derogatory notions deployed by outsiders to depict Haiti as a whole. Individuals who feared that the Haitian Revolution would have grave consequences for their own societies demonized Haiti, its people, and its recent history. In Cartagena, with Spanish officials preoccupied with the arrival of ideas of liberty and disobedience, merchants and slaveholders also fell to scaremongering. José Ignacio de Pombo, who had trained as a lawyer, was one of the most successful merchants in Cartagena and a leading member of the local political and business elite. Around March 1804, Pombo wrote that "sixty thousand brave Frenchmen, able to conquer any Kingdom in

Europe," had been the victims of the "law of the Saint-Domingue Negroes."[37] Referring to the defeat of France's armies by the forces who had founded Haiti, Pombo posited that this state of affairs in the Antilles had to be regarded as a lesson for slaveholders in Spanish territories.

In Pombo's view, the triumph of the former slaves in Haiti seemed to announce a turbulent future for people like him—free, white, and well-off. He claimed that the new Haiti could be impossible to destroy and would soon turn people of European descent throughout the Americas into its "tributaries." The implication was that Haiti would achieve a political power beyond its merit, exercising vengeful influence abroad. Considering that Pombo saw black people as "our most irreconcilable of enemies," it comes as no surprise that he would make such claims. Moreover, it seems almost natural that, just a few years later, he would distance himself from radical revolutionaries in Cartagena who proved willing to welcome foreign people of color in their port town.[38]

Cartagena had barely remained immune to the political and economic crisis that began in earnest in the early 1790s. Slaves, former slaves, and sailors of color had arrived from the French Caribbean in the wake of the Haitian Revolution; the governor had foiled a plot allegedly led by "French Negroes"; and magistrates and other white inhabitants had displayed a growing sense of alarm about these developments. The next challenge materialized after Napoleon Bonaparte's invasion of Spain in the spring of 1808. With the mother country in deep turmoil, a window of opportunity was thrown open for people in Cartagena to push for political reforms and independence. Cartagena would soon become a republic with egalitarian aspirations and a privateering policy equal to the task. Foreign seamen too would play a key role in unraveling over three centuries of Spanish government in Tierra Firme.

3

Cartagena de Indias and the Age of Revolutions

IN 1533, SPANISH conquistador Pedro de Heredia and his followers found a strategically located and well-protected bay on the northern coast of South America. It seemed like the perfect base from which to launch raids on vulnerable indigenous communities whose gold posed an irresistible temptation. Spaniards settled on the spot and named their new town Cartagena de Indias. A military outpost with two hundred people living in a few thatched huts, this settlement would grow into a prominent city. By 1611, Cartagena had become a crucial pivot in transatlantic trade, a stronghold in the Spanish defense against foreign encroachment in the Caribbean, and the seat of several Iberian institutions, including an Inquisition tribunal.[1]

Spanish authorities gradually fortified Cartagena, enclosing the city with walls, bastions, and forts. Loyal to the Spanish monarchy for generations, Cartagena's inhabitants, rich and poor, celebrated the births of princes and princesses, the deaths of kings, and the wartime triumphs of Spain against its enemies.[2] The city itself withstood attack from the French and British no less than six times between 1543 and 1741. But the legitimacy of the Spanish monarchy slowly eroded, and Cartagena's conflict of interests with the viceregal capital, Santa Fe, as well as its domestic tensions, intensified across the 1700s.

Santa Fe and Cartagena were the two most important cities in the New Kingdom of Granada. The capital city since 1550 and the viceregal court since 1739, Santa Fe was home to the highest justice tribunals and top administrative offices and educational institutions. Cartagena, with its coastal location and strategic character, was home to the most significant military garrison. It was the capital of one of the largest provinces (also named Cartagena, with about 120,000 inhabitants in 1780) and had a dynamic and rapidly growing merchant sector. The local merchants, however, found little political space to promote their own initiatives. Merchants and bureaucrats from Santa Fe strictly regulated Cartagena's trade with foreign ports, imposing limits on other enterprises too. By 1795, leading merchants were intensely lobbying viceregal and metropolitan authorities to expand free trade policies and foster economic growth.[3]

Cartagena's merchants were not the only residents anxious for change at the turn of the century. Free artisans of color, a group that had also recently expanded, held strong aspirations of their own. Although some artisans could potentially afford education at colleges and universities for their children, their status as people of African descent—with slave ancestors, slave relatives, and the stigma of presumed illegitimate birth—prevented them from getting academic degrees, much less becoming priests or holding political office.[4] Elites' anxieties about people of color pushing for privileges intensified following the Haitian Revolution, with its real and imaginary effects on Tierra Firme.[5]

It was Napoleon Bonaparte's 1808 invasion of the Iberian Peninsula that accelerated demands for economic, political, and social change. Well positioned to take advantage of the ongoing Spanish troubles, Cartagenan merchants declared that the "crumbling" edifice of the Spanish monarchy could be saved only by opening the ports to trade with "all friend and neutral nations of the Americas."[6] As authorities continued to reject full-out free trade policies, the merchants simply began to defy commercial regulations in 1809.

following page:
Figure 2. A Plan of the City of Carthagena,
1772. By John Andrews. Courtesy of
Biblioteca Luis Ángel Arango (Bogotá).

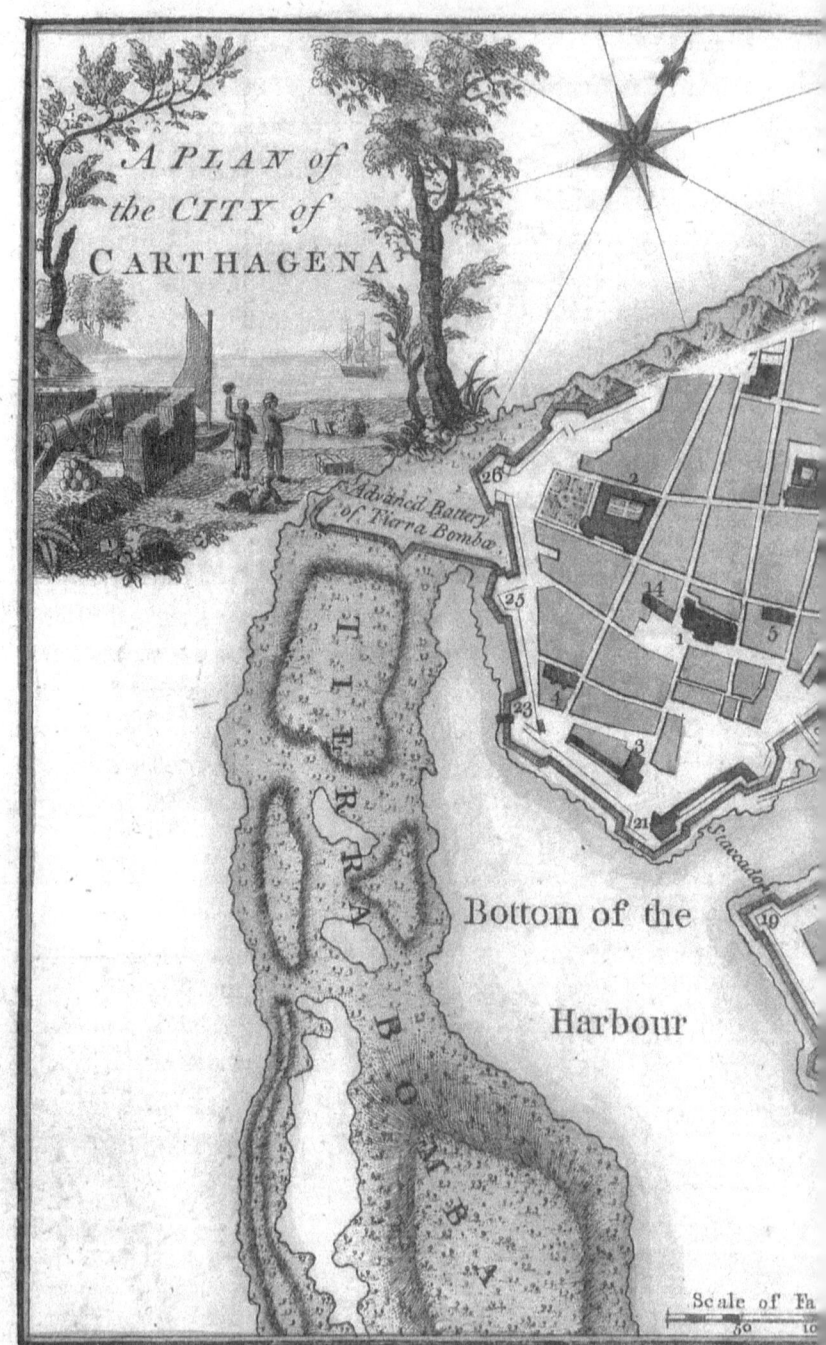

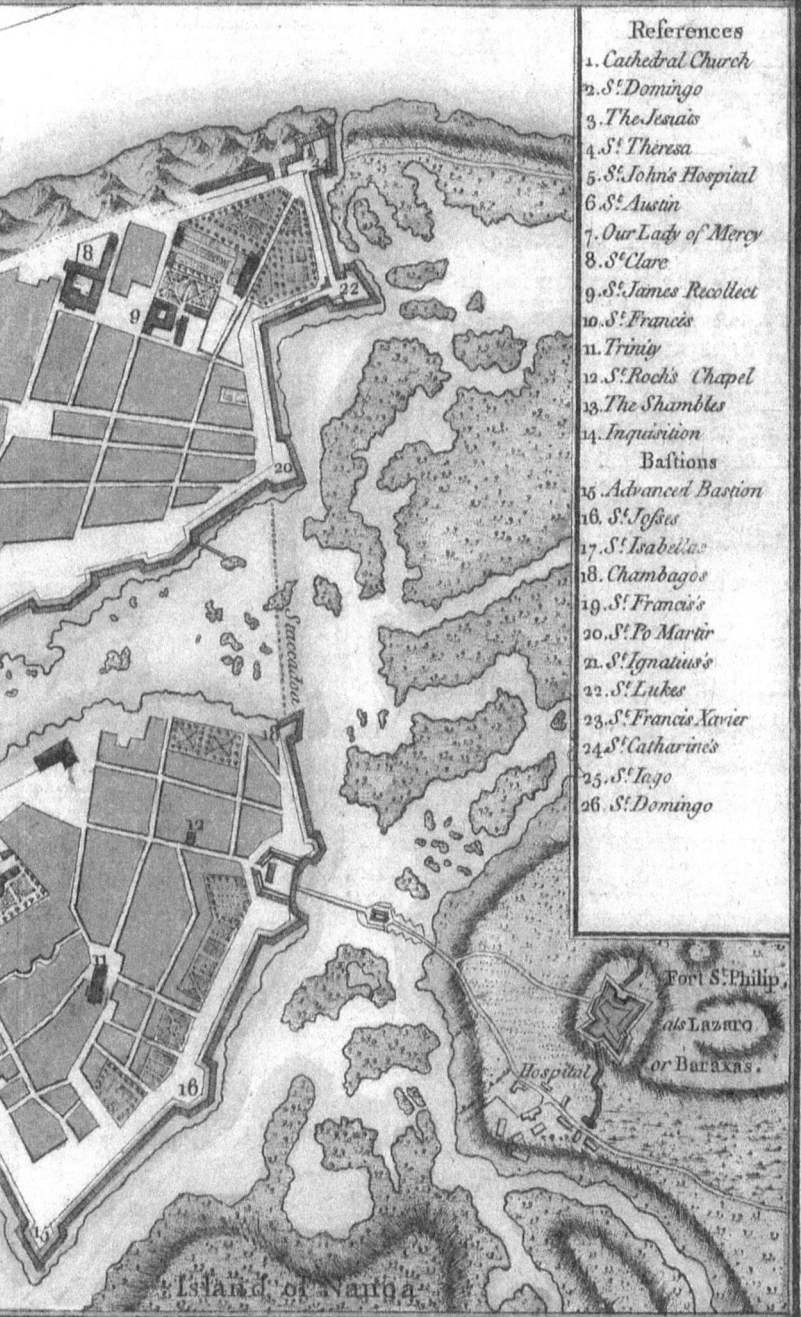

Merchants and their allies even staged a coup against the Spanish governor in mid-1810, but refused to declare independence from Spain, seeking to safeguard and increase their social and economic privileges as Spaniards.

The maneuvers against the Spanish governor took place with the vital support of free people of color and artisan leaders. These commoners, however, recognized that the merchants' agenda would neither meet their expectations nor end discrimination. Free people of color thus formed an alliance with more liberal patricians, and together they pushed the revolutionary process into a new, radical direction. On November 11, 1811, they forced the autonomous government to declare absolute independence.[7]

Over the following months, radical leaders would consolidate the State of Cartagena, an independent republic governed by a liberal constitution. This constitution abolished the old privileges, upholding the principle of legal equality for male residents and welcoming foreigners, people of color included, who wished to reside in Cartagena and obtain Cartagenan citizenship.[8] Along with growing trade and other maritime international connections, this open-door policy attracted scores of newcomers, including privateering outfitters and Afro-Caribbean sailors. Radicals had laid the basis for independence from Spain, facilitating in the process the arrival of outsiders who would allow them to mount a maritime defense of their social and political achievements on land.

FOLLOWING BONAPARTE'S INVASION of the Iberian Peninsula in the spring of 1808, a crisis of sovereignty profoundly shook the Spanish world. Napoleon pressured the Spanish king to abdicate the throne, installing his brother Joseph Bonaparte as the new monarch. But scores of Spaniards rose up against the French, pledging allegiance to the deposed Ferdinand VII, now Napoleon's captive in a French castle. Mutinies began on April 18 in the city of Burgos. Starting on May 24, local elites across Spain formed self-governing bodies known as *juntas* to rule in the name of the absent king, coordinating resistance against the French and managing internal political affairs.[9]

Across the Atlantic, authorities in Tierra Firme tried in vain to prevent news of developments in Spain from spreading throughout their jurisdictions.[10] Many subjects soon realized the gravity of the situation, refusing to recognize Joseph Bonaparte as their monarch. What the next step should be, however, was not altogether clear. Even viceregal authorities in Santa Fe hesitated to make firm determinations, unintentionally providing room for local officials elsewhere to make their own decisions. In this context of uncertainty, provincial governors, members of city councils, and other elites responded in diverse ways, many of them acting only in defense of their own interests. A variety of possible solutions would emerge as fresh reports arrived from Spain.[11]

In Cartagena, merchants would take advantage of the unusual situation to push their agenda for economic reform. Cartagena's merchants resented elites and viceregal authorities from Santa Fe for enforcing policies that prevented them from doing business in non-Spanish countries, or allowed them to do so only in exceptional circumstances. Cartagena's merchants also faced increasing competition from smugglers along the coast of Tierra Firme, whose illegal business seemed impossible to stop.[12] The merchants openly advocated for free trade with Jamaica and the United States, seeking access to cheaper goods, lower taxes, and more effective ways to undermine smuggling. They lobbied for authorization to import foreign cargo when warfare slowed down Spanish trading.[13]

Trade in flour, an essential good in a city of about twenty thousand people and dozens of bakeries, epitomized the clash between Santa Fe's central authorities and Cartagena's autonomist merchant sector. Leading families in Santa Fe who owned wheat-growing estates managed to force Cartagena merchants to buy flour from them. But this was expensive, poor-quality flour from wheat grown far off in the mountainous Andean interior, which took at best a month to arrive in Cartagena. By contrast, cheap barrels of fresh Pennsylvania flour were available for purchase in Jamaica. The trip by sea to this British island and back could be accomplished in less than ten days. Against Spanish regulations and directives from Santa Fe, some merchants from Cartagena secretly bought North American flour in Kingston, participating in the thriving smuggling business.[14]

While smuggling barrels of flour had previously occurred through complicated subterfuges at the docks, or under cover of night and in secret spots on shore far away from the city, smugglers and merchants felt emboldened in the wake of the Napoleonic crisis to defy regulations openly. On April 12, 1809, a Baltimore schooner carrying flour and other foodstuffs arrived in broad daylight, with no legal authorization. The *Hetty*'s consignee in Cartagena was the merchant Juan de Dios Amador. A member of the city council, a substantial taxpayer, and a relative by marriage to preeminent local businessman Pombo, Amador was truly a leading patrician.[15]

Amador was one of the most well-traveled and knowledgeable merchants in town. Following a trip to Spain as master of the *San José*—most likely a merchant ship belonging to or chartered by his father—Amador had lived in Barcelona during the early 1790s. He made a second trip to Europe later that decade, arriving back in Cartagena in December 1800. On his way home, Amador had stayed in Baltimore for several months, engaging in business transactions and most likely working on his English-language skills.[16] With contacts in Spain, the United States, and Jamaica, Amador was in a position to influence his colleagues, helping them emulate his new approach to trading openly with foreigners.

Over the weeks following the arrival of the *Hetty* in April 1809, other US merchant vessels continued to sail into Cartagena's harbor. In Santa Fe, the viceroy's reaction was no surprise. He ordered the transactions to stop, threatening Cartagenan merchants and bureaucrats with punishments and fines.[17] But the merchants controlled the city council and held sway over the customs officers and the acting provincial governor. On September 28, the governor actually au-

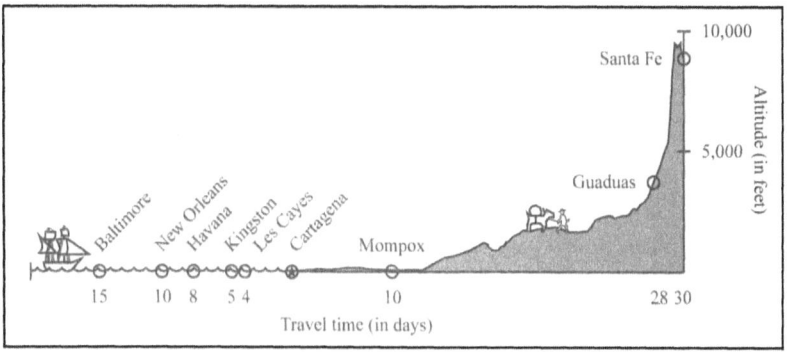

Figure 3. Travel Time and Elevation Profile relative to Cartagena. By Eric Schewe.

thorized trade with US ports and the importation of foodstuffs from non-Spanish places.[18] With this legally thin but effective endorsement of free trade, the merchants had scored a significant victory.

The situation, however, became more complicated the following year. By the end of April 1810, people in Cartagena learned that French forces had gained the upper hand in the Spanish conflict, with an improvised and seemingly illegitimate regency council as acting sovereign. Although it remained impossible to tell to what extent the regency could command respect and bestow authority, Cartagena's new governor, Francisco Antonio de Montes, hastened to swear allegiance to this new governing body. Like Spanish bureaucrats and military commanders elsewhere, Montes probably feared that locals would take advantage of the regency's weakness and ambivalent standing to push for further reforms, home rule, or perhaps even independence. Members of the city council, on which merchants had representation, carefully raised their voices against Montes.[19]

Montes's fears were not altogether unwarranted. Cartagena's leading merchants formed a coalition with José María García de Toledo, a landowner and a city council member who enjoyed the respect of most local patricians.[20] Working to curtail the governor's authority, Toledo's coalition gradually took over local public affairs and most of the province's administrative business. The governor did not hesitate to call these developments a "revolution," even trying to enlist the help of British authorities in Jamaica to thwart the movement. But Toledo and his allies finally deposed Governor Montes on June 14, 1810.[21]

The coup against Montes had important military and political implications. Toledo's coalition now controlled Cartagena's military garrison, the most important Spanish stronghold in Tierra Firme. In the past, central authorities in Santa Fe had deployed soldiers from the Cartagena garrison to the interior of the viceroyalty to quell unrest or suppress insurrection. Toledo's control of this force, therefore, left the viceroy and other high-ranking administrators unable to enforce their authority.[22] Local elites in several towns now felt free to strike without fear of military repression, establishing autonomous governments, deposing the incumbent authorities, or otherwise curtailing their power. By the end of July, autonomist leaders in Santa Fe had formed their own junta, deposing the viceroy himself. Nobody came to his rescue. The entire viceroyalty and neighboring Venezuela were in turmoil.[23]

These changes in government throughout Tierra Firme were not a centrally coordinated movement but rather a series of atomized revolutions. Caracas had set up a junta on April 19, 1810. Thirty-seven towns followed suit between April 1810 and June 1811. Fractured into multiple sovereignties resulting from disparate provincial revolutions, Tierra Firme would mutate, between 1811 and 1815, into several independent states. Cartagena became one of these autonomous polities. These states interacted with one another, signing agreements of amity and commerce or waging war. They also experienced internal conflicts.[24]

The mutation of Cartagena from Spanish province into independent republic took place gradually. At first, Toledo's coalition shied away from declaring absolute independence from Spain. Conservative merchants feared that independence would bring the local economy to a halt. Cartagena's economic dynamism was propelled in part by its public budget, and over half of this budget came from an annual subsidy that Spain required other provinces to deliver to Cartagena. This money, or letters of credit later paid by the subsidy, was used to pay soldiers, officers, bureaucrats, and artisans on the public payroll, who in turn used it to pay for different goods and services. Most of the money thus eventually ended up in merchants' pockets. If Spain managed to liberate itself from the French, merchants could potentially gain access to free trade in exchange for continuing their political allegiance while keeping the earnings from the subsidy. However, when subsidy-paying provinces turned into autonomous polities, their leaders refused to continue to allocate money for Cartagena. The subsidy would all but disappear by the end of 1814.[25]

Uncertainty about risks to their patrician standing was yet another reason that conservative leaders rejected absolute independence for Cartagena. Toledo's coalition aspired to obtain home rule while leaving the social hierarchy intact. Under Toledo's plan, the historical privileges enjoyed by Spaniards and people of Spanish descent would continue to exist, keeping poor people and families of African descent out of local and provincial government, and giving no redress to slaves, of whom there were over two thousand in town and about eight thousand in the rest of the province. But artisans of color and a few radical white patrician allies were developing different plans. They would push the revolutionary process into a radical direction, preparing the ground for Cartagena's social transformation and its engagement with foreign revolutionaries, adventurers, and scores of Afro-Caribbean sailors working as privateers.

IN THE DECADES leading up to 1810, Cartagena's artisans (masons, bricklayers, carpenters, blacksmiths, coopers, tailors, seamstresses, bakers, sculptors, painters, goldsmiths, and silversmiths) had benefited from the public budget. They had built and maintained walls and bastions, mended soldiers' uniforms, cooked for officers and bureaucrats, and manufactured and repaired jewelry for the rich, as well as sacred art for the churches and chapels in town. But local patricians had allowed them little to no voice in politics, and Spanish regulations had kept them from attending colleges and universities. Even those who had entered the militias, showcasing their loyalty to Spain, rarely became officers. Outspokenly building on their military status and economic relevance, however, they started to claim, if not equality for all, privileges for people of color who had some standing.[26]

In spite of their commitment to the hierarchy, Toledo and other conservative leaders understood that they could not aspire to true control of Cartagena without support from the artisans and the urban poor, whose social and demographic relevance could not be ignored, especially because crowd action was an effective tool. Toledo had already turned to commoners and their leaders to back his maneuvers against Governor Montes. Pedro Romero, a blacksmith of color, had effectively deployed his influence with the artisans and other plebeians by organizing a mutiny against Montes. On June 19, 1810, Toledo ordered the raising of two militias, one white and one of color, known as the Patriotic Volunteers. Toledo and Romero coordinated the volunteers of African descent, mostly artisans who lived in Getsemaní, a neighborhood just outside of the city's main precinct with access to the bay and the docks. Romero took the rank of colonel.[27]

Conservative patrician leaders, however, continued to oppose the political aspirations of Romero and other commoners. After they received news of the juntas in Spain and across Tierra Firme, beginning in April 1810, commoners favored the creation of a similar governing body in Cartagena, seeking to open up spaces for emerging voices. By contrast, Toledo had favored simply replacing the Spanish governor with government by local notables. Aware of their own strength, artisans and the urban poor began to demand the establishment of a junta in which city commoners, as well as rural inhabitants, would be represented. Popular pressure prevailed, and a local junta was formed on August 14, 1810.[28]

The Cartagena junta, however, proved unable to reconcile the opposing agendas of patricians and plebeians. The junta could not even stop the internal friction within Toledo's group, as *peninsulares* (people born in Spain) and *criollos* (people of Spanish descent born in the Americas) came to blows. In early February 1811, an alleged conspiracy to overthrow the junta was discovered.[29] With individuals born in Spain singled out as traitors, most peninsulares left the city for Santa Marta, a port town to the north of Cartagena. Aware that Toledo had allowed the conspirators to leave the city freely, artisans, soldiers, and other commoners lost the little confidence they had in him, expressing their resentment of "European Spaniards" and local "aristocrats." The tensions between the shrinking white elite and free people of color became more evident.[30]

Animosity against Toledo's remaining conservative allies reached a climax in late October and early November 1811, when news came from the Cortes of Cádiz, a national assembly in Spain formed to fix the troubled monarchy. To the great dismay of people of color, the Cortes had decreed that no person of African ancestry was worthy of Spanish citizenship or the right to vote. This was a tremendous blow for people of color, who now contemplated whether absolute independence from Spain was the only way to advance their own struggle for political standing.[31]

As their outlook radicalized, Romero and other leaders found new allies among the ranks of the patricians. A man of egalitarian and anti-Spanish convictions, the merchant Gabriel Gutiérrez de Piñeres, working in tandem with his brothers, came forward as a supporter of privileges for people of color and of independence from Spain. Drastic in its opposition to Spain and outspoken in its critique of Toledo's conservative approach, this coalition decided it was time to take the revolution to its logical conclusion.[32]

Piñeres, Romero, and their allies made their move on November 11, 1811. After taking over the armory and securing control of the city, Romero and other leaders, along with a crowd of armed men and women, marched on the governor's palace, where the junta was in session. Under threat from the crowd, junta members yielded to the demand for a declaration of absolute independence from Spain. The junta signed a declaration stating that Cartagena, by right and in fact, was a "free State, sovereign and independent," with all the privileges of "free and independent nations."[33] The radicals had triumphed and Cartagena was now poised for true revolutionary action. Cartagena was about to be transformed into an egalitarian republic with increasing maritime connections, including transactions with privateering sailors active in Caribbean and Atlantic waters.

IN THE WAKE of the unprecedented events of November 1811, the radicals hurried to build a new political system for Cartagena. Elections were held and a constituent assembly formed in early 1812. Free people of color voted, obtaining representation in the assembly. Romero, along with other individuals of mixed African and European ancestry historically denied the right to participate in government, became legislators. Romero's son, Mauricio José Romero, joined the government as commissioner of "public health."[34] These leaders would put their imprint on the emerging new State, fostering legal equality for people of color. They would even welcome to Cartagena foreigners of color, including so-called French Negroes, whom Spanish bureaucrats and many local notables had so fervently despised in the recent past.

On June 14, 1812, the constituent assembly approved a political charter, formally establishing the State of Cartagena. Although pro-independence criollos participated in the drafting of the Constitution, it was the leaders of color who pushed for its most radical principles. A "representative republic" administered by three separate branches of government, the State of Cartagena recognized no corporate, inherited, or aristocratic privileges, declaring "the idea of legal equality" as "right, just, and natural." All male free citizens, regardless of color or social background, would now be equal before the law.[35]

Figure 4. Seal of the State of Cartagena de Indias, 1812.
Courtesy of Archivo General de la Nación (Bogotá).

Besides a strongly articulated idea of legal equality, other principles also made the Constitution of Cartagena the most original and radical among the several constitutions drafted in Tierra Firme during these years.[36] The 1812 charter abolished the slave trade to Cartagena, though it did not abolish slavery itself. Slaveholding patricians like Toledo, who was a member of the assembly, very likely pushed against proposals for the abolition of slavery. The assembly, however, did order the government to consider the use of public funds for the gradual manumission of slaves, obliquely supporting the idea that slavery should eventually disappear altogether.[37]

The Constitution abolished the Inquisition, which had been in place in Cartagena for two hundred years. Besides enforcing Catholic orthodoxy, the Inquisition had also policed ideological and political affairs on behalf of the Spanish crown, preventing the circulation and reading of so-called "prohibited books."[38] It had also censored works written by local people and, in collaboration with Spanish officials and authorities in Santa Fe, prevented Cartagenan merchants from operating a printing press for business purposes. After the end of the Inquisition, Cartagena witnessed a surge in printing activity. Between 1811 and 1815, at least two printing workshops operated in the city. No fewer than six newspapers circulated in independent Cartagena.[39]

Finally, the Constitution of 1812 achieved a change in policy that would help attract immigrants to the new State. While the Spanish government had always tried to exclude foreigners from its territories, most recently banishing French-speaking people in the wake of the French and Haitian Revolutions, the Constitution expressly allowed the "admission and settling of foreigners" in the State of Cartagena. As long as they practiced a trade or established a useful "industry," outsiders were free to move in, to set up shop, and even to become naturalized citizens.[40] By 1814, the city would be teeming with sailors from Haiti, revolutionaries from Venezuela and France, adventurers and merchants from the United States, businessmen from Jamaica, and refugees and émigrés from all across Tierra Firme and the Caribbean.[41]

Trade with ally and neutral ships showed clear signs of growth soon after Cartagena established its welcoming policies. In 1813 alone, seventy foreign ships dropped anchor in the Bay of Cartagena. Meanwhile, Cartagena's own fleet multiplied from about five vessels operating in 1809 to sixty-nine by the end of 1813. Merchant ships visiting Cartagena were registered in British, French, Portuguese, Swedish, Haitian, and US port towns. Even two large naval frigates stopped in Cartagena in 1813—one Prussian, the other French.[42]

While trade with the British and contact with Jamaica were particularly robust, trade with the United States was also significant.[43] Some Cartagenan merchants traded with colleagues in Baltimore. Notarial documents and press reports from New Orleans show that commerce also occurred between Louisiana and Cartagena. Ready to depart from New Orleans on April 10, 1813, the sloop *Joanna* planned an itinerary that would take her first to Les Cayes, in Haiti, and then to Cartagena. The merchant ship *Hamilton*, commanded by Captain Thomas Barret, was registered in Cartagena and made trips to Haiti and New Orleans. Bertrand Casterés, a resident of New Orleans, owned and captained the schooner *Revenge*. Laden with foodstuffs, she set sail for Cartagena in the fall of 1813. The Cartagena merchant schooner *Mulita* (Little Mule) departed for New Orleans on July 9, 1814.[44]

Both for economic and political reasons, some pro-independence merchants and political leaders showed enormous appreciation for Cartagena's growing trade with the United States. Commercial contact with US citizens may have embodied an ideological link with a republic worthy of emulation—one that could even become a natural ally. Cartagenan leaders fantasized about the United States, with its storied American Revolution, famous founding documents, and liberal institutions, picturing it as the protector of their independent republic. Moreover, with the arrival of US privateers in Cartagena in mid-1812, the American connection expedited the consolidation of yet another radical project, the establishment of Cartagena's own privateering policy.

4

The American Connection

ON OCTOBER 29, 1812, the US merchant schooner *Caroline* set sail from Cartagena to Baltimore. As had already become usual for ships bound for North America, the *Caroline* carried both merchandise and a few passengers. This time, one of the men on board, a Venezuelan lawyer named Manuel Palacio Fajardo, was leaving Cartagena on an important mission. An ardent fighter for Spanish American independence, Fajardo was traveling as a diplomatic envoy of the State of Cartagena to the United States. He had instructions to seek US government recognition of the independence of Cartagena, and to secure material help for the State, preferably in the form of guns and ammunition.[1]

Cartagena's plan to obtain help from the United States built on preexisting contacts with the American republic. Some of Cartagena's leaders admired the United States, sought to emulate its political and economic development, and actually had direct contact with that country, including with American merchants and privateers. Fajardo's mission, which would yield only partial results, was nevertheless built on Cartagena's tangible American connection. Even before Cartagena's revolutionary transformations and declaration of independence, some of the most cosmopolitan members of the local elite felt enthusiastic about the Anglo-American world. The well-traveled merchant Juan de Dios Amador, the foremost local expert on US affairs, engaged in trade with the United States and thought of the American republic as the ideal political model for Tierra Firme. He belonged to a sector of the merchant elite with growing pro-independence feelings.[2]

Crucial political and economic considerations underpinned excitement about the United States in Cartagena, as well as the expectation of American support for the State. First, after the atomized revolutions that broke up the viceroyalty between 1810 and 1811, Cartagena's leaders promoted US-inspired federalism as a means of re-aggregating the now-independent provinces into a larger polity. Cartagenan leaders hoped that this approach would neutralize Santa Fe, where the old elite expected to lead a new but still highly centralized government. Revolutionary Cartagena advocated for and indeed helped materialize the idea of a union of autonomous provinces modelled after the United States. Second, as Cartagena's military defense drained the public treasury, the government took the bold step of establishing a privateering policy, issuing letters of marque to outfitters willing to attack Spanish shipping on its behalf. The American connection was crucial in this regard too, for it was US privateers who first proved ready to utilize letters of marque from Cartagena.[3]

The intersection between US and Cartagena privateering was somewhat coincidental. US merchants had begun to visit Cartagena openly as early as 1809. But in the late summer of 1812, US privateers began to visit too. In June of that year, the United States declared war on Great Britain, sparking US privateering in the Caribbean. Privateersmen operating out of port towns like Baltimore and Charleston sailed to the Bay of Cartagena, where the revolutionary government allowed them to refit, resupply, and launch their hunts for British-flagged ships. Seamen operating as privateers on behalf of the United States probably helped inspire Cartagena's privateering venture. Moreover, the diplomatic agent Fajardo had instructions to issue letters of marque in US ports now teeming with privateers.[4]

Nevertheless, American privateers would soon be replaced by privateersmen of other nationalities. The presence of Haitian sailors (who worked on US as well as Cartagenan privateers) quickly expanded, along with that of French and French Caribbean officers and outfitters. The Parisian Aury and his Haitian crewmen would become emblematic of the French and French Caribbean presence aboard Cartagenan privateers, yet Aury's association with Tierra Firme also began to materialize at this time, thanks to the American connection. He was first recruited on behalf of Cartagena in the United States, where he took one of the letters of marque brought to Baltimore by Fajardo.[5]

While Cartagena revolutionaries had a somewhat romanticized perception of the American Revolution and the early republic, the United States, US citizens, and US-flagged ships did inspire and would directly influence the development of the State of Cartagena. Cartagena's most radical stances, from its declaration of absolute independence to its federalism and privateering tactic, were shot through with references to the United States and intricately linked with American citizens and other individuals on US soil. Independent Cartagena also resembled the United States in its extension of citizenship to maritime personnel, including sailors of color.[6] Although this policy largely served the pragmatic and legal exigencies of privateering, the contrast with Cartagena's very recent past was not negligible, as political belonging had been largely restricted to Spanish subjects before independence.

THE HISTORY OF the United States and its early republican institutions became key paradigms among some members of the Cartagena elite. Still remembered in the early 1800s, the American Revolution operated as something of a model for anti-colonial struggle. Local patricians also praised the United States' economic policies and federal political system. The American republic seemed to provide an ideal blueprint for the future development of independent Tierra Firme. Although he did not favor absolute independence from Spain, the merchant Pombo extolled US economic policies. He was relatively well informed about US affairs from reading works by Thomas Jefferson and reports to the US Congress by Albert Gallatin, a successful New York merchant and the secretary of the treasury from 1801 to 1814. Pombo wanted Cartagena to build direct contacts with the United States. It was important to draw inspiration from the republic of the North, but Pombo also wished to extend to white American citizens the warm welcome previously denied to them in Cartagena.⁷

Amador, who happened to be Pombo's brother-in-law and who sided with the pro-independence sympathizers, had even stronger links with the United States, more forcefully embodying the American connection. Amador spoke English and maintained direct trading relationships with merchants in New Orleans and with Baltimore merchant John McFadon, who had outfitted the *Hetty*, the first ship to defy Spanish regulations openly, in 1809.⁸ Amador had probably met McFadon during his stay in Baltimore. From McFadon, Amador received not only merchandise but also books for his own use and for sale to others. Amador sometimes forwarded these books to yet a third US enthusiast in his extended family, Miguel de Pombo y Pombo. In a personal letter to Miguel, dated July 30, 1811, just a few months before Cartagena's declaration of independence, Amador wrote that nothing short of a federal political system "could make these provinces flourish, build their happiness," and "gather their strength."⁹

Amador and Miguel's commitment to US-inspired policies took the shape of specific intellectual and political projects. In his mid-1811 letter, Amador promised to personally distribute a Spanish translation of the US foundational documents that Miguel was about to complete. This translation, published as a book in December 1811, included Spanish versions of the American Declaration of Independence (1776), the American Articles of Confederation and Perpetual Union (1777), and the US Constitution (1787). By May 1812, Amador had received twenty-eight copies of the book. These were presumably sold to other merchants and US enthusiasts in Cartagena.¹⁰

Pushing against the centralizing projects of their historical enemies in Santa Fe, the leaders of independent Cartagena found US political culture particularly useful. Each state of the American union was its own country, people like Amador reasoned, and perhaps the old Spanish provinces of Tierra Firme could move in a similar direction, becoming independent entities. He also felt, however, that these small republics should be bound up in a larger sovereign polity capable of raising armies to keep foreign domination at bay. In his letter to Miguel, who was originally from the southern province of Popayán, Amador specifically invoked the North American example. He hoped, Amador told Miguel, to see Popayán "free of tyrants so that it can become the Pennsylvania or the Virginia of our Federation."[11]

Drawing on the model of the United States, rather than on Spanish institutions and legal principles alone, Cartagena's leaders quickly positioned themselves as the political vanguard of Tierra Firme during the early struggle for independence. On September 19, 1810, to counteract the efforts by centralists seeking to reunite the fractured viceroyalty under Santa Fe government, the Cartagena junta had invited other provinces across Tierra Firme to a general congress. The junta hoped that this institution would in turn install a "federative system" of government. Independent from outside political influence and free of despotism, each province would have the autonomy to pass its own laws, establish its own justice tribunals, and build its prosperity. On November 27, 1811, representatives from Antioquia, Cartagena, Neiva, Pamplona, and Tunja signed an Act of Federation, establishing the United Provinces of New Granada. Other provinces joined the federation in 1812.[12]

Following plans first developed and debated in Cartagena, local and provincial elites elsewhere in Tierra Firme thus came together to form a sovereign entity broadly based on the example of the United States. Cartagena's American connection, however, was underpinned not just by emulation and adaptation, but also by actual commercial and political contact, setting it apart from its sister provinces. US citizens set up residence in Cartagena soon after its independence. People moving back and forth between Cartagena and places like Baltimore and Philadelphia helped establish relatively strong links between North America and Tierra Firme. Besides Amador and his associates, other individuals embodied this connection as well. On US Independence Day in 1812, aboard the merchant schooner *Caroline*, some of these individuals ritualized the political bond between the United States and the State of Cartagena in a public ceremony.

This civic festival commemorating the independence of the United States, most likely the first of its kind in South America, was presided over by a US citizen. He celebrated the memory of George Washington, toasting the government of his country, the US Constitution, and the cause of "freedom all over the world." In typical

Figure 5. The United Provinces of New Granada, 1812. By Eric Schewe. Adapted from Daniel Gutiérrez Ardila, *Un Nuevo Reino: Geografía política, pactismo y diplomacia durante el interregno en Nueva Granada (1808–1816)* (Bogotá: Universidad Externado de Colombia, 2010), 291, map 11. Courtesy of the author.

fashion, he toasted "our kind countrywomen," lamenting that distance was presently depriving him of "the pleasure of their charms." The locals toasted Benjamin Franklin, Tom Paine, and Thomas Jefferson, and honored "the first representatives sent to Philadelphia by the Northern Provinces." In a poem commissioned for the occasion, a local writer expressed Cartagena's hopes of growing in prosperity with the protection and friendship of the United States.[13]

The presence of US seafarers in Cartagena increased after the United States declared war on Great Britain in mid-June 1812.[14] This conflict, the War of 1812, which would last until 1815, led to an expansion of privateering activity in the Caribbean. US privateers came to regard Cartagena as an ideal spot from which to launch their aggressions on British shipping. Tierra Firme's shores had become an important destination for British merchant ships after the American Revolution, and commerce between Tierra Firme and Jamaica had grown, thanks to Cartagena's free trade policies. Furthermore, independent Cartagena allowed US privateers to enter the bay to refit and purchase provisions.[15]

Armed American schooners and their crews, which included sailors from places like Haiti, became relatively commonplace in Cartagena. In early 1813, four such vessels could be seen at anchor in the bay, with their men surely visiting inns and taverns in town. The schooners were the *Snap Dragon*, with a crew of ninety; the *Two Brothers*, recently arrived from Les Cayes with seventy-five men on board; the *Lady Madison*, with a company of forty-five sailors; and the *Saratoga*, which had arrived in Cartagena to refit after being damaged in an engagement with the *Raquel*, near La Guaira.[16] Cartagena's president Manuel Rodríguez Torices, vice-president Gabriel Gutiérrez de Piñeres, and their colleagues realized that they could hire US privateers to work on their behalf.[17] The American connection would turn out to be essential in the conception and launch of Cartagena's privateering policy, which was perhaps the State's most radical move against Spain after declaring independence.

AT THE TIME that it declared independence, Cartagena had no navy of its own and very limited control over seagoing vessels and maritime personnel under its jurisdiction. Although Spain had stationed a naval commander in Cartagena, deploying a small fleet known as the *guardacostas* to keep contraband traders off the coasts of Tierra Firme, most of the defense budget went to the army. A large and costly defense infrastructure—walls, bastions, and batteries—made Cartagena a stronghold, but one that lacked a substantial and effective seafaring force in spite of its strategic coastal location. To guarantee that inhabitants of Cartagena working in the fishing and coastal maritime trades would be available for service in times of naval warfare, Spain had established a recruitment system known as the *matrícula de mar* in 1779. This policy failed to enforce conscription meaningfully.[18]

Moreover, Cartagena's elites worried that sea captains from neighboring port towns or operating in secret landings could more effectively carry out smuggling activities and even legal trade with places like Jamaica. In 1808, Cartagena merchants reported, inaccurately, that the viceroyalty could not deploy a significant merchant fleet. The four viceregal port towns (Riohacha, Santa Marta, Cartagena, and Portobelo) together had only ten vessels at best, most of them small schooners and bilanders. Merchants also complained that local maritime personnel lacked the "art" for sailing these ships efficiently.[19] But coastal trading and smuggling were prevalent along the coast, with both local and foreign maritime workers connecting Tierra Firme to the outside world. Cartagena's elites and authorities were in no position to control those sailors.[20]

Without a reliable source of seafarers, the State of Cartagena, and by extension the larger polity of the United Provinces of New Granada, was unable to enact maritime defense tactics, let alone maritime attacks on Spanish forces. This was a serious strategic concern for revolutionaries. As the most important stronghold on the Caribbean shore, Cartagena was considered the key to Tierra

Firme—and, indeed, to all of Spanish South America. It had to be defended at all costs for the sake of revolution there and elsewhere.

Unfortunately for pro-independence forces, the risk of counter-revolutionary royalist attacks emanated not from the Iberian Peninsula—engaged in a war against the French occupation—but from three close neighboring enclaves still under the control of Spanish authorities. First, many of the merchants and military officers who left Cartagena after independence, most of them peninsulares, had relocated to Santa Marta, Cartagena's immediate neighbor to the north, contributing to growing pro-Spanish sentiment there.[21] Second, exiled viceregal authorities from Santa Fe had relocated to nearby Panama. Royalist forces in Panama and Santa Marta kept in communication, coordinating seaborne and overland attacks on Cartagena. Finally, pro-Spanish forces controlled Cuba throughout the crisis, with Spanish authorities on the island coordinating their anti-revolutionary efforts with royalists in Tierra Firme.[22]

All but encircled by hostile forces, Cartagena soon had to face battle. After May 1811, Cartagena's relationship with Santa Marta had deteriorated, leading to a low-intensity war that would drag into 1813, fought mostly along the Magdalena River—Cartagena's natural and political border with Santa Marta. Meanwhile, Spanish vessels harassed shipping and coastal trade into and out of Cartagena. To make matters worse, the conservative coalition led by José María García de Toledo regrouped in September 1812, launching an uprising in Cartagena's hinterland. Toledo and his rural allies took over the agricultural district known as the Tolú and Sinú plains, cutting off the city from food supplies for a few months. Lastly, the Santa Fe centralists did not join the United Provinces, creating instead their own polity, the Free and Independent State of Cundinamarca. Hostilities between Cundinamarca and the United Provinces broke out in December 1812.[23]

Financing the defense of Cartagena from internal and external enemies proved expensive. The war with Santa Marta further depleted an already shrinking budget. On the brink of economic and political catastrophe, and in dire need of cash and weapons, the newly born State of Cartagena needed both an effective tactic to undermine Spanish power and new sources of revenue.[24] When American privateers began showing up in the Bay of Cartagena in mid-1812, the outlines of possible cooperation became clear. Perhaps foreign seafarers could come to the rescue of Cartagena's political and financial fortunes. If Cartagena and the United Provinces were truly sovereign polities, then they had the right to sponsor armed ships to attack their enemies, achieving through private naval warfare the goals they could not accomplish through public means. The decision was reached by October 1812. Cartagena adopted a privateering policy, issuing its own letters of marque with the blessing of the United Provinces of New Granada.[25]

US privateers present in Cartagena were not only a source of inspiration for Cartagena's new policy, but also the first potential privateers to hear about it. Some of those privateers decided to switch from US-sponsored to Cartagena-sponsored privateering. Some captains and outfitters took Cartagena's letters of marque mainly because Cartagena allowed them to take a bigger share of the prize money. Moreover, the operations were comparably smoother and entailed less risk, as Spanish ships remained easier targets than the heavily guarded, more sophisticated British merchant fleet (their target under US colors).[26] Some captains even dared to combine commissions from the United States and Cartagena, which was illegal under international law. Such was the case of the *George Washington*, the first ship known to have received a privateering commission from Cartagena.[27]

A privateer schooner out of Norfolk, Virginia, the *George Washington* was commanded by Captain S. Sisson. While Sisson seems to have concentrated on anti-British privateering, he mainly cruised off the coast of Tierra Firme and eventually obtained a letter of marque from Cartagena. George Little, the first lieutenant on board this vessel, later wrote a memoir about "life on the ocean." Little claimed that Captain Sisson had planned to sail under either US or Cartagena colors, depending on whether a potential prize was British or Spanish. According to Little, the officers rejected this plan, as sailing under more than one flag, albeit a common practice among privateers, amounted to piracy. The captain, however, secretly took a Cartagena letter of marque and a Cartagena flag. Coming within sight of a Spanish schooner a few weeks later, Sisson produced the document and the flag, ordering his men to take the Spanish craft. Upon returning to Cartagena, Little and the second lieutenant demanded to be discharged with their share of the prize money. They walked away with 1,800 dollars each, which they used for the purchase of a coppered schooner. A few days later they sailed to New Orleans, taking cargo and passengers.[28]

At first, only a few of the existing US privateers seem to have been willing to take letters of marque from Cartagena. The State therefore decided to advertise its privateering policy directly in US port cities, hoping to attract seafarers and further utilizing its American connection. Manuel Palacio Fajardo, Cartagena's diplomatic envoy to the United States, was charged with the mission of recruiting privateers in places such as Baltimore and Philadelphia. When he left for the United States on board the *Caroline* at the end of October 1812, Fajardo carried with him blank letters of marque that he planned to fill out and issue to privateers interested in sailing under Cartagena colors.[29]

While in the United States, Fajardo came across lawyer Pedro Gual, yet another anti-Spanish agitator from Venezuela with contacts in Cartagena. Fajardo and Gual joined forces, managing to meet with Secretary of State James Monroe in December 1812. While Monroe declined to support the revolutions of Tierra Firme, Fajardo obtained permission from the French ambassador to travel to France and present his case in Paris.[30]

Holding onto the as-yet-unissued Cartagena letters of marque, Gual traveled to Baltimore, which was rapidly turning into a cen-

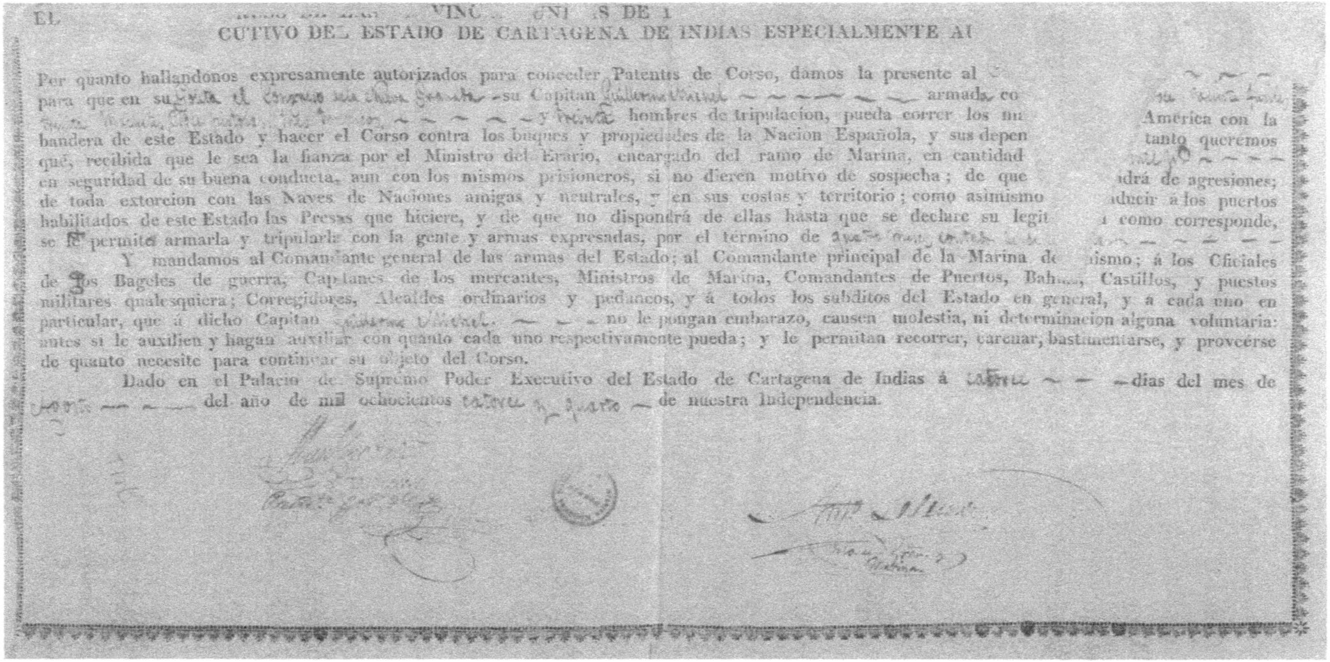

EL ———————— VINC————ÓNI——S DE 1————
CUTIVO DEL ESTADO DE CARTAGENA DE INDIAS ESPECIALMENTE AU————

Por quanto hallapdonos expresamente autorizados para conceder Patentes de Corso, damos la presente al ——————— para que en su————— el Cherres su ———— Sr—h—, su Capitán ———————— armada, co———— ————————— ————— ————y ———— hombres de tripulacion, pueda correr los ma—— bandera de este Estado y hacer el Corso contra los buques y propiedades de la Nación Española, y sus depen ———, recibida que le sea la fianza por el Ministro del Erario, encargado del ramo de Marina, en cantidad —drá de agresiones; en seguridad de su buena conducta, aun con los mismos prisioneros, si no dieren motivo de sospecha ; de que —ducir á los puertos de toda extorcion con las Naves de Naciones amigas y neutrales, y en sus costas y territorio: como asimismo ————— como corresponde, habilitados de este Estado las Presas que hiciere, y de que no dispondrá de ellas hasta que se declare su legit— se ——— permite armarla y tripularla con la gente y armas expresadas, por el término de dos —— ————— ————

Y mandamos al Comandante general de las armas del Estado, al Comandante principal de la Marina de —————ismo; á los Oficiales de sus Baxeles de guerra; Capitanes de los mercantes, Ministros de Marina, Comandantes de Puertos, Bah———, Castillos, y puestos militares qualesquiera; Corregidores, Alcaldes ordinarios y pedáneos, y á todos los súbditos del Estado, en general, y á cada uno en particular, que á dicho Capitán ————— ————— no le pongan embarazo, causen molestia, ni determinación alguna voluntaria: mates si le auxilien y hagan auxiliar con quanto cada uno respectivamente pueda; y le permitan recorrer, carenar, bastimentarse, y proveerse de quanto necesite para continuar su objeto del Corso.

Dado en el Palacio de Supremo Poder Executivo del Estado de Cartagena de Indias á ————— ——— dias del mes de ———— ——— del año de mil ochocientos catorce y 4.º ——— de nuestra Independencia.

Figure 6. Letter of Marque issued by the State of Cartagena, 1814. Courtesy of Archivo General de la Nación (Bogotá).

ter of anti-Spanish activity. Aury, who had previously encountered trouble in New Orleans, Savannah, and Charleston (as discussed in the Introduction), was also in town. Although US neutrality laws prohibited the outfitting of privateers in American ports, Aury had traveled to Baltimore with the hope of sailing again.[31] A proposal to work for Cartagena must have seemed to the ambitious Frenchman like a particularly well-timed opportunity to return to revolutionary privateering.

It was the spring of 1813 when Gual and Aury struck their deal. First, Gual filled out a letter of marque, authorizing Aury to sail the privateering ship *San Francisco de Paula* (formerly the *Whiting*) on behalf of Cartagena. Aury took a couple of prizes and then sailed south with Gual, arriving in Cartagena in May. By August, Aury had received a commission as commodore, the rank of ship captain with authority over a small flotilla.[32] As he would later tell his relatives in a letter from Cartagena, it had been by sheer chance that he had ended up in this South American "free province."[33] His attachment to Tierra Firme and the struggle for Spanish American independence, however, would grow through the following years.

Other privateers came from the United States to Cartagena in early 1813. The *Lady Madison*, a ship out of Charleston, South Carolina, operated originally under a US letter of marque, but eventually worked for Cartagena.[34] The *Kingston Packet* also sailed under Cartagena colors. Manned by "Americans, Frenchmen and Spaniards," she was owned and operated by Philips and Cohen, two colleagues of Captain Sisson.[35] Philips did not enjoy much luck as a privateer, or in any case did not persevere in the enterprise. He managed to capture only two prizes, leading him, according to a report from Kingston, to consider returning to his "old trade of turtling," the latter comment perhaps more mocking than accurate.[36]

Because Cartagena opened its doors to both British shipping and US privateering, incidents occurred that generated political tension. For the British, Cartagena seemed to be acting at cross-purposes by trading with Jamaica while at the same time facilitating attacks on vessels flying the colors of Great Britain or carrying British cargo. For example, the *Lady Madison* was a US privateer cruising in company with the *Eagle* out of Charleston and Les Cayes. These ships captured the *Catharina* and the *Portshire*. The *Catharina* had been registered in Cartagena and was sailing under a Cartagenan flag at the moment of her capture, but her captors likely knew that she belonged to British subjects.[37] Such operations underscore Cartagena's bold approach to free maritime activity out of its port, but they also confirm that Cartagena's authorities found it difficult to oversee and keep under control every single seagoing initiative in their jurisdiction.

While both British and Cartagenan officials tried to keep up an appearance of neutrality, some privateers simply played the game by their own rules, going rogue when they thought a gamble might pay off. The Cartagenan privateers who took the British schooner *Rover*, which had departed Kingston bound for India, are a good example. The privateers sacked the *Rover* and gave a beating to her captain. A Kingston press report on this episode sarcastically titled "Carthaginian respect for the British Flag" blamed the government of Cartagena for failing to provide restitution to the *Rover*'s captain. Hoping to file a claim and recover part of his losses, the captain traveled to Cartagena after the attack. However, the report claimed, "the satisfaction given was to pay for the plundered muskets, and let the master remain with his beating, as an equivalent for his detention, consequent expenses, and defeating the object of his voyage there."[38]

Another article published in Kingston similarly expressed British frustration, even suggesting that Cartagena's privateering could be construed as piracy. This time, the British complained that their flag had been insulted and British neutrality with regards to Cartagena disregarded when one of their merchant schooners, after leaving the Bay of Cartagena, had been immediately chased by the privateer *Providencia*. "We have repeatedly had occasion to notice the improper conduct of the Carthagenian privateers," asserted the report, "not from a desire to reflect on that Government, but with the intention of reprobating and endeavoring to put down all piratical acts."[39]

Yet, the British seemed willing to acknowledge that Cartagena should defend its independence as best it could. In exchange for this informal gesture of support, the newly independent State was expected to respect British shipping or else risk accusations of piracy from authorities in Kingston. Land-bound bureaucrats in both Kingston and Cartagena, however, could not guarantee that their maritime agents would honor neutral or friendly vessels. This difficulty became even clearer as Cartagena's privateering forces swelled in 1813, becoming not just more numerous but also heavily French Caribbean.

ALTHOUGH THE PRESENCE of US privateers in the Bay of Cartagena was instrumental in sparking the State's privateering policy, seafaring men from other backgrounds soon sailed to Tierra Firme in search of Cartagena letters of marque. French and French Caribbean officers and sailors, already aboard US privateers operating out of Cartagena, quickly replaced their US colleagues, becoming by far the most prevalent people among Cartagenan privateers. Spanish authorities in Cuba, keeping themselves relatively well informed of these developments, believed that Francophone seamen supported not just Cartagena but other emerging Spanish American revolutionary movements across Tierra Firme and elsewhere.[40] Up to 1816, most of the foreigners involved in the revolutions of Tierra Firme appear to have been French-speaking people. Some came from the French colonies and former colonies, others directly from France.[41] Some traveled to Tierra Firme inspired by Cartagena's stand against Spain, but some were simply seeking jobs and economic gain. Others, like Aury, combined both impulses, desiring both revolutionary glory and material fortune. Regardless of their goals, they all worked shoulder to shoulder.

On board the Cartagenan privateer schooner *Bellona*, outfitted in 1814, Commodore Aury worked with a former slave, the Haitian sailor Ignacio the Younger. Other French- and Kréyol-speaking sailors commanded and manned vessels flying the colors of independent Cartagena. Vincent, Boutin, Fleuri, and Pierxin appear as the family names of captains on board Cartagenan privateers, though it is difficult to track down the full names of those men. Pierre Yolet, Jean Gara, Jean Detruie, Pedro La Maison, Pierre Marie, and Pierre Charriol, also Cartagenan privateering captains, left paper trails that offer a little more detail.

While most officers seem to have been white Frenchmen, people of color from the French Caribbean had a larger numerical presence aboard Cartagenan privateers. The outfitters and officers of the *Bellona* and the *Criolla* seem to have been originally from France. Besides Aury, the outfitters included a man known as Monsieur Dibü, and the officer corps included Pierre Charriol.[42] Nevertheless, the Afro-Caribbean presence was particularly noticeable among the crewmen, as most of the sailors on the *Bellona* and the *Criolla* came originally from Haiti.[43]

Cartagena's open-door policy, and most importantly its privateering endeavors, thus fostered the welcoming of individuals who would have fitted under the label "French Negroes." Feared and derided by patricians and bureaucrats, and accused of conspiracy against slavery and the Spanish government when authorities foiled an uprising in 1799, foreigners of African descent and enslaved ancestry were now the protagonists of Cartagena's privateering experiment. Moreover, along with other French- and English-speaking people, individuals of color from the Antilles often became naturalized citizens of Cartagena. They lent a cosmopolitan air to a city that had been almost hermetically sealed to foreigners for many generations, embodying Cartagena's radical shift from restricted subjecthood under Spanish legal traditions to more inclusive citizenship under the 1812 Constitution.[44]

Inclusion of Afro-Caribbean and other foreigners through citizenship in independent Cartagena, however, had an important instrumental dimension. While some foreigners might have aspired to become citizens of Cartagena for ideological reasons, others might have done so for legal and tactical purposes only. Cartagena authorities required foreign officers taking their letters of marque, and foreign sailors manning their ships, to become naturalized citizens of the State.[45] Most sovereignties issuing privateering commissions required naturalization, as this could shield their privateers from accusations of piracy by other countries.

Some Cartagenan privateers interrogated by British bureaucrats in Kingston declared that they were naturalized citizens of the State of Cartagena. Juan Francisco Pérez, originally from New Orleans, was a resident of the island of Margarita. A victim of the intense political turmoil on the island, Pérez had to emigrate, leaving his family behind. He became a naturalized citizen of Cartagena and engaged in privateering activities as owner and first officer of the privateer schooner *Carthagenera*. Pierre Yolet, the captain, was originally from Aiguillon, southeast of Bordeaux, France. After the British ship *Sappho* took their craft in 1813, these men testified before the maritime authorities in Jamaica. According to his testimony, Yolet had resided for several years in Spanish territories, most recently becoming a "naturalized subject of Cartagena." He further mentioned that the fifty-six men on board the vessel had likewise become naturalized citizens of Cartagena.[46]

André Ranché, owner of the *Défenseur de la Patrie*, a privateer schooner nicknamed *Caballo Blanco* that began a cruise on July 10, 1814, was also a naturalized citizen of Cartagena. Originally from Basse-Terre, on the French island of Guadeloupe, Ranché had resided for many years in Cuba and Tierra Firme. He settled in Cartagena after the declaration of independence, setting up shop as an outfitter of privateers. He obtained Cartagenan citizenship and became integrated into the local maritime community. From

José María Guerra y Posada, he purchased a schooner. Ranché also signed a work contract with a likely slave or former slave named José Joaquín, hired to cook on board the ship. Ranché may have recruited most of his sailors in Cartagena itself, including Captain Jean Baptiste Pemerlé, a Haitian man born in Les Cayes who had moved to Cartagena in 1812.[47]

People of color from the French Caribbean like Captain Pemerlé not only resided in Cartagena but also obtained Cartagenan citizenship, if only for pragmatic reasons. Some natives and longtime residents of Cartagena were pleased to work with them; others saw the arrival of foreigners and people of color in a negative light. Before independence, José Ignacio de Pombo had advocated for free trade and the opening of Cartagena to the outside world. But he remained selective about who should settle in Cartagena. He declared that authorities should not encourage non-Catholics and people of African descent to immigrate. In Pombo's view, Cartagena needed to be renewed not with "barbarian" slaves or people of color, but Swiss, German, Flemish, Irish, and Italian working families, all free and Catholic.[48]

The revolutionary transformation of Cartagena and the challenges faced by the new State propelled politics and social change in a direction quite different from the path envisioned by patricians like Pombo. In the wake of a radical political alliance that included free people of color pushing for political privileges, Cartagena not only drew on the services of some non-Catholic foreigners but also entangled itself with the masterless Caribbean. For it was former slaves and descendants of slaves who, in their capacity as sailors and citizens, formed the backbone of Cartagena's privateering policy.

Nevertheless, Cartagena accommodated foreigners of color with hesitation. While sailors were encouraged to apply for citizenship for instrumental reasons, conservative individuals likely continued to resent their claims to political belonging. Moreover, sailors employed in privateering stayed in Cartagena only for short periods of time, as their cruises required them to be away for several months. Like other maritime workers, privateers had ambivalent links to societies on land. Decidedly transient and often irreverent, sailors frequently clashed with authority figures, defying the hierarchies meant to maintain discipline on sea and political stability on shore.

5

Detachment from the Land and Irreverence at Sea

JOSÉ MIRANDA, A NATIVE OF Cartagena, died at sea in 1814. A sailor by trade, Miranda had signed on for a cruise on board *Le Chasseur*, nicknamed *El Nariño*, a Cartagenan privateer that set sail on March 21, 1814, at three in the afternoon. The ship's logbook has survived. From its entries, duly written every day by Captain Jacques Cyran, we learn that Miranda's last four days were miserable. Afflicted with what Captain Cyran called a *fluxion de poitrine*—most likely pneumonia—Miranda expired on May 9. The next day, at five in the afternoon, the captain and the crew paid their last respects and committed Miranda's body to the deep.[1] This is all we know of Miranda's life.

At first glance, it may seem paradoxical that José Miranda enters the historical record at the end of his days and out at sea, from where he never returned. However, Miranda's death and resting place epitomize the fate of common sailors in the Caribbean; it was not uncommon for them to be born, spend considerable time, and die at sea. To most non-sailors, these ships' denizens must have seemed completely detached from the land.

An intense connection to the sea set sailors apart from most other social groups. Among those who worked on ships in the 1700s and 1800s, many felt at odds with institutions, ways of life, and political communities on land. Most seamen had roots, relatives, and friends somewhere on shore, to be sure, but individuals who were escaping slavery or were particularly fond of the ocean and shipboard life saw time spent on land as a necessary evil. Some of them distrusted and disrespected people who, not acquainted with the seas, ignored the complicated tasks necessary to keep a ship afloat.[2] Known among landbound people for their irreverent attitudes and odd superstitions, common sailors at times even defied maritime officers and other people in positions of power.[3]

Political identification among sailors also differed from political identification among people more permanently tied to land. Sailors sometimes identified with specific countries, but not necessarily because they had been born in them. Rather, their sense of identity came from being born on or spending long stretches of time aboard ships flying the colors of those countries. Moreover, sailors used expressions of political identification in instrumental ways, claiming to be citizens or subjects of a certain sovereign when this suited their immediate needs, most importantly when they hoped to avoid punishment for piracy or to escape recruitment by force. Consequently, authorities second-guessed sailors' political allegiances, and many people on land found their sense of loyalty to be rather tenuous.[4]

For bureaucrats, officers, and merchants who had to rely on maritime workers to advance their naval and commercial interests, sailors' attitudes and ways of life raised serious concerns. Sailors defied social and political rules, including those of respecting hierarchy. In some cases they even mutinied. Moreover, sailors—especially those engaged in privateering—could easily escape the grasp of people on land. Sailors thus posed real challenges to their employers. But with their knowledge of the sea and maritime trades, seagoing people also offered great advantages in times of war.

From the vantage point of the State of Cartagena de Indias, an emergent polity with no respectable sea forces of its own, hiring foreign privateers was a risk worth taking. Although they could be difficult to control and their allegiance seemed unclear, privateers had the potential to take Cartagena's challenge to Spain to a new level. Their ability to crisscross jurisdictions, their maritime expertise, and even their irreverence and political flexibility made them ideal agents for defending the State by attacking Spanish interests overseas.[5]

Detachment from the Land and Irreverence at Sea [77]

MOST SEAFARERS BEGAN their lives on board when still very young—sometimes in childhood, by today's standards. Like workers in other preindustrial trades, seamen during the Age of Sail started out as apprentices, and aspiring sailors were advised to begin their apprenticeships early. After a certain age (for many, during their teen years), it would be more difficult to overcome motion sickness, or to learn "the art of slicing and knotting, the general rudiments of rigging, the proper way of going aloft—grasping the shroud and not the ratlines—and a host of other more complicated operations."[6]

Some sailors were even born at sea. While people on land could recall a town as their place of birth and, in the case of some Christians, a church where they had been baptized, the primordial memories of some seamen reached back not to a town or a city but to a specific ship. Even if they had not been born at sea, some seamen had a sense of nationality founded not on having been born or lived in a country but on long stretches of time working under a specific flag. Two cases of maritime officers whose ships were taken by the British afford some evidence of this. John Syerr, the captain of the *26 October 1812*, said that he was "born at sea under the British flag."[7] Juan Carrère, captain of the *Rosa*, told British maritime authorities in Jamaica that he was single, born in Saint Domingue, and had "no fixed place of residence." "Having followed a seafaring life for fifteen [years]," Carrère added, he "considered himself a British subject having been in the employ of British subjects."[8] Though perhaps they were invoking British subjecthood as a way of finding fairer treatment in Jamaica, these two seamen chose to talk of themselves in a way that placed their political identification in a world of intense geographic mobility, and at the crossroads of circumstance and free will.

In the early modern era, political belonging and allegiance (in the form of vassalage or subjecthood) emanated, at least in theory, from place of birth. If one was born within the realms of the king of Spain, one owed gratitude and "natural allegiance" to the Catholic monarch. This condition followed people from birth to death and could only rarely be changed.[9] In a context dominated by such a strong connection between place of birth and political allegiance, detachment from the land garnered sailors a bad reputation among territorial authorities. Bureaucrats often depicted sailors accused of piracy as enemies to all nations—people with no real home or true country. Seamen understood their liminal position quite well, either embracing it or simply regarding it as a natural characteristic of their trade. In 1699, a mutinied sailor said that "it signified nothing what part of the World a man liv'd in, so he Liv'd well."[10] Another sailor born at sea once said that he considered himself "as not belonging to any particular nation."[11] The sailor Francisco Díaz, from the Cartagena privateer *Bellona*, who was spared sentencing for piracy in Panama in 1816, said that he had been born in Coro, Venezuela, but had no fixed place of residence since he was a "sailor by trade."[12]

Sailors' detachment from the land not only unfolded in matters of political belonging but also manifested itself in matters of everyday communication. While people on land regularly observed hierarchical deference when talking to others, outside commentators and sailors themselves admitted that pirates, privateers, merchant sailors, and naval seamen often talked irreverently, even to their superiors. Seagoing individuals not only used lingos and tones distinct to their profession, but were known to joke, insult, and curse constantly. Cartagena's privateers were typical representatives of these behaviors, which had evolved over several hundred years along with the transformations of the maritime professions.

Even within European naval forces, common sailors at times did not acknowledge or abide by all the formalities and exigencies of rank separating them from officers. Before the consolidation of European navies, most sailing ships had operated as mobile workshops run by craftsmen. The men were led by a master who often came from within their own ranks. They had internal hierarchies, but they also worked on principles of brotherhood. In the process of building their navies, early modern authorities grafted landed military and political hierarchies onto the less rigid social world of the workshop-ship, challenging a preexisting order in which little space existed for a martial way of life. Many sailors tenaciously held on to their previous practices as new hierarchies and work dynamics emerged.[13]

The introduction of wages to remunerate seamen also gave sailors a relative advantage for defying authority. Because payments in money mediated between tars and employers, the expanding paternalist authority of investors and captains became somewhat vulnerable. Sailors could walk away at the end of their contracts, and they often took officers and merchants to court over wages in arrears. A contract and a salary—as opposed to bonded labor or payments in kind—increased the room for irreverence toward superiors with authoritarian inclinations. Among privateersmen, however, the share system was common, with each seaman on board taking a part of the prize money at the end of each cruise.[14]

Irreverence and bravado were powerful weapons for all sorts of seamen in different sets of circumstances. For common sailors, bold and defiant language came in handy when dealing with officious superiors. It was also crucial when confronting abusive officers and greedy investors. For privateering captains, irreverence was an idiom for sharply expressing political convictions or commitments. During and after battle, irreverent and heretical outcries characterized the seaman's fighting persona, underpinning the performance of his ideal of manhood.[15]

The taking of the British schooner *Favourite* by privateersmen in 1814 furnishes a good example. This merchant vessel was en route from Grand Cayman Island to Montego Bay, in Jamaica, when attacked by a Cartagenan privateer. After capture, the commander of the privateer instructed Captain Haynes of the *Favourite* to supply him with a pilot versed in coastal navigation off the complicated shores of Cuba. Haynes refused to cooperate. Indignant, he explained that if he agreed to deliver one of his pilots, he would become an accomplice in the capture of other British and Spanish vessels. He raised his voice and further explained his understanding of the situation: the privateer was acting on behalf of a "self-assumed Government, not acknowledged by any power." Infuriated, the privateer captain ordered his men to offload all the merchandise (a tortoiseshell cargo) and set the *Favourite* on fire. He gave the crewmen a boat, and as they rowed away the privateer captain screamed "the most opprobrious epithets to them respecting the British, and said that Carthagena was an independent State, which did not care a damn for any offense that might be taken against what she did."[16]

Cartagena's privateers were thus embedded in a long maritime tradition of irreverence and bravado. Take the *Bellona*'s Ignacio the Younger. A few weeks after running aground on Escudo de Veragua Island, off Panama, this sailor found himself thrown into jail and accused of piracy. Asked by local authorities why he had boarded what Spain deemed to be a pirate ship, Ignacio answered that he did so simply because he was a sailor. Still, Ignacio added a twist to his straightforward answer, invoking the Devil to explain why he would serve any master, though by implication only on his own terms: even if the "great Devil" himself took the form of a ship, Ignacio said, on that very ship he would come aboard and go a-sailing.[17]

Ignacio's boast also suggests just how many cultural traditions influenced seagoing individuals. For one, his words may afford a glimpse of the worldview of men and women of African ancestry from the Caribbean who were close to the sea and the maritime trades. Among peoples from West and Central Africa, water, water-spirits, and watercraft had important spiritual dimensions, some of which survived even in the context of New World slavery.[18] Throughout the Francophone world, "Great Devil"—*grand diable* in French—was a common expression. The meaning of these words, however, changed over space and time.

Several possible meanings can be linked to the notion articulated by Ignacio.[19] As an irreverent, everyday life expression, people used *grand diable* to characterize someone or something as particularly big and strong. This might be close to Ignacio's idea of the devil turning himself into a ship, therefore rendering that vessel not only extraordinarily powerful but also highly dangerous. Running through oral traditions that drew on folk tales and images from Christianity, the connection between the devil and watercraft was a common topic among seagoing or riverine Romance language-speaking peoples. A French privateer taken by the British in 1811 was named the *Grand Diable*. In the province of Cartagena, the largest river boat running the trade between the city of Cartagena and the inland Magdalena River ports of Mompox and Honda was named *El Gran Diablo*. The pride of her owner, the powerful Marquis of Santa Coa, this boat took thirty oarsmen to propel her.[20]

Ignacio's words might have been taken quite literally to refer to Lucifer. Maritime historians suggest that religious heterodoxy was common among sailors with Christian backgrounds, who tended to be irreligious, skeptical, and anticlerical. Pirates took these attitudes to further extremes, turning typical skepticism into a peculiar antireligious militancy.[21] Nevertheless, the notion of heterodoxy refers to an outsider's normative vision, and thus the concept presumes the universal value and coherent essence of "religion," most commonly from the point of view of Catholicism or Protestantism.[22]

Like other people, sailors who invoked the devil simply performed practices and held convictions emanating from ongoing processes of cultural cross-fertilization and tension. It was generally people in authority—officers, bureaucrats, priests, planters, and merchants—who accused sailors of religious deviation and otherwise portrayed them as abnormal or even criminal.[23] Unfortunately for sailors, especially for those involved in privateering, it was not difficult for outsiders to find excuses to hold them in low regard. Besides being seen as irreverent and coarse, privateers were also seen as people too prone to bend the rules of politics and war during their maritime endeavors. As sailors switched jobs from regular to irregular warfare with the same agility that they might show when switching the flags of their ships to fool the enemy, land-bound authorities second-guessed their loyalty, often drawing on preexisting notions about seamen's bad behavior and questionable integrity.

FROM THE VANTAGE point of state agents, sailors always moved between the blurry lines separating lawfulness from criminality, and loyalty from treason. Authorities on land felt uneasy about people who switched bosses often, and Spanish bureaucrats in particular disliked people who rubbed shoulders with people from other nationalities. Not only did sailors change employers after their contracts expired, but they also switched from engagements as regular sailors on merchant or navy vessels to working as privateers—in which case they stood awfully close to accusations of piracy. New jobs were often accompanied by a new flag flying from the mast. Sailors in the Caribbean, where so many "nations" stood within close proximity, toiled under different colors during their working lives.

For many bureaucrats, every sailor was a potential privateer or a potential pirate. Take the case of the Spanish administrator Juan José Ruiz de Apodaca. Experienced in naval architecture, navigation, and maritime governance, he suspected that sailors aboard Spanish ships taken at sea by Cartagenan privateers would abandon their allegiance to the Spanish monarchy if it suited them. Even the European navies, after all, were plagued by sailors' indiscipline and desertion.[24] When the Spanish frigate *Neptuno* returned to Havana in August 1815 after being taken by a Cartagenan privateer, Ruiz de Apodaca ordered that the sailors be fed, sheltered, and then sent to Santa Marta. Before letting them go, however, the bureaucrat wanted each man to be interrogated. He wanted to find out whether the seamen had been transferred to the capturing privateer ship and what work they had done aboard, "for it may well be that they became party to the privateer, in which case they are delinquents."[25]

In reality, however, things were not as clear-cut as they looked in Ruiz de Apodaca's assessment. While on land it could be relatively easy to throw defeated enemies into jail or otherwise immobilize them after battle, in Caribbean waters it was common, indeed necessary, to set politics aside after one side emerged victorious. After a battle at sea, it was not unusual for the crew of defeated vessels to come aboard the victors' ships. When this happened, crewmen did not necessarily climb aboard as prisoners. A sailing ship could not afford to become a jail. It was too enclosed a space and too complicated a machine. Instead, the defeated sailors were temporarily integrated into the social body of the privateering crew, and they had to do their share of the hard work needed to stay afloat and moving.

Perhaps with the exception of captains, every defeated seaman who went aboard a victorious privateer had to find a task to do on board. José Vigre, a sailor of color who was taken on board the *Bellona* for about a month, for example, worked side by side with the very sailors who had defeated him and his colleagues. Vigre would later refer to the sailors on the *Bellona* as "compañeros" (partners). This did not mean he had pledged allegiance to Cartagena, thus becoming "party" to the privateer, as Ruiz de Apodaca might have thought. It only meant that Vigre had been neither a prisoner nor a loiterer on the *Bellona*.[26] But for people on land, and especially for government officials, the imperative of distinguishing among nationalities was too strong, and often a hard thing to accomplish when it came to sailors.

An outside observer would have noted little difference between Vigre and the regular crewmen of the *Bellona*, perhaps none at all. They wore similar clothes, received equal food rations, worked together under the same captain, and spoke of one another as partners. Nevertheless, sailors who found themselves in Vigre's situation (working shoulder to shoulder with their supposed enemies) did not usually take long to leave their host ships. In most cases, they were free to go after adjudication of the prize. In some instances, they simply walked away from port, while on occasion they had to push their luck and break free. Vigre soon found the chance to leave the *Bellona* and tried his best to make it back home to Puerto Rico. While riding at anchor in Naranjo Bay, on the northeast coast of Cuba, the *Bellona* waited for news on two Spanish ships getting ready to depart from a nearby anchorage. The privateers were intent on taking these two ships. As they waited, one of the officers went on shore for a quick hunting trip, bringing with him Vigre and other sailors. Once on land, the officer ordered his subalterns to gather firewood. At the first opportunity, Vigre took off and ran some three leagues into the woods.[27]

Sailors were typically in the midst of changing circumstances, and thus had to keep their wits about them at all times, often having to come up with ways to deceive and trick others. This was especially true for those engaged in warfare. As it was difficult not only to distinguish sailors' nationalities but also to discern the nationalities of ships, especially from afar, sailors ingeniously used different maritime flags and pennants with tactical purposes.

ALL SEAGOING CRAFT had to deploy a flag and a set of pennants to identify their country of origin, the nature of their commission and, in the case of naval ships, their rank. However, crews usually carried the colors of several nations on board. All Cartagenan privateers flew the flag of the State, featuring three concentric rectangles—red, yellow, and green—with a white eight-point star in the center. And, like almost every other privateer, Cartagenan privateers always carried several flags representing different polities. Seamen used flags both for defensive and offensive purposes. By flying friendly colors within sight of unfriendly ships, enemies could be tricked into either approaching without caution or moving along unconcerned. Some seamen used flags that were less prominent in the Caribbean in order to be left alone. Such was the case of the *26 October 1812*, which sailed under Portuguese colors "to avoid capture." In the 1812 capture of the Spanish *Nuestra Señora del Nevis*, a schooner that had set out to sea from Riohacha, in Tierra Firme, the privateering crew, predominantly Spanish-speaking people, deceivingly showed British colors.[28]

Opportunities to attack with the advantage of false colors were not rare. Although the oceans are vast, skippers keep close to known routes, use the "highways" afforded by sea currents and the wind, and usually sail to known shores. Maritime craft thus tend to congregate around the same spaces. During the Age of Sail, in fact, it was relatively common for vessels to "speak" to one another at sea:

crewmen hailed and communicated with crewmen on board other ships, exchanging oral information and even written correspondence. In mid-1814, a Cartagenan privateer flying Spanish colors successfully lured a Spanish ship within gunshot range. Right before opening fire on their would-be prize, the privateersmen struck the Spanish flag and hoisted the flag of Cartagena.[29] A few years before, another Spanish ship, the *Blanche*, nicknamed *General Monteverde*, was sailing under Spanish colors between Santiago de Cuba and Puerto Cabello when she was taken by an American privateer near Jérémie, in Haiti. On board, however, the *Blanche*'s crew also had British flags. The British *Sappho* later captured this prize.[30]

Political inclinations played a role in the use of flags too. According to a press report from September 1815, a small schooner manned by "a most motley crew" of "various languages and various complexions" showed no colors before attacking the *Prospero*, but soon afterward "hoisted the Carthagenian flag."[31] For the Cartagenan privateersmen to show their true colors in the middle of the attack, or close to completing it, seems to have been more of a political statement than a practical need. Louis-Michel Aury himself proudly raised what he once called "our flag of independence"—Cartagena's flag—on the *Bellona*. But he also brought on board flags from several other sovereignties and monarchs.[32]

Before sending ships to port for adjudication, privateers sometimes replaced the prize's flag with the colors of their commissioning sovereignty. After four hours of battle, the Cartagenan privateer *Caballo Blanco* prevailed over the privateer brig *San José de la Unión*, with a Spanish letter of marque issued in Havana. The victors hoisted Cartagena's colors on their prize's mast, but she was later taken by the British *Variable* and sent to Kingston.[33] At this point, the ship's flag was probably changed again, this time to a British ensign.

Although they seemed detached from land and were seen as people of questionable or insubstantial political character, some sailors deployed a strong sense of identification with specific polities. Sometimes they pushed against the idea that they had no real homes or firm loyalties. Nevertheless, they did so with tactical purposes in mind. After he was imprisoned in Panama on the piracy charge, Ignacio the Younger emphasized his political allegiance and place of residence, stating that he considered himself a subject to the authority of Pétion, the president of the Republic of Haiti, where he lived when not at sea. Apparently well versed in the pitfalls of a trial for piracy, Ignacio made other instrumental claims about politics and justice, hoping to avoid a negative outcome, demonstrating his keen perception of judges and jurisdictions on shore.[34]

First, given that Haiti had not declared war on Spain, Ignacio had to explain why, as a Haitian citizen, he had participated in privateering against Spanish ships. His argument was that, as a sailor, he had no way to make a living other than plying his trade. From this, he concluded that he was free to "sail under any flag." Second, Ignacio knew that Spain did not recognize Cartagena's sovereignty, so he also had to explain why he had joined the complement of a ship flying illegal colors. His explanation was that he had gone on the *Bellona* only after witnessing many other people of "more talents" than himself doing the same. As a "poor and ignorant" sailor, Ignacio claimed he was in no real position to break the law or cause any offense by sailing aboard a State of Cartagena–sponsored privateer.[35] He had simply followed an example set by his social betters.

Ignacio's self-portrayal as a poor and ignorant workman was a clever, albeit unsuccessful—he was found guilty of piracy—component of his argument.[36] In legal systems based on Roman law—like both the Spanish and French legal traditions, which Ignacio seems to have been familiar with—lawyers could claim that a defendant's "rusticity" and ignorance diminished their culpability. Considered too poor or weak to know their own shortcomings, rural inhabitants, women, children, slaves, and Indians could be portrayed as offenders against God or the monarch without being fully at fault. Knowledge of this line of argument may have been available to many people. In the end, however, people adopted this defense or pursued others based on their idiosyncrasies or individual assessments of their situation. This is underscored by the difference in strategy, content, and tone in the depositions of Ignacio's colleagues. His colleague Hilario, for instance, plainly denied awareness of the *Bellona*'s privateering plans.[37]

Even if many sailors privateering on behalf of Cartagena identified with other countries (at times strongly, at times tangentially), or simply ignored the implications of their activities, their actions at sea constituted Cartagena's maritime power and embodied the policies of this revolutionary polity. This power was based on a largely borrowed contingent of seamen whose attachment to Cartagena was tenuous or very recent. Nevertheless, as the polity authorizing privateering under its colors, Cartagena tried to exercise a certain degree of control over its privateers. Outfitters and captains had to negotiate and renegotiate the terms of their commissions with Cartagena bureaucrats. On occasion, Cartagenan authorities even demanded services from their privateers that went beyond regular expectations, such as the gathering and relaying of intelligence. Maritime actions were thus never really fully detached from landbound interests.

VERY FEW DOCUMENTS detailing the negotiations between the State of Cartagena and its privateering outfitters, officers, and common sailors have survived. However, the extant evidence indicates the growing complexity of these dealings. Early privateers like Aury had received letters of marque after direct negotiations with individual agents such as Gual. These more or less direct negotiations seem to have been prevalent in late 1812 and early 1813. As its privateering (and free trade) boomed later in 1813 and throughout 1814, however, the State of Cartagena set up maritime administration institutions, thus creating a layer of bureaucrats and brokers that aspiring privateers had to negotiate with in order to obtain their commissions.[38]

Cartagena's secretary of war and the navy was in charge of maritime jurisdiction. Operating under this secretary was the chief commander of maritime affairs, and below him there were notaries of the navy and their assistants. It was these notaries who made the maritime administration function, mainly through paperwork exchanges. These scribes pushed printed and handwritten documents from hand to hand, up and down the maritime administrative hierarchy. The issuing of letters of marque took place within this system, as did the adjudication of prizes and all the potential litigation after privateering cruises. When privateer captains officially reported the prizes taken at sea to the maritime authorities, notaries and their assistants assessed the value of those prizes, allotted shares of the prize money, and finally took the paperwork to their superiors, who approved (or rejected) the proceedings and signed the documents.[39]

While these administrative practices were meant to guarantee Cartagena's relative control over its privateers and access to its share of the prize money, they were also functional examples of Cartagena's independence. By installing its own maritime administration and following "proceedings" similar to those of admiralties in other countries, Cartagena's leaders claimed that their privateering policy was an "act of sovereignty" with international legal standing. By contrast, they also argued that Spanish privateering lacked the "formalities" to make it legal, painting Spanish privateers as mere pirates. While Spanish privateers operating out of Panama and harassing Cartagena shipping had no clear commissioning sovereign (because of the war in Spain), Cartagena's privateering had the backing of the United Provinces of New Granada. Part political propaganda, part legalistic analysis, these assertions by Cartagena nonetheless mirrored everyday maritime and commercial transactions taking place in the city and supervised by the State's naval authorities. Bureaucrats paid special attention to the sale and purchase of vessels meant to be outfitted as privateers, for these had to be owned by citizens or naturalized citizens of the State. This legitimized their use of the flag of Cartagena, creating firmer ground for the legality of Cartagenan privateering and further distinguishing it from piracy.[40]

One comparatively clear difference between pirates and privateers was that officers and maritime investors affected by the latter had the option of bringing complaints before officials with maritime

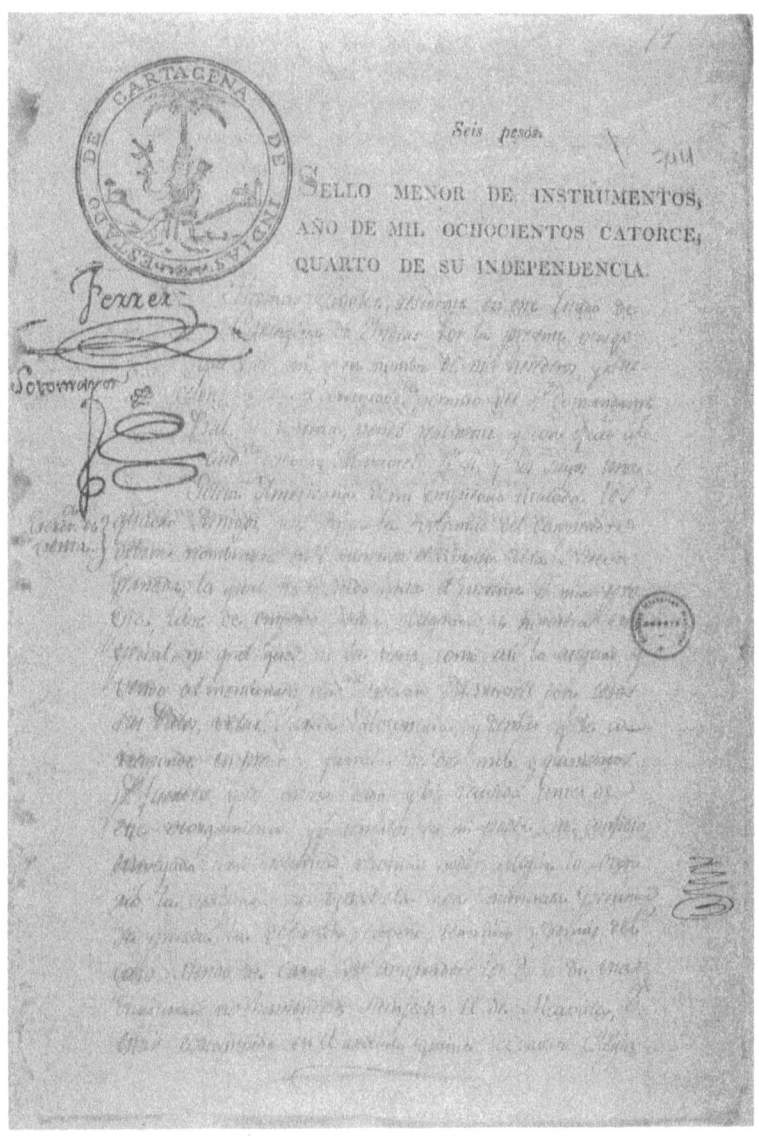

Figure 7. Bill of Sale for the American schooner *Four Brothers*, now the *Congreso de la Nueva Granada*, registered by State of Cartagena notary of the navy Nicolás Durango, 1814. Courtesy of Archivo General de la Nación (Bogotá).

jurisdiction. Privateers were expected to demonstrate the lawfulness of their exploits before maritime authorities. Victims of privateering, in turn, could expect to gain redress if enough evidence or influence was available to prove that a prize had been illegally taken. That is exactly what the businessman Charles Machin tried to accomplish in Cartagena, as he later described in his unpublished memoir.[41]

A struggling English merchant, Machin lost property in an attack by the Cartagenan privateer *Filantrópico* in 1813. Hoping to recover at least some of his goods, Machin sailed to Cartagena to present his case before the State's maritime authorities.[42] No further details of the case seem to have survived, but Machin's willingness to subject his case to the jurisdiction of this self-proclaimed republic is striking. This case suggests that other merchants probably took a similar path, engaging with the government of Cartagena and its maritime officials in largely the same ways they would with the British admiralty courts. Even if Machin did not personally recognize Cartagena's sovereignty, in practice he had to do so. After arriving in Cartagena and making his claims, Machin had to abide by the rules and the administrative practices of the State, and had no choice but to accept the final decision.

The hired seamen who worked as privateers for Cartagena also recognized, at least in practice, Cartagena's sovereignty. They too abided by the State's terms and procedures for the issuing of letters of marque. Moreover, some privateersmen were pushed to provide further help. They were at times expected by the leaders of Cartagena to participate in tactical and intelligence operations not directly related to privateering. Depositions from Cartagenan privateers before the British Vice-Admiralty Court in Jamaica show that the *Carthagenera* not only received a letter of marque from the revolutionary State, but was also involved in a naval blockade against Santa Marta. Against the wishes of her crew, the *Carthagenera* spent almost a month off the shores of Santa Marta before finally going out on her privateering cruise. Captain Joseph Clement of the *General Bolívar*, who shipped out of Cartagena on January 29, 1814, had a letter of marque authorizing him for privateering operations. He had also been directed to carry out a "mission in Venezuela." Or so Clement told New Orleans notary John Lynd, while giving no specifics on the nature of the mission.[43]

A relatively more consistent lead on missions of intelligence gathering by privateers comes from the *Défenseur de la Patrie*, also known as the *Caballo Blanco*. Although not a sailor himself, André Ranché, the owner of this privateering ship, had participated in at least five expeditions by the end of 1814. The fifth cruise, however, encountered complications—the ship was captured first by a ship flying US colors and later by the British *Onyx*. At the time of her second capture, the *Caballo Blanco* had both a privateering commission and a set of special instructions: her crew was to look out for Spanish ships bound for Cartagena and to relay intelligence on their moves.[44]

Although their work experiences, irreverent personalities, and ways of political identification made them feel or seem different from members of land-bound societies, seagoing individuals could never entirely escape the pull of the land. Besides having family and friends on shore, sailors had to rely on supplies exclusively found at harbors. The public policies and the maritime tribunals of various countries also kept privateers legally and financially connected to port towns such as Cartagena, Kingston, or Santiago de Cuba. Cartagena's own privateers and a whole host of other seagoing individuals often found themselves undertaking legal battles not only in Cartagena, but also before British maritime authorities in Jamaica or Spanish officials in eastern Cuba.

The *Défenseur de la Patrie* again furnishes a good example. Taken by a US privateer before falling prey to the *Onyx*, she had in theory already become US-owned. Her capture by the British was litigated in Kingston, where the owner was restored to his property after successful proceedings and the payment of court fees.[45] The schooner *Governor McKean*, out of Cartagena and bound for Philadelphia with a valuable cargo of platinum, indigo, barks, sarsaparilla, and tortoiseshell, was captured and taken to Santiago by a Spanish felucca. After negotiations, the Spanish let her go once her owner paid an impressive seven thousand pesos in ransom.[46] All the while, the common sailors aboard these ships waited in port before the vessels were released, sometimes centering their everyday lives around bars and inns, sometimes visiting family and friends, and often moving on to different ships for immediate employment.

While typically transient and relatively detached from the land, the privateers hired by the State of Cartagena played an important role in the life of this revolutionary polity. The outfitters, officers, and common sailors who fitted out, commanded, and manned the privateers at the service of Cartagena became a strong pillar and a strategic extension of this society on land. In the difficult construction of its sovereignty, the presence of the Cartagenan flag overseas lent Cartagena a not insignificant air of belligerent standing. Through the actions of its privateers, Cartagena posed a credible challenge to Spanish sovereignty by engaging in combat out at sea and, more importantly, threatening the booming plantation economy of Cuba. An island of paramount logistical, financial, and political importance for Spain, Cuba was controlled by slaveholders and merchants who watched with alarm a spate of privateer attacks on their vessels in mid-1813. The evidence from those events provides important clues to the dimensions and the regional impact of Cartagena's privateering policy.

6

Under the Walls of Havana

AT FIVE IN THE AFTERNOON on June 9, 1814, four ships under full sail appeared within sight of the Cartagenan privateer *Bellona*. Cruising off the island of Cuba, Captain Aury and his privateersmen figured the ships must be Spanish. They kept a close watch on the vessels, approaching them until they were within gunshot range by ten in the morning the following day. The brig *Descubridor* indeed raised a Spanish pennant and quickly positioned herself to defend the rest of the convoy, three Spanish merchant vessels, from the threatening *Bellona*. All the seamen aboard both ships stood alert at their battle stations. An engagement was imminent.[1]

The battle soon began. After two hours of fruitless exchanges of cannon fire, the *Bellona* found herself within boarding distance of her opponent. Aury's men tried to board the *Descubridor* on her port side, but they were effectively repelled twice by musket shot. At the same time, the *Bellona*'s sails were barraged with firebombs from the *Descubridor*. Aury's men then moved their heaviest cannon to the prow, rammed four loads of grapeshot into it, and aimed for a small artillery piece on the *Descubridor*. They fired at such close range that the blast pushed both ships apart. The men loaded again and fired, but this time the ropes lashing the cannon in place broke. With a loose cannon, damaged sails, and an exhausted crew, the *Bellona* had to beat a tactical retreat.[2]

Things were not as bad as they seemed, however. The *Bellona*'s crew were not novices, and managed to refit both rigging and artillery in little time. By two in the afternoon, they had caught up again with the Spanish brig, whose crewmen had clearly had enough. As the *Descubridor* tried to make her escape, the *Bellona* made chase, firing on her quarry no less than thirty times. At five in the afternoon both ships were again within gunshot. Aury ordered his men to fire another fourteen times. But a squall from the southeast enveloped his ship. Aury ordered the crew to strike the sails. As the Cartagenan privateer waited out the weather, the Spanish brig got away. But the effort had not been in vain, for the *Descubridor* had abandoned the merchant ships under her protection. Aury took the three defenseless vessels as prizes, which he sent to Cartagena. Laden with wine, olive oil, and other European goods, this catch yielded handsome revenues for Aury, his colleagues, and the State.[3]

Aury and his crewmen had cast off just weeks prior, heading out to sea from Cartagena on April 2, 1814. Their cruise turned out to be very successful. In addition to the *Descubridor*, the *Bellona* also engaged with the Spanish brig *Cupido*, four of whose sailors died at the end of the forty-five-minute combat. Moreover, by the end of the cruise in mid-July 1814, the *Bellona* had sunk twenty-three ships and dispatched six prizes to the port of Cartagena. Such significant accomplishments highlighted not just the skills of Aury and those who had sailed with him but also the growing maritime capabilities of the State of Cartagena.[4]

Proud of these results, Aury wrote an account of the cruise, which he presented to Manuel Rodríguez Torices, the president of Cartagena. Aury boasted of his actions, remarking on his "temerity," the damage caused to "the enemies of Independence," and the unlikely location of the attacks: "under the very walls and off the enemy shores of Havana." The account was published in the official gazette of the State. The *Bellona* must have been the talk of the town.[5] On October 24, Aury wrote with confidence to his relatives in Paris. Fortune, which had so far been elusive, Aury told his loved ones, had finally begun to favor him. Being a privateer was not only an honorable vocation—as he had insisted back in 1808—but truly profitable as well.[6]

The *Bellona* belonged to a larger group of privateer ships flying the flag of Cartagena, and Aury was counted among the many officers commanding these ships. Aury's remarkable seamanship and the actions by the *Bellona*'s crewmen were representative of Cartagena's privateering policy, enacted by a borrowed yet increasingly effective maritime force in the Caribbean. By the end of 1813, Cartagena's privateering initiative had successfully crystalized, attracting considerable numbers of seamen. Some were convinced anti-Spanish fighters, others were escaping slavery and other constraints, and most of them were interested in the prospect of prize money. Concentrating on attacking ships bound for Cuba or leaving this Spanish island, Cartagenan privateers directly helped undermine Spanish power, as Cuba remained a Spanish territory. Moreover, assaults on Cuban shipping tended to yield substantial revenue, thanks to the island's turn-of-the-century economic takeoff, which made vessels in Cuba's vicinity ideal prey.

Although attacking Spanish interests off the coasts of Cuba was economically motivated, it was also consistent with Cartagena's political principles and actions. Unlike Cuba, Cartagena became a separatist polity that did not follow the model of plantation agriculture, having even outlawed the slave trade to its territory. However, with their varied and complex backgrounds, interests, and outlooks, privateers sometimes acted in ways inconsistent with the political principles espoused by the State of Cartagena. While some sailors did indeed spread anti-Spanish sentiment and revolutionary ideas, sometimes they placed profit before principle, perhaps even participating in illegal slave trading to Cartagena. Thus, the figure of the privateer remains not only illustrative of the blurry lines between economic and political interests, but also of the ambiguities and tensions embodied by common sailors in the revolutionary Caribbean.

PRIVATEER SHIPS FLYING Cartagena colors seemed to have multiplied rapidly throughout 1813. The economic impact of Cartagenan privateering is apparent from several sources. Toward the end of May 1813, the Jamaica gazettes informed their readers that several privateers with letters of marque from Cartagena had captured a few

Spanish schooners.⁷ Appearing in print in early July, further reports noted that a Cartagenan privateer named *Dos Amigos* had boarded the *Catherine Anna*, while another privateer had captured two vessels near Puerto Cabello, in Venezuela, later sending them to Cartagena.⁸

In July and August, Jamaican papers informed the public of about fourteen Cartagenan privateers at sea. Recently arrived from New York, for instance, the *President* touched in Cartagena, immediately obtaining a privateering commission and setting out to sea. Apparently well versed in the shipping routes in and out of Cuba, the *President*'s seamen captured the Spanish brig *Aquiles*, which had left New York for Havana, carrying flour and other foodstuffs.⁹ Toward the end of the year, a Cartagenan privateer captured a Swedish ship from Gothenburg, bound for Cuba with naval stores.¹⁰

In Cartagena itself, members of the independent government and the public witnessed increasing numbers of prizes arriving in port for adjudication, including ships from far-flung places with valuable merchandise on board. A case in point is the Spanish brig *San Sebastián*, publicized in the local press. Taken by the privateer ship *Filantrópico*, she arrived on September 2, laden with boards, staves, and wine. On the same day, Cartagena saw the arrival of the *Nuestra Señora del Carmen*—another ship vanquished by the *Filantrópico*—which had set sail from Havana to New York with a cargo of sugar, baled tobacco, boxed cigars, and coffee.¹¹ The privateer *Once de Noviembre*—whose name celebrated the independence of Cartagena, which had taken place on November 11, 1811—finished a successful cruise in December 1813. Her six prizes included the Spanish schooners *Trinidad* and *Carmelita*, loaded with wine, tobacco, garlic, and other goods.¹²

The case of the merchant ship *Ciencia* provides a glimpse of other attacks on large ships with valuable cargo. Having left the Spanish port of Cádiz for Havana, the *Ciencia* fell prey to the Cartagenan privateer *San Francisco de Paula* in 1813. A three-masted frigate, the *Ciencia* carried considerable quantities of merchandise and was herself a valuable asset. Consigned to the merchant and slave-trading

Havana firm Cuesta Manzanal & Hermano, the cargo belonged to several Cádiz merchants.[13] Orchestrating attacks on this type of large transatlantic operation, Cartagena's privateers became a force to be reckoned with—a private irregular navy of significant capacity.

Although independent Cartagena's maritime archives did not survive, a trail of scattered documents attesting to privateers' actions indicates that, between 1812 and 1815, Cartagena authorized at least forty ships to privateer on its behalf. A few of these ships, as well as six other vessels presumably with Cartagena letters of marque issued in 1815, continued to attack Spanish shipping into 1816, after the defeat of the State of Cartagena.[14] The figure of forty ships suggests a very robust contingent of maritime workers attracted by Cartagena. Even allowing for the possible duplication of ships in the records—sometimes the same vessel would adopt a different name for each cruise—a large number of common sailors must have been working aboard Cartagenan privateers.

Like other privateers, Cartagena-flagged ships usually employed many more sailors than was typical on merchant vessels. Privateers needed the manpower to engage in battle and plunder. The prospect of prize money also attracted large numbers of sailors.[15] The *Popa de Cartagena* had a hundred-man crew and carried fifty muskets on board. Fifty-six seamen sailed on the *Carthagenera*. Around forty mariners manned the *Défenseur de la Patrie*, also known as the *Caballo Blanco*. The *Filantrópico* boasted a company of 130 men, although not all of them were necessarily on board at all times. Forty men worked on the *Centinela*, a ship that could accommodate even more sailors. According to an eyewitness named Antonio Suárez, 720 sailors manned the six-ship privateer fleet he spotted on Naranjo Bay, in Cuba—well over one hundred men per craft.[16]

With work contracts of three to five months at a time, sailors might labor on two or three different ships over the course of a single year. But even allowing for potential overlap of crewmen, in 1813 alone there could have been around a thousand seamen working under the flag of Cartagena. Supposing an average of 50 people per crew, the best evidence available suggests that well over 1,500 sailors would have worked aboard Cartagena-sponsored privateers between 1812 and 1815. Without official sources, however, these figures remain speculative. Nevertheless, the well-documented impact and extent of Cartagena's privateering, especially in the vicinity of Cuba, make these numbers seem plausible.

CARTAGENA'S BELLIGERENT PRIVATEERS deliberately concentrated on Spanish shipping in and out of Cuba, for several important reasons. First, Cuba's economy, increasingly based on plantation slavery, expanded dramatically at the turn of the century. Cuba thus offered the most tempting potential prizes: large transatlantic trading vessels loaded with produce, manufactured goods, and specie. Second, after the crisis of 1808, royalist forces had prevailed in Cuba, making the island a pro-Spanish stronghold (it would maintain its colonial status for the rest of the century).[17] Any maneuver against Cuba had the potential to undermine Spanish presence and power in the Caribbean. Finally, Cartagena was becoming somewhat of an antithesis to Cuba, as the two societies had taken different economic and political paths during this era. Cartagena's attacks on Cuba foregrounded its political rupture with Spain.

Cartagena's steps toward economic and social transformation contrasted with those taken by Cuba. Cuba's loyalists favored expanding plantation slavery, while separatists reluctant to adopt a plantation economy took over Cartagena. With a much smaller and less fertile hinterland, a comparatively modest merchant sector, and an economy that was not poised for dramatic change, Cartagena's patricians had realized, even before independence, that implementing plantation agriculture in their country might come with too high a cost and major risks.[18]

Overseas trade and non-plantation agriculture seem to have been the two pillars of the emerging economic blueprint in turn-of-the-century Cartagena. Even relatively conservative José Ignacio de Pombo concluded that the slave trade should be outlawed. This important member of the Cartagena elite proposed that free trade and free farmers should become the instruments with which to build the future wealth of Cartagena.[19] Unlike his counterparts in Cuba, Pombo believed that a thriving agricultural sector could be achieved by unbound laborers—that is, members of free rural families.[20]

Underpinned by economic interests and political calculations, Pombo's reasoning took both Cuba and Haiti into consideration. Pombo was no abolitionist. Under certain circumstances, he believed, slavery was perhaps necessary to sustain a thriving economy. Like some Cuban promoters of plantation slavery, he thought that it should be Spanish traders who profited from the trade in human beings, were it to continue. However, "in light of reason" and the Haitian Revolution, Pombo claimed that the massive importation of slaves could create the conditions for a general uprising in Cartagena that would destroy the slaveholding families.[21] Surrounded as they were by circumstances that made plantation agriculture a much safer bet, Cuban investors had reached the opposite conclusion about their island.[22]

Pombo's skeptical positions on slavery were in some ways motivated by general political and philosophical considerations. The slave trade, he stated, added fuel to the flames of "barbaric" African wars. The purchase of African captives by an "enlightened European," wrote Pombo, turned the former into beasts of burden, depriving them and their offspring of liberty, "the most sacred of rights." But with the principle of liberty having been ignored on behalf of short-term profit, the "natural" consequences of upholding slavery in the New World were already clear for everyone to see—the French had been violently overthrown in Saint-Domingue, where a dangerous black empire now seemed unstoppable. Forecasting a similar outcome for the British in Jamaica, Pombo anticipated that an uprising of slaves in that island would occur in response to the planters' greed and cruelty. The same fate awaited Cuba and other slave societies, unless "the introduction of Negroes is brought to a halt, and a system for extinguishing slavery in the Americas adopted."[23]

Expressing his ideas before the crisis of 1808, Pombo hoped that Spain would be the first among the European nations to abolish the slave trade and slavery altogether. Such a policy would demonstrate the Spaniards' humanitarianism and advanced culture. Moreover, it would give the rest of Europe a dignified lesson while transforming Spanish American possessions from slave emporia into "colonies of citizens"[24] Of course, Pombo imagined that these new citizens would eventually resemble him, for he hoped that miscegenation would dissolve the presence of black people, whitening out evidence of African roots. By contrast, Cuban planters relied on the presence of an African and African-descended slave force to propel their plantation experiment, maintaining that they could forestall revolt by avoiding political unrest and division among the masters, which they viewed as the real causes of the Haitian Revolution.[25]

By the time revolutionary Cartagena began to issue letters of marque, its political economy was radically different from Cuba's. Preying on commercial shipping in and out of Cuba seemed only logical, given the circumstances (Cuba was the richest Spanish island in the Caribbean). But Cartagena's irregular maritime war against that island also seems to represent the outcome of two divergent political processes, in turn reflecting economies that evolved within the limits and possibilities of two different geographical locations and demographic outlooks.

Cartagena's privateers thus attacked Cuban ships at a time when Cuban elites were aggressively moving to replace the now-disappeared Saint-Domingue as the premier Caribbean sugar producer. Merchants and authorities in Havana and other towns on the island, worried about their economic interests and political stability, could not afford to underestimate the naval threat from Cartagena. Over the course of the year 1813, Cuban elites constantly heard about ships taken as prizes by seafaring forces they sometimes referred to as "insurgent privateers." On that year, privateersmen took at least forty-one Spanish vessels: twenty-six schooners, six frigates, five brigs, two polacres, and two bilanders.[26]

According to a report published in Spain, during the last five days of September and first ten days of October 1813 alone, three ships en route from Spain to Cuba and six ships out of Cuba had been taken by Cartagenan privateers. They had also taken several coasting boats. People on board the vessels taken as prizes had later reported in Baracoa that thirty-two privateer ships had cleared out of Cartagena, intent on cruising against Spanish shipping off the north and south shores of Cuba.[27] Although this figure might be inflated, the challenge was real and present.

By year's end, people of means and power in Cuba, directly affected or otherwise worried about these relentless attacks, began to ponder seriously how to respond.[28] In October and November, they sent letters to Spain reporting on the many prizes taken by "revolutionary privateers." Perhaps exaggerating to make the matter appear even more urgent, officials claimed that privateering forces planned to take over the port of Baracoa, in the east. Cuba's captain general, Juan José Ruiz de Apodaca, approved the measures taken by the lieutenant governor of Baracoa, who had raised a small militia to defend the place from Cartagenan privateers. Worried about the king's purse, however, Ruiz de Apodaca suggested that the militia be disbanded as soon as the threat ceased.[29] Still, denouncing and persecuting Cartagena's privateers and other sea robbers helped officials showcase their loyalty to Spain—a pressing need in a time of political crisis, especially for bureaucrats who were known to engage in illicit activities and defraud the Crown.

Although it seems unlikely that they ever tried to occupy port towns in eastern Cuba, Cartagenan privateers certainly roamed around the island's shores. At times, they used bays and inlets to seek refuge and to jump on shore to acquire supplies like water, meat, and firewood.[30] The lieutenant governor of Holguín, an inland town with coastal jurisdiction over the northeast part of the island, alerted his superiors in Havana to the presence of privateers off Cuban shores. By the end of November 1813, authorities had deployed several ships expressly commissioned to chase and neutralize

Cartagenan privateers.³¹ In December, a Spanish Navy corvette and two schooners weighed anchor in Havana with instructions to "protect Spanish commerce from its predators."³² Soon afterward, sublieutenant Andrés Ramos had an engagement with a privateer flying the colors of Cartagena near the port of Baracoa.³³

In spite of these initiatives, merchants in Havana continued to worry about privateers preying on their vessels and pillaging their merchandise, ultimately concluding that the island's government could not cope with the problem. With the Iberian Peninsula still fighting a war of liberation against the French, merchants also knew that little more could be expected from Spain, even though metropolitan authorities were aware of the troubles caused by "insurgents." Official communications from Spain promised no help, instead encouraging Cubans to fend off the threat while trying to revive the "paralyzed" trade. The merchants decided to take matters into their own hands. They pulled together twelve thousand pesos and outfitted a small fleet to combat Cartagenan privateers plying the waters off Cuba. This force set sail from Havana in late 1813 or early 1814.³⁴

In February 1814, Spanish minister Julián Fernández de Navarrete, secretary of state and finance, expressed his gratitude for the merchants' efforts and their "patriotic zeal." He further recommended that Spanish privateers be outfitted in Cuba in order to root out the problem by destroying the Cartagenan privateers.³⁵ Attacks on Cuban shipping, however, carried on into 1816. As late as July of that year, authorities established a special tax to be collected by customs officials from Spanish and foreign merchant ships, to fund the fight against revolutionary privateers, this time referred to as "pirates infesting our shores and waters."³⁶ The merchants and planters themselves had suggested the tax. Still worried about maritime attacks, they had met in an open assembly and decided to foot the bill for a more robust naval defense of their interests.³⁷

While Cuban elites utilized their own resources to protect their property, the radical elites of Cartagena relied on foreign maritime operatives to restock the ailing treasury of the State, undermining

Spanish power in the process. Of course, private wealth and public revenue in Cartagena could not compete with Cuba's riches. However, Cartagena's reliance on privateering as a source of revenue (and as a way to tap Cuba's own wealth, via maritime robbery) also foregrounds the diverging paths taken by these Caribbean societies. Cartagena's privateering forces became a potent embodiment of the revolutionary State's stance against Spain, turning the waters off the island of Cuba into the ideal stage to perform their increasingly complex threat to Spanish power.

Nevertheless, the politics of revolutionary Cartagena did not neatly map onto the politics of its privateersmen. Outfitters, captains, and common sailors had their own convictions, and they assessed the evolving regional economies and the finances of privateering according to their own interests. Privateers who took letters of marque from Cartagena had taken, and would in the future take, similar commissions from other sovereignties and rebel polities. Some of those privateers were even willing to act as free agents—without official or semi-official commissions—dangerously getting closer to full-out piracy.[38]

Moreover, in spite of the robust presence of people of color with enslaved backgrounds among their ranks, Cartagena's privateers may well have disregarded the prohibition of the slave trade included in the Constitution of 1812. Although evidence on this is scarce, the involvement of Cartagena's privateers in slave trading is a good example of the discrepancies between the official policies of the State and the actions of its maritime forces. These discrepancies tended to unfold in very obscure circumstances, both out at sea and on Cartagenan territory. Privateers were a formidable tool for an emergent sovereignty like Cartagena, but keeping their actions under full control was impossible.

CARTAGENA'S 1812 CONSTITUTION outlawed the slave trade to the State, but preventing people from importing slaves remained a difficult task.[39] The general increase in trade, the arrival of scores of foreigners, and the rise of privateering itself made it difficult for authorities to police businesses and other affairs on and off shore. This was particularly true in the case of activities carried out by privateersmen, some of whom engaged in illegal transactions while in Cartagena or cruising under Cartagena's flag.

Some privateers, even if they may have been interested in undermining Spanish maritime power in the Caribbean and bolstering Cartagena's claim to sovereignty, did not show an inclination to abide by Cartagena's anti-slave trade policy. As men of complex and varied backgrounds and goals, privateers never played just one role—at times freedom fighters capable of near-heroic actions, they could also deal in enslavement and exploitation. People in Cartagena itself may also have tolerated and even encouraged the introduction and sale of slaves after 1812. Moreover, these developments were possibly linked, as some of the slaves introduced in Cartagena after 1812 may have arrived aboard vessels captured by privateers. The small schooner *Alta Gracia*, taken by the *Bellona* in late 1814, offers some clues on possible illegal slave trading to independent Cartagena.[40]

The *Alta Gracia* was a Spanish ship involved in the intra-Caribbean slave trade. Agustín Manguar, the owner of this schooner, had commissioned his agent, Joaquín Ferrer, to oversee the sailing of the ship from Puerto Rico to Maracaibo, in Venezuela. The ship carried merchandise to be traded for slaves in Tierra Firme. The slaves would then be taken to Puerto Rico. Everything seems to have gone smoothly until the *Bellona* intercepted the *Alta Gracia*, which carried a group of slaves (four men, six women, and a child). Aury, commanding the *Bellona*, ordered the four men to be taken on board. The women and the child—María Felipa, Vicenta, Felipa, Dolores, Juana María, Paula, and Paula's son, Ramón—remained on the *Alta Gracia*, which was to continue to Cartagena as a prize.[41]

On its way to Cartagena, however, the *Alta Gracia* lost its course and ended up stranded on a sandy beach in Escudo de Veraguas, a tiny island off the coast of Panama. The fate of the women and the small child remains unknown. What happened to the men transferred to the *Bellona* is also unclear. Since slavery itself remained legal in the State of Cartagena, Aury or his men could have sent captives there to be sold secretly to local buyers. For although the regional economy did not pivot on plantations, thousands of slaves did work in the city and in the countryside. Cartagenan privateers may have specifically targeted ships engaged in slave-trading activities, seeking to boost profits with this illicit side business.[42]

Cartagenan privateers also sold slaves outside of Cartagenan territory, closer to the thriving plantations of the US South. Although the evidence is not definitive, surviving proceedings from US federal courts suggest that most of the captives smuggled into the United States during the 1810s were brought in by privateers. Illegal slave trading by privateers took place on the Gulf Coast, near New Orleans and the cotton- and sugar-producing regions. The Cartagena-flagged privateer *Législateur*, for instance, unloaded 570 slaves in Louisiana. The slaves had been originally transported by the Spanish slave ship *Santa Rosalía*.[43]

Slavery remained close to the maritime world of privateers for other reasons as well. Many sailors were descended from slaves or had been slaves themselves, having obtained freedom or simply run away to try their luck at sea. Because of this background, captivity was a constant threat to them. Moving from one jurisdiction into another could mean moving from a society without slaves to a slave society, where the danger of re-enslavement always loomed large. After 1804, runaway slaves and former slaves could rely on Haiti's rejection of slavery and its hospitality toward people of color. But places such as Jamaica, Cuba, Louisiana, and even Tierra Firme were still a long way from the abolition of slavery.[44] In Haiti, it was easier to secure freedom, and also relatively easy to obtain employment in the maritime trades.

Shipping out of Haiti, however, could prove treacherous for people whose complexion, garments, habits, and ways of speaking gave away their slave ancestry or potential slave status. Where slavery existed, enslaved people represented capital as well as labor.[45] Slave traders eager to turn a handsome profit could kidnap people of color, sometimes acting in cahoots with local authorities. Other times, officials found it nearly impossible to ascertain a person's legal status, inadvertently facilitating the illegal enslavement of individuals and families.

In the case of maritime workers of color, it was particularly difficult to tell apart enslaved from free. Consider the case of the Spanish brig *Ana María*. After being intercepted by Cartagenan privateers during her passage from Bermuda, the *Ana María* dropped anchor in the Bay of Havana. On board were three black crewmen. Every ship arriving in port had to undergo a visit by a Spanish official. When the person in charge of this procedure, Pedro Hidalgo, came aboard, he asked the ship's captain, Juan Ambroses, whether the black sailors were free men or slaves. Perhaps trying to protect the three sailors, Ambroses proved unwilling or unable to give an answer. The three men must have been aware that their looks alone could land them on a Cuban plantation.[46]

Prison sentences also threatened the freedom of sailors who decided to work as privateersmen. If caught by Spanish officials, seamen hired to serve on vessels with anti-Spanish commissions could be tried for piracy. That was exactly what befell Ignacio the Younger, Hilario, Francisco, and Juan Esteban, the unfortunate *Bellona* sailors who had manned the *Alta Gracia* after it was taken as booty. After running aground off the coast of Panama, and enduring several days of thirst and hunger, they decided to row toward the continent, looking for water and food. They found provisions, but they also found trouble. Quickly spotted by locals, the shipwrecked seamen were thrown into jail, tried for piracy, and found guilty.[47]

Following standard Spanish judiciary practices, the accused sailors had a defender, Manuel José de Arce. It would be impossible to prove that these sailors had personally profited from stolen goods or taken anybody's life, he argued. Arce further insisted that although the crime of piracy was punishable by death, these particular men should be spared the gallows because they were "sailors by trade." Instead, they should be made to serve in the Spanish navy for a period of six years. On appeal, the sentence was revised to eight years of unpaid labor in the military facilities of Havana. Any lesser penalty would be unacceptable, read the sentencing, on account of the many "ravages" caused by "pirates" who had acted "under the protection of the Cartagena rebels."[48]

Only Francisco seems to have escaped forced labor in Havana. Francisco claimed that he was not a pirate, but rather a sailor taken prisoner by Cartagenan privateers when his ship was en route from Jamaica to Maracaibo. He had ended up in Cartagena, he asserted, where he had been forced to sail on the *Bellona*. Francisco managed to summon people to corroborate his story—three militiamen from the Free Colored Battalion in Panama. He was found innocent.[49] Whether Francisco was lying or telling the truth, his story illustrates how difficult it could be, even for Spanish officials, to categorize certain individuals as either "pirates" or privateers. People slipped in and out of these occupations and categories according to the changing circumstances of life at sea, which most individuals could hardly control.

Whether at sea or on land, life for sailors was risky, and the dynamics of politics and justice complicated and shifting. Francisco might have been on the *Bellona* willingly, but this did not necessarily mean that his allegiance to the State of Cartagena was undivided. Or maybe it was, but he was clever and lucky enough to avoid the fate of his colleagues, who were sent to Havana. There, in what seemed to Spanish authorities like the proper course of action, those sailors were forced into work that would shore up the very society they had undermined with their actions as privateers for Cartagena. Aury, their commanding officer, had once boasted that Cartagenan privateers successfully attacked Spanish interests "under the very walls" of Havana.[50] Now a few unlucky sailors had to pay the consequences.

Although Cartagena-sponsored attacks on vessels in and out of Cuba caused much alarm among Cuban elites for economic reasons, Cartagena's privateering tactic had an equally distressing political dimension: the State's privateers were finding safe haven in Haiti. Having expelled the French and dismantled slavery, Haitians posed a potential threat to Spain, one that materialized with their support of revolutionary provinces like Cartagena. Of Cartagena's tactical and political allies, the Republic of Haiti would indeed demonstrate the most unwavering commitment to the struggles against Spain in Tierra Firme.

7

Haiti

The Beacon Republic

THE PRIVATEERS WHO TARGETED Cuba as a Spanish enemy of Cartagena identified the Republic of Haiti as a natural ally. With Haitians both facilitating and participating in Cartagenan privateering, this Republic would prove more helpful in sustaining Cartagena's revolution than the United States, which some Cartagena leaders had hoped would become their foremost protector. Cartagena's emerging closeness with Haiti stood in contrast to its rejection of Cuba. Inhabitants of Cartagena who had family ties or commercial interests in Cuba remained cut off from their relatives and associates there.[1] The opposite was true for those with connections in Haiti. Led by President Alexandre Pétion, a man of color, Haiti rejected slavery, welcomed foreigners of African descent, and deployed an anticolonial stance, affording protection to anti-Spanish privateers and revolutionary agents.[2]

Privateering stimulated Cartagena's contact with Haiti, as many privateersmen frequented Haitian port towns to recruit sailors and refit their ships. However, contact between Cartagena and Haiti went beyond privateering logistics, moving well into the terrain of political and diplomatic relations. Cartagena sent a Frenchman named Pierre Antoine Leleux as a representative before Pétion in March 1813.[3] Cartagena seems also to have authorized three other agents in Haiti. Pétion, interested in fostering "the independence of the New World," quietly authorized direct trade with Cartagena and tactically prohibited trade with Spanish military personnel.[4]

Pétion's Haiti remained officially neutral with respect to the conflict between Spain and its New World territories. Nevertheless, the good relations between Haiti and Tierra Firme revolutionaries were clear to many people, with anti-Spanish sympathizers praising Haiti as a generous republic. Haiti was a beacon, efficiently providing assistance in the complicated waters of revolution.[5] The Haitian port town of Les Cayes became a revolutionary entrepôt, hosting political agitators, revolutionary fighters, and privateers. In July 1813, the Jamaican press reported that fourteen foreigners had departed Les Cayes on board the schooner *Duchess of Manchester*, bound for Cartagena and ready "to join the Standard of Independence."[6]

Relationships between Tierra Firme and Haiti, advanced by citizens, agents, and privateers of the State of Cartagena, would have important consequences for future political and military developments, with Haiti becoming a refuge for many after the fall of Cartagena in late 1815. Those who landed there, however, did not share the same convictions about revolutionary action. Amid internal conflicts, political clashes, and faltering revolutions, Simón Bolívar and his allies offered a different tactical approach and an alternative political conception of the struggle against Spain. This emerging perspective threw into question Cartagena's federalist policy and would eventually lead to reevaluating the need for, and legitimacy of, the revolutionary connections with Haiti's vibrant port towns.

LES CAYES FUNCTIONED as the epicenter of the collaborations between Haiti and Tierra Firme. A seafaring community located on the southern shore of Haiti, Les Cayes buzzed with legal and illicit seaborne commerce going back several generations. People there knew where and how to get their hands on merchandise, and how to operate the vessels to move it around. With the right contacts and enough luck, outside operatives could utilize Les Cayes as a reliable source of both supplies and seagoing personnel.[7] For Cartagenan privateers, Les Cayes soon became one of their most frequent ports of call.

The town of Les Cayes had grown in size and economic activity over the course of the eighteenth century, from just 80 houses in 1751 to 329 houses in 1776, reaching over 700 by 1790. Located on a corner of the central market square, the colonial administration building in Les Cayes housed an admiralty tribunal, established in 1779. According to the French planter and lawyer M. L. E. Moreau de Saint-Méry—author of an authoritative description of the French colony later published in Philadelphia—France had established the admiralty court following a request by French merchants.[8]

As Moreau de Saint-Méry put it, the town owed its very existence to its port.[9] Separated from the north of the colony by a mountain range, Les Cayes found a different way to connect with the outside world. In spite of the complicated, unpromising nature of its bay, which made it difficult for the harbor to shelter big ships, Les Cayes relied heavily on waterborne communication and trade. Before the Haitian Revolution, around fifty deep sea vessels arrived annually from France, around thirty vessels from the United States, and a few from Spanish and Dutch territories. Although much of the merchandise brought in by sea found its way elsewhere, some of these supplies were crucial for both town dwellers and the inhabitants of Les Cayes' rural hinterland, a countryside replete with sugar, coffee, indigo, and cotton plantations.[10]

Les Cayes' overseas connections were not limited to long-distance trade with Europe. In fact, as most of the European trade in Saint-Domingue took place in far-off Cap Français, the inhabitants of Les Cayes had to rely on supplies from other Caribbean societies, including Cuba, Jamaica, and Tierra Firme. Privateers and diplomats working for Cartagena helped strengthen connections with Les Cayes, but they themselves were building on preexisting contacts between the continent and the islands. For although in theory every French colony had to limit itself to communicating only with other French territories and France, Les Cayes' separation from the north of the colony and its relatively late development as a plantation society stimulated early connections with neighboring port towns. Bowing to the pressure of local needs, the French government officially authorized some foreign shipping into and out of Les Cayes in 1784. Locals could now legally trade for wood and foodstuffs from abroad.[11]

After the southern Republic of Haiti came into existence in 1806, seaboard business and political activity continued apace in Les Cayes. This included the sale and refitting of ships, trade in all sorts of maritime supplies, and the hiring of seamen. Privateers seem to have been particularly attracted to this port town. The harbor saw not only many prizes brought in by privateers, but also the arrival of ships in distress. An American ship robbed by a French privateer in 1811 sailed to Les Cayes after her mishap. The following morning, a report on the episode reads, the American captain "was not a little surprised to find the robber at anchor alongside of him."[12] Cartagenan privateers would soon come to Les Cayes and nearby places in southern Haiti.[13]

Records regarding the *Bellona* and other Cartagenan privateers offer some clues to the tactical and even personal importance of southern Haiti for privateersmen. The Haitian sailor Ignacio, the man who would later face charges of piracy in Panama, had been born in Port-au-Prince. His family resided there. He left for independent Cartagena, where he joined the crew of the *Bellona* for a privateering cruise beginning in mid-1814. But he would return again to his homeland, as Captain Aury ordered his men to sail to Jamaica and later to southern Haiti. The *Bellona* stopped near Les Cayes, where Aury had the schooner's foremast repaired and recruited more seamen, including Hilario, a native of Les Cayes.[14] The *Lady Madison*, which had begun to operate with a privateering commission from Cartagena the year before, also dropped anchor at Les Cayes on several occasions.[15]

Further testimony comes from depositions made by Captain Pedro Bruno, and by supercargoes José Buadas and Francisco Romero. Working aboard the Spanish ship *Rosita*, these seamen set sail from Santa Marta on December 24, 1815, bound for Kingston, where they loaded a cargo of dry goods before casting off again. Attacked and defeated by the *Popa de Cartagena*, the *Rosita* was taken to a place near Les Cayes, where both privateer and prize arrived on the night of January 10, 1816. The outfitters of the *Popa de Cartagena* arrived the following morning, having traveled overland from Les Cayes. Two of the outfitters went on board, and the convoy was joined by another privateer, the *Centinela*. Together they made for Aquin, to the east, where they arrived two days later.[16]

The outfitters quickly realized the *Rosita*'s cargo had a value of forty thousand pesos. The privateers decided to sell the merchandise immediately. In order to do so without leaving traces that could give away the original owners, they decided to erase all the marks and seals on the bundles and crates. After rewrapping the merchandise, they labeled it again with false seals. The cargo was sold to a French merchant who traded between Les Cayes and Jamaica. He paid thirty thousand pesos.[17]

Bruno, Buadas, and Romero watched as the merchandise was then loaded onto an American-built merchant schooner, manned by US citizens but with no flag to show her country of origin. The three witnesses thought this was the same ship that, flying Spanish colors, had been captured by Cartagenan privateers off Portobelo two years prior, carrying military supplies and stores at the time.[18] Even if they were mistaken, their testimony rings true. In regions of intense maritime activity like southern Haiti, it was common to see vessels changing owners, nationality, rigging, and even names. A case in point is the American-built schooner *Caroline*. Purchased in Les Cayes by Juan Francisco Pérez, a naturalized citizen of Cartagena and one of its privateer outfitters, the *Caroline* was immediately renamed. Because she was destined to become a Cartagenan privateer, her new owners christened her the *Carthagenera*.[19] Similar transactions must have taken place in port towns like Les Cayes and Aquin, which welcomed not only privateers but also other people with republican and anti-colonial convictions.

Unlike the British island of Jamaica, the Republic of Haiti sealed itself more effectively from Spanish spies and operatives.

Therefore, Cartagenan privateers and other antagonists of the Spanish monarchy operated relatively unhindered there. Refugees from the increasingly violent conflicts plaguing Tierra Firme (both from New Granada and Venezuela) who could afford to move to various Caribbean islands did so, with many aiming for Haiti as the safest destination. According to a note of gratitude to the Republic of Haiti, published by Venezuelan émigrés in Cartagena, Pétion and private citizens—including members of the Masonic lodge of Les Cayes—afforded the refugees protection and shelter. The note described Pétion as "distinguished" and "virtuous," remarking on the humanitarian example set by his country during this difficult time.[20]

After Spanish forces began closing in on Cartagena in mid-1815, people involved in the revolutionary movements there looked for asylum in Haiti, including Simón Bolívar, a Venezuelan who had first arrived in Cartagena with Leleux in mid-1812. With Pétion's help, Bolívar would eventually become supreme leader of the anti-Spanish movement in northern South America. But the rise of Bolívar and his allies took shape against the backdrop of the internal conflicts that plagued Tierra Firme after 1810, which would continue to divide revolutionary leaders seeking shelter in Haiti.

BEFORE ARRIVING IN independent Cartagena, Lieutenant Colonel Simón Bolívar had begun his political career as a would-be diplomat in Great Britain. Dispatched on a mission to London on June 9, 1810, by the Caracas junta, Bolívar was a rich patrician and a man of letters who had previously visited Europe. The emerging pro-independence leaders of Caracas, who had launched their own quest for autonomy after the Napoleonic crisis of 1808, believed that their envoy could potentially obtain British support for an independent Venezuela. Although Bolívar did not achieve this goal, he further acquainted himself with European politics and made important contacts. In London, for instance, Bolívar met Francisco de Miranda, a Venezuelan defector and an early supporter of Spanish American independence. He also met Leleux, the Frenchman who would go on to become a naturalized citizen of the State of Cartagena, its secretary of war and the navy, and its diplomatic envoy to Haiti.[21]

In early September 1810, Bolívar left London and departed for Venezuela, where he encountered an increasingly difficult situation. Throughout the country, Spanish and pro-Spanish forces resisted the movement for independence, with the conflict taking on the character of a bitter civil war. In 1812, the early Venezuelan revolutionary impetus was crushed. On March 26, a devastating earthquake decisively altered the situation. It occurred on Maundy Thursday—the second anniversary, by Catholic reckoning, of the establishment of the Caracas junta. The earthquake killed thousands, with Caracas taking overwhelming damage and revolutionary soldiers killed under the rubble. In a fateful coincidence, regions dominated by pro-Spanish forces escaped almost unscathed. With the tragedy effectively publicized as proof that Providence opposed revolution, scores switched allegiances or otherwise began to view the political transformation with suspicion, and even fear. The revolutionaries capitulated on July 25, 1812.[22]

Following the fall of pro-independence forces in Caracas, dozens of Venezuelan patriots, including Bolívar, fled to Cartagena. Most of them had never been there before. They intended, however, to build relationships with the local revolutionaries, seeking to obtain their aid in the liberation of Venezuela. Already engaged in a low-intensity but politically and economically devastating conflict with loyalist Santa Marta and centralist Santa Fe, the leaders of Cartagena and the United Provinces of New Granada could not afford to protect foreign revolutions. These conflicts, however, provided a perfect stage for the Venezuelan émigrés—mostly military men—to showcase their political convictions and fighting skills. If they could bring about victory for Cartagena and the United Provinces, then these polities would be in a better position to contribute to the cause of Venezuela.[23]

The Venezuelans' plans soon began to crystallize. Through the press and in public and private conversations, émigrés like Bolívar voiced their opinions on the political future of Tierra Firme. In their view, the multiple sovereignties that had emerged with the atomized revolutions of 1810 and 1811 should eventually coalesce into a single, larger state. The Venezuelans therefore pushed forward a new perception of how to wage war. They believed that the present conflict was not a chivalric war to be fought by moderate militias, but rather an international clash that required professional armies, with disciplined, full-time soldiers prepared to engage in direct, sustained combat. Mercy toward enemies was to be rarely deployed and deserters were to be shot.[24]

The Venezuelans seized their first opportunity to practice their doctrine and showcase their commitment to the cause. Under Bolívar's orders, a core group of young professional soldiers, accompanied by fresh recruits, played a crucial role in a fleeting but politically relevant defeat of Santa Marta, completed in January 1813. Building on this triumph, Bolívar obtained resources from the United Provinces and pushed the struggle back to Venezuelan soil. He led a rapid and successful campaign across the Andes, facing little resistance and gaining some support among local population along the way. In early August 1813, a triumphant Bolívar entered Caracas.[25]

Relentless royalist counterattacks soon followed, however, leading to a generalized war in Venezuela. Most people in Venezuela, much to the patriots' chagrin, remained on the side of Spain. In early September 1814, Bolívar fled the country, which had become ravaged by months of bitter fighting. With royalist forces back in control of Venezuela, Bolívar and other patriots emigrated for a second time to Cartagena. Bolívar did not stay there for too long. He traveled to the highland city of Tunja, near Santa Fe, to offer his services directly to the Congress of the United Provinces of New Granada. The federalists granted him the rank of captain general and gave him the mission of defeating the Santa Fe centralists, which he accomplished on December 12, 1814. With possession of the old viceregal capital, the

United Provinces not only increased their political weight but gained access to money, military supplies, and soldiers.[26]

Feeling increased confidence in Bolívar and his soldiers, the United Provinces' leaders now planned to defeat Santa Marta once and for all, authorizing Bolívar to take over that city and expecting Cartagena to provide soldiers, guns, ammunition, and other supplies. But Juan de Dios Amador and Manuel del Castillo, the governor and the military commander of Cartagena respectively, refused to support Bolívar's operations. Amador despised Bolívar's outspoken opposition to federalism. Castillo had clashed with the Venezuelan over military differences during the 1813 Santa Marta and Venezuelan campaigns. Other Cartagenans blamed Bolívar for the fall of Venezuela, which had made Cartagena more vulnerable to Spanish attack. Some simply balked at orders from abroad—even those emanating from the Congress of the United Provinces, in which they had representatives.[27]

Bolívar, however, was determined to gain access to Cartagena's resources to launch his attack on Santa Marta. In spite of the presence of many of his countrymen and his own sister within the walled city, Bolívar took drastic measures. He had Cartagena under siege by the end of March 1815. But the plan to force Amador and Castillo to comply with the United Provinces led nowhere. While disease and desertion dwindled Bolívar's army, Castillo's forces, now needed to protect the city, abandoned important positions along the Magdalena River, the border with Santa Marta. Santa Marta forces then began to enter Cartagenan territory.[28]

With Venezuela under Spanish control and Santa Marta's royalists rapidly moving into undefended Cartagenan rural areas, most people realized that the situation was ripe for a general Spanish counterattack.[29] Ferdinand VII was effectively back on the Spanish throne and, with war on the Iberian Peninsula at an end, metropolitan authorities finally seemed in a position to deal decisively with the troubles across the Atlantic. In Cartagena, rumors of a Spanish military expedition on its way to Tierra Firme were confirmed in mid-April 1815. Internal strife had to be brought to an end so that the State could prepare to defend itself. On May 8, 1815, Bolívar signed a peace agreement with Castillo. The Venezuelan left for Jamaica the following day.[30]

Bolívar eventually moved to Haiti, which continued to be the safest place for revolutionary émigrés.[31] Other political leaders and scores of refugees would flock to Haiti after the fall of the Cartagenan republic. Once again, privateersmen such as Aury facilitated this movement across the sea. They had been there during the State of Cartagena's difficult early months, and they were there for its death. But among the émigrés and others who reached Haiti, including Aury, the internal conflicts that had divided them in Tierra Firme changed their perception of Bolívar, with consequences that would reach a climax in Les Cayes.

8

"Horrors of Carthagena"

AFTER FIVE YEARS as Napoleon's prisoner in France, Ferdinand VII had returned to Spain in the spring of 1814. Determined to crush both liberal reformers at home and pro-independence forces in the overseas territories, the restored monarch had first dismantled the emerging parliamentary government, keeping his liberal detractors under control. The analogous tasks to be accomplished in South America became Ferdinand's overseas priority. The mission to restore monarchical government in the Spanish Indies would begin in Tierra Firme. With that region under control, Spain could then reinforce its presence in Peru and suppress autonomist forces active in Buenos Aires and Chile. Spain assembled the Expeditionary Army of Tierra Firme, with over twelve thousand men and dozens of ships. General Pablo Morillo y Morillo commanded this force. He had excelled on the Spanish battlefields during the war against Napoleonic occupation.[1]

Stymied by continuing internal conflict, pro-independence leaders found it difficult to organize and finance the defense of Cartagena. As Morillo's forces tightened the rope around Cartagena, its leaders, always innovative and willing to take risks, would make efforts to keep their republic afloat. Utilizing their mercantile American connection, they tried in vain to keep the city supplied with flour from the United States. Relying on their federative membership with the United Provinces of New Granada, they requested monetary resources from Santa Fe. Desperate for protection against a mighty enemy, they even invited Great Britain to annex Cartagena as a colony.[2]

Privateers and other maritime personnel carried out important tasks during the desperate defense of Cartagena. They protected strategic spots near the city and tried to undermine Spanish forces. But piercing Morillo's blockade proved difficult, and defeating it impossible. As the siege dragged on, some privateers remained in the city. In early December 1815, privateering commanders planned and carried out the evacuation of Cartagena. All the efforts of its leaders had been futile in the end. The moment had come to rely one last time on foreign mariners who could brave the sea, and Spanish artillery, to bring Cartagenan citizens out to safety somewhere in the Antilles.[3]

Revolutionary leaders who left before the siege or were evacuated by privateers, surviving what the US press would later call the "horrors of Carthagena," managed to regroup in the Haitian port town of Les Cayes. Haiti functioned as the crucial port in the middle of a tempest of counterrevolutionary repression that threatened to completely quash the different movements for independence. Exiled revolutionaries rallying around Bolívar forcefully cast their cause as an epochal struggle of continental proportions. They obtained the full support of Haitian president Pétion to launch an expedition against Morillo's forces.[4] But not all individuals with anti-Spanish sympathies shared a desire to follow Bolívar back to the continent.

In a reprise of the internal conflicts that had characterized the early revolutions in Tierra Firme, intense confrontations would take place among the émigrés in Haiti in early 1816. As tensions flared up again at Les Cayes, Aury and other privateers—perhaps more attracted to maritime warfare than to liberating any specific geographic regions—opposed Bolívar and relocated their operations to the Gulf of Mexico. Meanwhile, those who had stayed in Cartagena or fallen prisoner to Spanish forces would experience the counterrevolutionary retaliations of Morillo, the implacable architect of Spain's last stand in northern South America.

MORILLO'S EXPEDITIONARY ARMY set sail from Spain in early 1815. In April, Morillo made landfall on Margarita Island, just off the coast of Venezuela, immediately moving onto the mainland. If Tierra Firme was the stepping stone to regaining possession of the continent, Cartagena was the key to the reoccupation of Tierra Firme. By the end of July, Morillo had reached Santa Marta. There he organized and dispatched three different forces with the goal of occupying neighboring Cartagena. One division left on July 28. This force would move overland to the town of Mompox, secure Cartagena's hinterland, and cut off supplies to the walled city. This group would try to join up with forces coming in from Venezuela. On August 5, the army's vanguard began moving into Cartagenan territory from the north, with a plan to cross the Magdalena River, penetrate the countryside, collect supplies from locals, and get as close as possible to the city. With orders to blockade the Bay of Cartagena, seaborne forces set sail on August 12. Morillo had begun a frightening, large-scale encirclement operation.[5]

By the end of August 1815, large swaths of Cartagenan territory had come under Spanish control, with the city effectively blockaded by sea and land. According to a Spanish military account of the operations, Morillo refused to send an envoy or negotiator to the besieged city, claiming that the local leaders were not "worthy of such military transaction," for they had "atrociously insulted" the king with their rebellion. Moreover, the rebels had proven their "stubbornness" by setting ablaze entire towns and rural properties in the vicinity of Cartagena in order to deprive Spanish forces of food and other supplies. If the foreign soldiers lacked food long enough, the leaders of revolutionary Cartagena calculated, they would soon be decimated by disease in the tropical climate.[6] Toledo, the very man who had first opposed absolute independence from Spain, had his haciendas of Guayepo and Barragán set on fire so that Morillo would not be able to feed Spanish troops off his land.[7]

Although each side planned to drive the other to defeat by starvation, military skirmishes did take place in the outskirts of the city, as well as in several important positions near the bay. The fighting over the logistically critical island of Barú was bitter. For part of September, Cartagena kept communication with and effective control over this island. From Barú, cattle, poultry, and fish could be brought into the city. But the Spaniards moved onto the island. On September 22, Cartagena's forces tried to retake Barú with a seaborne operation carried out by eight schooners and five hundred men. Morillo's forces prevailed. Cartagena's last source of food disappeared.[8]

Other crucial resources would soon disappear as well. Although by now it must have seemed almost impossible to figure out how to put cash to good use, Spanish forces cut off Cartagena from its last source of money. On September 23, south of the city and up the Sinú River, Spanish forces caught up with and quickly defeated a group of Cartagenan officers, soldiers, and citizens, confiscating sixty-three thousand pesos sent over from Santa Fe by officials of the United Provinces of New Granada. Manpower was quickly eroding, too. Out of the 3,600 men originally recruited to face Morillo's attack, fewer than half were actually prepared for combat. Many soon died or were made prisoners by Spanish soldiers. One Spanish victory led an officer, Francisco Sanarrusia, to take his own life.[9]

Conditions within the walled city began to deteriorate rapidly. Overflowing with displaced people from the ravaged countryside, the besieged city found it difficult to provide enough food and safe shelter for everybody. With the Spanish successfully controlling maritime and terrestrial supply lines, hunger and disease began to set in by the end of September. The siege was to last for two more agonizing months.[10]

With the siege requiring more time than Morillo had anticipated, he modified his plans in order to accelerate the inevitable, beginning a series of artillery barrages. The bombardments destroyed several buildings and killed many people. Terrified, hundreds looked for refuge under the vaults and bastions of the defensive walls. The situation was desperate. Governor Amador also changed plans. He promoted the idea that the State of Cartagena, facing imminent ruin, should place itself under the "protection and guidance of the king of Great Britain."[11] He sent a diplomatic commission to Jamaica with orders to negotiate possible annexation with the British vice-admiral in Kingston. If Cartagena were to join the British monarchy as one of its colonies, desperate leaders believed, forces from Jamaica would soon come to their rescue. Although the commission managed to sail passed the maritime blockade, reaching Jamaica, no official in Kingston dared grant such an audacious request.[12]

The last few weeks of the siege were a nightmare. Unprecedented inflation appeared alongside scarcity. Flour barrels reached 150 pesos. A chicken could be sold for as much as sixteen pesos, an egg for four pesos. People ate their horses, mules, donkeys, cats, and dogs. To fend off hunger, many boiled and ate any piece of leather they could lay their hands on. Shoes, boots, saddles, bags, and even scraps from trunks and chairs became potential nourishment.[13] Plants that otherwise would have been rejected were consumed in desperation. In the words of historian José Manuel Restrepo, who spoke to siege survivors and read documents concerning the final weeks of independent Cartagena, "Hunger and its inseparable companion, plague, took scores of people to their graves every day; everywhere, nothing could be seen but pale men, extenuated women, and beings in agony. On several occasions, during the changing of the guard, officers discovered that sentinels had died during their watch."[14]

Governor Amador may have harbored the hope that his business contacts in the United States could come to remedy the situation. Although the details remain unclear, notarial records from New Orleans show that a consignment of flour worth twelve thousand dollars was ready to ship out of that port as early as mid-June. The flour had been loaded onto the *Caremarí*, which belonged to Amador. On June 19, however, the New Orleans District Court impounded the vessel and later sold it at auction. The notarial documents do not mention the reason for this.[15] In any event, if Amador and his associates in Cartagena were the consignees of the flour cargo, they waited in vain for its arrival. The *Caremarí* remained in New Orleans as late as April 23, 1816.[16] Although other craft had been able to successfully defy the Spanish blockade, bringing in some supplies, by early November 1815 maritime trade had ceased altogether.

Cartagena still had a small fleet in the bay, including several privateer ships, but these vessels were occupied with the defense of the city. Personnel aboard these ships fought over certain positions on the shore and nearby islands. On November 12, Cartagena's maritime force of about thirteen craft, including schooners, bilanders, and large canoes, attempted an amphibious assault on Spanish forces in the vicinity of Caño Loro, on Tierra Bomba Island. Even a Spanish account speaks of this battle as a fight unfolding "in a horrendous fashion," lasting "all day long." The attack continued with less intensity over the following two days. Spaniards soon brought to bear all of their available maritime power in the area. The much smaller and poorly supplied Cartagena fleet could accomplish nothing against such a mighty enemy. This was the last battle fought by the State of Cartagena.[17]

A strange stillness then followed. Artillery fire ceased. The comings and goings of sentinels and scouts, the skirmishes around the bay, the near-suicidal missions launched by the patriots—all ceased suddenly and for good. Independent Cartagena had lost impetus. Spaniards simply waited for capitulation. On December 5, civilians suddenly began emerging from the walled city. They slowly walked passed the Spanish line on several points and went on. Most were wretched-looking women and children who had all but died. They had been starved out of the city.[18]

For these people—common inhabitants of the city and rural areas—the last few days inside the walled city must have been horrific. Three hundred people had died on December 4 alone. On that day, a meeting of military officers and political leaders had made the final decision. Lieutenant Governor Juan Elías López Tagle gave orders to evacuate the city the following day. Commoners could try to reach safety and food somewhere in the countryside, while patricians and political leaders would brave the blockade and sail to exile in

Kingston and Les Cayes. Aury was ordered to coordinate the maritime evacuation. Other privateers also participated in the effort.[19]

On the morning of December 5, the seamen began to ready the ships. Quickly after, that very afternoon, they cast off. Enduring heavy fire from Spanish forces as they tried to leave the bay, they broke through several hours later. As it was still a young moon that night, the relative darkness was helpful. The wind was also favorable. The patriots managed to sail away. Further trouble nonetheless awaited them out at sea.[20] The fair weather abruptly changed a few hours later. The fleeing convoy encountered a serious storm and dispersed. Several hundred refugees perished. In a personal letter written by Amador, the leader-turned-political-refugee stated that the evacuation had been "as disastrous as any recorded in history." Newspapermen in the United States obtained a copy of the letter, translated it, and published it under the headline "Horrors of Carthagena."[21]

Although exact numbers are not available, thousands of people seem to have emigrated from Tierra Firme to the Caribbean islands during these months. The forced migration began with the arrival of Morillo's Expeditionary Army, a few months before the siege of Cartagena, and continued through the final evacuation. In April 1815, people on board the schooner *Carmen*, about to depart for Jacmel, in southern Haiti, had witnessed scores of small vessels arriving in Curaçao from the continent. As the *Carmen*'s captain put it, this happened as a "consequence of the arrival of the Spanish Expedition."[22] The evacuation of Cartagena later that year seems to have been the most tragic of a series of emigrations of people fleeing the war.

Many individuals and families who had been involved in the Revolution of Cartagena and the consolidation of the independent State suffered from Morillo's vengeful policies. Leaders and supporters of the independence movement who stayed in the city, as well as those who left but were later captured in Spanish territories and sent back to Morillo, lost their property, endured judicial scrutiny, and suffered political persecution. Dozens were tried for high treason, found guilty, and shot. The first victims, a group of thirty-five commoners, were followed by a group of nine patricians, including Toledo. Many others were shot or hanged.[23] As they moved inland, Spanish forces would replicate this strategy for months to come. Hundreds faced firing squads or were sent to the gallows. By early 1816, independent Cartagena was gone, and the United Provinces of New Granada disappeared quickly after, along with most of its political leaders.[24]

SOME SURVIVORS OF Cartagena's exodus did manage to regroup in Kingston and Les Cayes, the two places they had originally meant to go to for their exile. In the wake of the Spanish reoccupation of Cartagena, the refugees viewed Kingston and Les Cayes as logical places for rebuilding their lives or continuing their fight.[25] Located within relatively easy reach of Tierra Firme, Haiti and Jamaica were linked to Cartagena by sailors, merchants, and smugglers well before the political upheavals. Communication and travel between Cartagena and the islands had been consolidated further after independence, when many people participated in free trade and privateering operations. Amador, a survivor of the exodus, felt particularly welcomed in Kingston, where, he wrote, "the emigrants are treated by the government and the inhabitants with humanity above all praise."[26]

Jamaica was a place where refugees could eke out a living or rebuild their privilege. Beginning with the American Revolution, when thousands of royalists poured in from places like Savannah and Charleston, and continuing through the arrival of refugees from Saint-Domingue during the Haitian Revolution, this British island had become a destination for people fleeing war and political conflict. In Jamaica, free people of color from the French colony established a mutual aid society called the Société de Bienfaisance to help some of their arriving brethren in distress. But Kingston was also a locus of enslavement, where women and children freed by the

Haitian Revolution found themselves subordinated to new "masters" who sought to claim them as property.[27]

It remains difficult to ascertain what sort of treatment émigrés of color from Tierra Firme were afforded in Jamaica. However, Catholic parish records from Kingston indicate that some of those who arrived as slaves continued to enjoy the limited privileges they had in Spanish jurisdictions. Juan Reyna and María de la Cruz Barrera, for instance, were the slaves of a man from Mompox, within Cartagenan territory, who had settled in Kingston. Assuming it was their own wish to get married, Juan and María were allowed a Catholic wedding in October 1816.[28]

The Republic of Haiti became the preferred place for many of the most radical revolutionaries who evacuated Cartagena, including scores of privateers and political leaders of color like Pedro Romero, the craftsman who had played a crucial role in the early revolutionary process. Although Romero died in Haiti, others managed to survive and to continue their struggles. Bolívar himself, having survived an assassination attempt in Jamaica on December 10, 1815, quickly relocated to Haiti. There he encountered surviving Cartagena refugees, including some friendly to him and others who resented him for laying siege to Cartagena the year before. Some rejected his opposition to the federal form of government previously adopted by Cartagena and the United Provinces of New Granada.[29]

With the backing of President Pétion of Haiti for a large-scale attack on Morillo's forces, Bolívar began a campaign to recruit sympathizers for his cause. But he was determined to rely on the principles of centralized leadership and government, and he himself would be "the measure of the revolution."[30] Bolívar's potential role as supreme leader for the liberation of the entire Tierra Firme territories was seriously questioned by many. The ensuing debate over Bolívar's merits would be intense, and its consequences lasting. For although Bolívar eventually became supreme leader of the coming expedition, some privateers like Aury refused to follow him. Perhaps they intuited that Bolívar would move more firmly toward regular war, and that Bolívar's eventual triumph would leave little political room for irregular, multinational crews of privateers—a triumph that, in any case, was still far from certain.

SEEKING SHELTER IN Haiti after the fall of Cartagena, Aury had already reassembled a privateering fleet and found himself refitting at Les Cayes in early 1816. Aury's fleet included the ships *Republicano*, *Estrella*, *Júpiter*, and *Plancha*, and a schooner carrying eighteen cannon outfitted by Pedro Luis Brión, a merchant from Curaçao recently turned anti-Spanish fighter. The *Bellona*, which had been taken by the British brig *Carnation* before the beginning of Morillo's blockade, now rejoined this fleet. Aury's associates had recently recovered her in Kingston.[31]

Spanish authorities in Santiago de Cuba obtained intelligence that revolutionaries from Cartagena and other places in Tierra Firme had gone into exile in Haiti, where they remained active. Leaders from Venezuela, including Bolívar, operated out of Les Cayes and in alliance with Pétion, Spanish sources indicated. Although very little evidence of this survives, it is possible that in early 1816 privateer ships were getting ready to cruise against Spain with the Republic of Haiti's political support and logistical help. Bolívar and others may have issued letters of marque against Spain to privateers in the area, especially those based in Les Cayes.[32]

The conflict with Spain, however, was now framed as a truly epochal struggle—as the liberation of an entire continent that would begin with the retaking of Tierra Firme. This gave traction to proposals for a more centralized and militaristic approach. In the wake of Morillo's implacable counterrevolutionary campaign, anti-Spanish leaders opposing federalism could now paint the early, atomized revolutions and provincial states as mistakes not to be repeated. Local and regional sovereignties held together by a powerless federal government could lead only to civil strife at best, and to Spanish triumph at worst. The growing popularity of this new approach became known to Spanish authorities. From Spanish mariners present in southern Haiti, officials in Cuba learned that some revolutionaries had become more ambitious in their plans, pulling together resources for a continental invasion, rather than limiting themselves to privateering attacks or holding onto small and ephemeral revolutionary enclaves.[33]

The information came from the crewmen and officers of the *Rosita*, a Spanish ship. They gave further details on the plans they had heard about, much of which turned out to be accurate. At anchor near Aquin, in Haiti, the Spanish sailors had heard from some British sailors working for Bolívar that the dispersed Cartagena émigrés planned to regroup in Les Cayes, where they would assemble an expedition with the goal of retaking Tierra Firme. With help from Pétion and funds raised by Bolívar, they planned to take over strategic port towns along the entire coast of Tierra Firme, including Riohacha, Santa Marta, and Portobelo.[34]

Alarmed by this information, authorities in Santiago relayed the intelligence to Juan José Ruíz de Apodaca, the captain general of Cuba, as well as to Morillo in Cartagena and to officers in Santo Domingo, Santa Marta, and Maracaibo. Authorities in Santiago sent word to Haiti complaining about what they called the "protection and asylum given to Cartagenan privateers in the department of Les Cayes."[35] In possession of further details about the planned expedition, thanks to revolutionary correspondence intercepted by his men, Morillo vehemently raised the issue in a written protest to Pétion.[36]

In his letter to the Haitian president, Morillo seemed especially concerned about an alleged supply of firearms that had recently arrived in Les Cayes. These could be used by anti-Spanish forces, he feared. In his answer to Morillo, Pétion acknowledged that the State of Cartagena had ceased to exist, which minimized the threat, and insisted that his government was continuing to observe a policy of neutrality. He was determined to prevent privateering and other illegal activities in Haiti's port towns. Pétion further assured the

Spanish general that the Cartagena émigrés were but a few, and that his government had forbidden the outfitting of military expeditions to foreign territories in its jurisdiction. In reality, however, Pétion afforded extensive protection and help to Tierra Firme revolutionaries.[37]

Unlike Morillo, authorities in Havana had a less dramatic perception of the situation. Ruiz de Apodaca thought that the revolutionaries did not have the strength to put together an expedition. He believed that, after the disastrous evacuation of Cartagena, anti-Spanish partisans lacked the logistical capacity to mount a successful operation.[38] Bureaucrats in Santiago and Cartagena took the potential threat more seriously, because they continued to receive news of a growing fleet in Les Cayes.[39] The viceroy Francisco de Montalvo (who now resided in occupied Cartagena) nonetheless remained skeptical about this potential expedition. He doubted Bolívar's ability to gather the necessary resources or the will to launch the expedition.[40]

Bolívar, however, had found strong support in Haiti. In exchange for Bolívar's promise to free the slaves and abolish slavery in the Spanish territories he was to liberate, Pétion had secretly supplied ammunitions, arms, and men.[41] Bolívar had also made contact with merchants willing to advance money and supplies. Nevertheless, his leadership remained a matter of debate. Some of the patriots gathered at Les Cayes resented Venezuelans, refusing to forgive Bolívar for his attack on Cartagena. Others expressed federalist visions for the future of Tierra Firme (as opposed to the centralist vision espoused by Bolívar), and many had disagreements over rank and authority. Some were inclined to re-spark the struggle against Spain elsewhere.[42]

Joined by veteran fighters, new recruits, and some privateers who had previously held commissions from the State of Cartagena, Bolívar solidified his leadership and launched the expedition. They landed on Margarita Island on May 3, 1816. The fighters soon moved onto the Venezuelan mainland, but proved unable to make any significant inroads. Staggering tactical errors, miscalculations, and treason led the expedition to retreat by the end of July. Bolívar had to rush back to Haiti. A new liberation project had clearly begun to take shape, but military triumph continued to elude its leaders.[43]

Although Spanish authorities had information suggesting that Aury had participated in the failed expedition, the French privateer had in fact not been part of the operation.[44] Aury seems to have been ambivalent about following Bolívar to the continent and eventually mutating from commodore into general. In a private letter, he expressed his love for Cartagena, "our state" in the "Republic of New Granada," and therefore his inclination to bind his struggle to the land. But at Les Cayes he opposed the idea of directly attacking Tierra Firme.[45] Instead, perhaps under pressure from his men and financial partners, Aury favored a plan to take over Old Providence Island. This tiny island off the coast of Nicaragua could be more easily turned into a new Cartagena, a privateering heaven that would yield profits as well as smaller but continuing victories against Spanish targets.

Perhaps more interested in privateering business than taking over countries, the sailors on the *Bellona* and other privateers working with Aury chose not to sail for Venezuela. Instead, they established contact with Mexican revolutionaries, obtaining letters of marque from José Manuel de Herrera, a priest advocating for Mexican independence based in New Orleans. Aury's fleet then reoriented its operations toward the Gulf of Mexico.[46] For the time being, Aury's struggle against Spain remained partially detached from the land. By contrast, Bolívar persisted in his plans to retake Venezuela and then liberate the whole of Tierra Firme. His followers would have to work for another three years before any significant advances were made. In the meantime, Aury and his men would encounter a different set of circumstances in the Gulf of Mexico.

The lives of the foreign privateers and the seafaring people of color who had sailed under the flag of Cartagena did not revolve exclusively around the fate of Tierra Firme. They stayed on the move, becoming protagonists of multiple connected and entangled histories, some of which had little to do with the politics and warfare unfolding in northern South America. Facing challenges of their own, embedded in their own cultural traditions, and possessed of their own political convictions, they were, above all, common people trying to make a living at sea. In the process, sometimes they had to assert their own autonomy and freedom, by rough means if necessary. They could rob, mutiny against, and even kill their employers and officers with the same determination that they applied to attacking merchantmen at sea. Cartagenans fleeing Morillo aboard privateers, and even Aury himself, would get a taste of this in due course.

9

Robbery, Mutiny, Fire

NEWS OF THE SIEGE OF Cartagena by Pablo Morillo and the evacuation of the city in early December 1815 circulated widely. The fate of the refugees and the role played by privateers in their evacuation became the most common topics of conversations about those events. In a personal letter written in Kingston, Jamaica, in early 1816, Juan de Dios Amador negatively described the evacuating ships: lacking water and food, they were unprepared to meet the needs of so many refugees. Addressed to his nephew Francisco García del Fierro—yet another merchant and a signatory of Cartagena's 1812 Constitution who left town before the siege—the letter contained shocking details about the fate of the refugees.[1]

Under favorable conditions, a traveler departing from Cartagena could make it to Kingston in less than a week. In the wake of the evacuation of Cartagena and the hardships that followed, it took Amador thirty-four days to complete this trip. On January 15, 1816, when he first sat down to write the letter to his nephew, Amador looked back on the human tragedy he had barely survived and wrote that "the greatest weight of the common calamity seems to have fallen on our family." His sister María, his niece Pepita—García del Fierro's wife, who had given birth just three days before the evacuation—and other relatives who had left on the US schooner *Drummond* remained unaccounted for. By February 11, when Amador resumed writing his letter, he had received news. Forced to look for provisions near Portobelo, in Panama, the *Drummond* had been spotted and captured by Spanish privateers. Spanish officials threw Amador's relatives into jail and later shipped them to Cartagena, along with many other refugees.[2]

Although Amador felt the weight of the "calamity" falling on his own shoulders, Cartagena's tragic evacuation involved hundreds of people. Amador's letter recounts the particular tragedies of many "other vessels of the emigration." Seventy-five people starved to death during the *Constitución*'s passage to Jamaica. Even more people died on board the *Grand Sultan*, while the *Two Brothers* foundered just off the shores of Jamaica, "but so suddenly that only seventeen persons could be saved out of the great number that were on board." The *General Bermúdez* ran aground on the southern coast of Cuba, "with only twenty-three cadaverous persons remaining, of one hundred and twenty-three." While the *India Libre* was able to reach Jamaica, she arrived "in the greatest distress." Over eight hundred people who had left on the *Estrella* remained stranded on Old Providence Island. Nothing was known of the *Concepción*. "Such are the misfortunes," wrote Amador, "that have succeeded the mortality of so many days of famine which at last obliged us to emigrate."[3]

The misfortunes suffered by Cartagenan political leaders and regular citizens during the evacuation were partially blamed on some of the privateers and other skippers who participated in the operation. Writing about the *India Libre*, Amador mentioned that, after barely making it to Jamaican shores, the captain "took by force what he pleased from the emigrants." Placing his own family center stage in the narrative of the "common calamity," Amador described how he himself had been the victim of robbery by the very men his State had recently authorized to rob from Spain on its behalf.[4]

Following the dramatic change in the balance of power at the end of 1815, some privateers had decided to make the best out of a difficult and confusing situation. They experienced the end of the Cartagenan republic in less traumatic yet equally complicated ways. As privateers' destinies were not altogether attached to Tierra Firme and the political outcomes there, they simply had to look for new bases of operation (which they would find on the Gulf of Mexico and the US East Coast), new employers, or other opportunities for gain. Because privateering sailors rarely deployed unconditional loyalty to their commissioning states, often clashing even with their own outfitters or commanding officers, some felt their bond to the citizens of Cartagena had been dissolved, making their former allies fair game.

While Bolívar later accused Aury of embodying privateering degradation, things were not that clear cut. Aury had found a certain measure of glory and fortune in privateering, but he would come to second-guess his commitment to this particular calling. And although he had worked with other privateering agents for several years, Aury himself clashed with privateering sailors and officers, experiencing their bitter rejection as he tried to set up a new privateering enclave after the fall of Cartagena.

WHEN THE LEADERS of the State of Cartagena decided to evacuate the city on December 5, 1816, Amador left the bay aboard the privateer schooner *General Castillo*. In total, eighty people came aboard. All of them, Amador claimed, endured not only hardships and a terrible storm but also robbery by the ship's captain, William Mitchell. As Amador told his nephew, the captain "despoiled us of all our money, gold, silver, jewels and precious stones," and then "put us on shore in the island of Providence." Amador's intended destination was Jamaica. It took him several weeks to finally make it to Kingston. Some of his relatives had followed equally complicated paths. García del Fierro's mother, siblings, nephews, and nieces, who had left on the brig *Hope*, made it to Grand Cayman barely alive. Their intended destination was New Orleans.⁵

After dropping off the refugees on Old Providence, off the coast of Nicaragua, Captain Mitchell seems to have moved on to San Andrés, just to the south of Old Providence. There, several sources suggest, he killed the Spanish governor, intimidated local troops, stole cattle, took one hundred slaves, and temporarily occupied the island. Archbeld Mikella, a local resident, claimed that Mitchell had also killed nine of the fourteen soldiers detached to this small corner of the Spanish Indies. According to newspaper reports from Kingston, Mitchell used the flag of Cartagena during his attack on San Andrés, and hung the governor by the neck from one of the masts of the *Comet*.[6]

Anglo-American sources provide a little more information on the *Comet*, though unfortunately they have little to say about the fate of the refugees. A Charleston newspaper reported on Mitchell's arrival in San Andrés and Old Providence. According to this account, Mitchell had entered port alleging that his ship needed to resupply water.[7] From the logbook of the US warship *Boxer*, which captured the *Comet* on April 7, we gather that Mitchell was still flying the colors of Cartagena when the *Boxer* approached his vessel. Timothy Gay, in charge of the *Boxer*'s log, wrote that at the time of her capture the *Comet* carried fourteen slaves, gold, and silver. The slaves, according to Gay, had been stolen in San Andrés after the murder of the governor.[8]

Not all privateers who participated in the evacuation of Cartagena abandoned or robbed the refugees. Aury provided full aid to those he took on board his ship. But when he and his sailors reunited with surviving refugees in the south of Haiti, Aury insisted that his expenses during the Cartagena evacuation be paid. This demand became entangled with the bitter debate over Bolívar's leadership in the plans to retake Tierra Firme. Sponsored by Pétion and with a growing following, Bolívar secured supreme command of the revolutionary forces gathered in Les Cayes. Aury and many others, however, favored the idea of a ruling council rather than a supreme leader. He also did not take well Bolívar's choice of Pedro Luis Brión for naval commander. As Brión had only recently joined anti-Spanish forces, Aury looked down on him, considering him but a junior captain. Aury would not let authority over his ships and men go to Brión.[9]

Larger differences in strategy and ways of life seem to have pitted Aury and his men against Bolívar and his followers. Bolívar had grand aspirations. He devoted himself to the idea of liberating Caracas and the rest of Venezuela and Tierra Firme, cementing an alliance with some leaders from New Granada interested in defeating

Morillo. This would be the foundation for continental liberation. Aury, perhaps yielding to pressure from his sailors and associates, insisted that instead of turning the struggle into a land invasion the patriots should continue a privateering course of action. For maritime personnel relatively detached from the land, the idea of transitioning from sailors into soldiers for an indeterminate period of time must have raised serious concerns. Accustomed to the ways of the sea, both in peace and during wartime, and coming out of a privateering bonanza under the auspices of the State of Cartagena, Aury's men had little intention of joining Bolívar's experiment.[10]

Parting ways with Bolívar, Aury and his men shipped out of Les Cayes. Aury took command of the *Bellona*, leading an eight-vessel privateer squadron, but he was forbidden to operate in the name of Tierra Firme revolutionaries.[11] Although tension had built among Aury, his officer corps, and his common sailors, they would continue to work together for a few months. They headed to the northern coast of Cuba, where they captured the Spanish ship *Aguilar*. A crewman on the *Aguilar*, Antonio Suárez, was taken aboard the *Bellona*. This sailor established communication with those who spoke Spanish among Aury's men. From them, Suárez learned that the privateers planned to take the corvette *Diana* and every other Spanish ship entering and leaving the port of Havana "until commerce is destroyed." They then planned to sail around Cape San Antonio to meet up with another seven privateer ships coming from the southern shores of Cuba. After joining forces, they expected to attack Alvarado, a port town not far from Veracruz, in Mexico.[12]

José Vigre, another man who found himself aboard the *Bellona* at this time, also spoke with sailors and later claimed to have heard from them that Aury planned to attack Baracoa, in Cuba, and then move on to the Gulf of Mexico.[13] In June 1816, Aury's fleet did indeed head toward the Gulf of Mexico, planning to carry out further attacks on Spanish shipping on behalf of Mexican revolutionaries. Cuban shipping, however, continued to be attacked by other privateers through the remainder of 1816. After Cartagena disappeared as a privateering haven, privateers (and the investors backing their operations) became even more active in places like New Orleans and Baltimore, where they outfitted and launched cruises against Spanish shipping.[14]

AFTER THE FALL of independent Cartagena, Spanish authorities in the Caribbean stepped up their defense against privateers. Early in 1816, Morillo sent a squadron out to sea with orders to bring privateer attacks under control. The squadron managed to capture two enemy ships.[15] The bulk of the active privateering vessels, however, successfully avoided Spanish ships. Spanish officials praised the capture of the privateer *Margariteña*, an exception to this trend. Under a US captain named Osman, the *Margariteña* had earlier taken a Spanish slave ship with African captives on board, as well as a British schooner carrying cattle.[16] The *Margariteña* arrived in Havana on October 5, 1816, as a prize of the Spanish schooner *Santa Isabel*. On learning the whereabouts of the *Margariteña*, captain José Cepeda, commander of the merchantman *Santa Isabel*, had decided to give her chase, beginning in the early morning of October 3. Around eight in the afternoon, Cepeda was in sight of the *Margariteña* and ordered the successful attack.[17]

The capture of the *Margariteña* was advertised east of Havana as a major triumph against the privateers. Maritime trade and transportation in and out of this part of the island had suffered the effects of anti-Spanish privateering in recent years. The governor of Santiago sent news of this "glorious action" to the inhabitants of Baracoa, Holguín, Bayamo, Puerto del Príncipe, Trinidad, and Matanzas. In his letter to those districts, the governor wrote that the "entire Spanish people" felt a justified indignation against privateers, an "enemy race" afflicting Spanish trade and inflicting so much suffering on the island. Spaniards should now rejoice in the capture of this privateer.[18]

The happiness and officiousness on the part of Santiago's governor seem unwarranted, and perhaps self-serving. Privateers would continue to plague Spanish shipping with almost complete impunity, not only from the shores of Tierra Firme but also from US shores.[19] In 1816, privateer ships outfitted in Anglo-American port towns preyed on commercial vessels in and out of Cuba. In September, the owners of the brig *San Andrés* lobbied José Cienfuegos and Alejandro Ramírez, Cuba's captain general and general intendant respectively, imploring them to try to bring the situation under control. The merchants petitioned Cienfuegos to communicate with Spain's diplomatic envoy in Philadelphia. They hoped for the diplomat to put some pressure on US officials in that city, making them cease their de facto protection of privateer vessels engaging in what the Spanish called *piraterías*—piratical actions.[20]

But there was not much Spanish diplomats could do. The United States maintained a position of neutrality with respect to the conflict between Spain and anti-Spanish insurgents, and privateers managed to take advantage of this neutrality effectively. Anti-Spanish naval, military, and political action—both in the open and secretly—became prevalent in US Atlantic port towns, most importantly in Baltimore. This city's commercial and maritime success—not yet eclipsed by the rise of New York City—made it a particularly attractive town for all manner of troublemakers. Local merchants—some of whom harbored anti-monarchical inclinations—soon found it lucrative to illegally invest in anti-Spanish privateering joint ventures. With letters of marque from Argentine, Venezuelan, and Mexican revolutionaries (all now following the model first set by the State of Cartagena), privateers shipping out of Baltimore tended to target big merchant ships traveling between Europe and Cuba. Profits were truly handsome.[21]

Anti-Spanish privateering, however, did not operate exclusively out of the East Coast. A tradition of piracy in the Gulf of Mexico and contested sovereignties in the area made the shores of Texas and Louisiana particularly useful for Aury and other privateersmen. But both coasts remained connected, as conspirators and privateers moved back and forth between ports and harbors in the North Atlantic and the Gulf of Mexico. In September 1816, the Spanish consul in Baltimore reported that several ships had left Baltimore for Matagorda, on the coast of Texas, carrying insurgents ready to join their colleagues in the Gulf, where they would build a new base of operations. The US press reported that Aury had already established a stronghold in Matagorda.[22]

In a dramatic twist of events, after Aury reappeared on the coast of Texas, he was placed on the defensive against his own men, most of them people of color.[23] Many Afro-Caribbean sailors had chosen the path of the sea in part to escape from arbitrary bureaucrats, officers, and masters.[24] But the maritime trades demanded obedience too, and at times exposed individuals to harsh forms of discipline and punishment. Aury's anti-Spanish project and aspirations for profit, which necessarily rested on his sailors' willingness to obey him and to respect hierarchy, would be seriously compromised after his men mutinied in opposition to his increasing demands and abusive attitude.

ACCOMPANIED BY PEOPLE who had privateered with him on behalf of Cartagena, on board some of the same ships that had just recently flown Cartagena's colors, and along with some new men he had recruited at Les Cayes, Aury began to cruise off the coasts of Texas and Louisiana in the summer of 1816.[25] Setting out to sea from Matagorda Bay, Aury raised serious concerns among Anglo-American merchants. In New Orleans, a growing emporium of trade, contraband, and slavery, some residents feared that merchant ships coming in and out of the city could fall prey to Aury and his associates. In September, it was rumored that Aury had taken the schooner *Swift*, which had left New Orleans for Nassau, in the Bahamas. The schooner, however, had made it safely to her destination.[26]

Many people in the United States showed support for anti-Spanish privateering. A Baltimore newspaper note sympathetic to Spanish American independence asserted that people spread rumors about privateering agents to discredit "Mexican patriots," a label that fit Aury only loosely, but plausibly enough from the vantage point of some outside observers. The editorialists urged their readers not to pay attention to the rumors, for patriots like Aury followed the rules of war in their struggle against Spain and had orders not to break the laws of the United States.[27] In practice, anti-Spanish insurgents and investors involved in privateering activities did break the law on a regular basis, relying on smuggling and other illegal activities to boost profits.[28]

People in port towns like New Orleans and Baltimore closely followed news about Aury's activities in the Gulf Coast. In the fall of 1816, news spread that Aury's squadron had been destroyed. Word of this development first reached New Orleans at the end of September, when a Galician sailor named José Peña arrived in town in very poor shape. Before the Spanish consul, he declared that he had been taken prisoner by Aury's men, who had then mutinied against Aury and other officers, destroying six ships and eight prizes they had recently taken. The confusion had given Peña the opportunity to break free, and to head immediately to New Orleans. The Spanish sailor claimed that Aury had died in the mutiny, killed by his own men.[29]

Aury was not dead, but his men had in fact tried to get rid of him for good. Peña, making his escape during the chaos, had had little ability or time to gather details on how things unfolded. But he managed to give a rough account. According to Peña's testimony, it all began when six of the eight prizes taken by Aury ran aground while entering Matagorda Bay. Determined to salvage the merchandise on board the grounded vessels, Aury pressed his sailors to work harder than they had anticipated or were willing to tolerate. Although it remains difficult to verify Peña's testimony with other sources, he claimed that Aury had made his men work in a most "cruel" and "inhumane" fashion, mistreating them in word and deed. Aury had even denied his men food rations.[30]

It may be the case that Peña and the Spanish consul were exaggerating, trying to depict Aury in the most negative light possible. Whatever the circumstances were, however, Aury and his men did come to blows. It is not difficult to imagine that excessive work after a mishap triggered the confrontation. Under normal circumstances, unloading cargo required long hours of exhausting work from maritime personnel. Unloading grounded vessels off shore, with no proper infrastructure to facilitate the work, must have been a risky task.

A group of Haitian sailors led the move against Aury. Before coming to Matagorda, Aury had recruited new sailors at Les Cayes with the promise that they would take prizes at sea and sail them to New Orleans, where they would divide up the proceeds. Instead, the sailors found themselves working as stevedores in difficult circumstances. Along with the fresh recruits, Aury's small naval force included sailors who had worked with him for some time, most recently operating from Cartagena and the south of Haiti. These veterans seem to have had accumulated grievances against Aury dating back to the conflict with Bolívar at Les Cayes. The veterans sided with the Haitian recruits against Aury.[31]

One night in early September, the conspirators moved ahead with their plan to strike against their captain. The crew on board the *Criolla*—seventy men later described as "black" and following the orders of one Bellegarde Batigne—had all sailed under Cartagena colors. Conspiracy became mutiny when these men detained and tied up their officers. Officers on other ships heard the noise from this action. One of the captains, the man in charge of the *Bellona*, sent a detachment of men on a small boat to find out what the trouble was. They approached the *Criolla* and requested permission to board. When the mutineers denied permission, the officer on the small boat announced that he had orders to climb aboard the *Criolla*. With the advantage of their elevated position, the men on the *Criolla* opened fire, lighting up the night and finishing off the officer and almost every other soul on the boat. Afterward, mutiny quickly spread across the rest of the fleet.[32]

Meanwhile, Aury remained on shore inside his tent, protected by a temporary fort he had previously ordered built. The men on land, however, had already sided with the mutineers. Upon hearing firearm discharges from the *Criolla*, they stormed Aury's quarters and demanded his surrender. When Aury resisted and reached for his sword, one of the mutineers shot him three times. Aury received injuries to both his hands and his chest.[33]

The sailors assumed Aury was dead and left him bleeding on the ground. They detained the remaining officers and gathered all the firearms, ammunition, and other supplies, as well as Aury's personal effects and all the merchandise unloaded from the grounded vessels. The sailors loaded everything on board three ships. The officers were given one ship and set free to go wherever they pleased. Free from what they viewed as the tyranny of Aury and his officers, the sailors on Matagorda Bay were now ready to make for Haiti with the booty. Before heading out to sea, they set the *Bellona* ablaze.[34]

Similar to what slaves in Saint-Domingue had done during the Haitian Revolution, these Haitian sailors used the power of fire to do away with the instruments and symbols of their oppression.[35] Hailing from a world in which exploitation and abuse had been trademarks of planters, slave drivers, state agents, and maritime authorities, these men chose to strike, shifting the balance of power in their favor. Seafaring could lead to freedom or autonomy, but these gains were relative to the authority of others and could be lost again. The masterless Caribbean was thus not a place but an ongoing social struggle.

When the labor regimes aboard sailing ships came to resemble slavery much too closely, sailors could defy, challenge, or even destroy the yoke of hierarchical subordination binding them to their captains and officers. But it remained impossible to do away with the tension between autonomy and subordination. Even mutineers necessarily granted some authority to those among them who would serve as captains, and they would eventually join the crews of other ships. Bound for Haiti, Aury's former sailors looked to a country where they could enjoy a certain measure of safety, and where they could easily ship out again. They listened to the call of the land, and they would be detached from it again.[36]

Having left Aury for dead in a lonesome spot on the coast of Texas, the rebel sailors also left behind what remained of their connections with the privateering and republican experiment of Cartagena. Their engagements with Aury and Tierra Firme revolutionaries were but episodes of their longer odysseys. Aury himself moved on after the events of Matagorda. Having recovered from his injuries, he soon found yet another revolutionary enclave and base of operations. Across the Florida Peninsula, on Amelia Island, he would participate in a new ephemeral privateering republic, striking an alliance with freshly recruited Haitian sailors.

On Amelia Island, revolution and privateering took off in familiar ways, with multinational crews, attacks on Cuban shipping, and the participation of anti-Spanish partisans known to Aury from his Cartagena days. However, the hemispheric context had begun to shift, and privateering and small republics now saw their political legitimacy fading. On Amelia Island, Aury and his colleagues stood dangerously close to the state of Georgia. The dream of Spanish American liberation would clash with the reality of Anglo-American slavery and US expansionism. In Tierra Firme, a centralized, militaristic government rose with the establishment of the Republic of Colombia. Led by Bolívar and his loyal followers, Colombia would reject Aury—and Afro-Caribbean privateers—as old rivalries and continuing prejudice came home to roost in the wake of military triumph over Spain.

Epilogue

From Amelia Island to the Republic of Colombia

PEDRO GUAL, THE ANTI-SPANISH agitator and diplomat from Tierra Firme who had hired Louis-Michel Aury in the spring of 1813, returned to the United States some time before the 1815 Spanish siege of Cartagena. In the North American republic, Gual advocated for Spanish American independence and conspired against the Spanish monarchy. After the defeat of Cartagena, Gual became convinced that the liberation of Spanish America had to be triggered from abroad. Eager to capitalize on the relative freedom of movement and substantial resources available in the United States, he realized that neighboring Spanish Florida could serve as an ideal stepping-stone for the southward expansion of republicanism. Most of the Florida Peninsula posed serious difficulties for Spanish administrators, offering safe havens for conspirators, privateers, and smugglers.[1]

Along with other international conspirators, Gual soon fixed his attention on Amelia Island, at the mouth of Saint Mary's River, the border between Georgia and East Florida. Gregor McGregor, a Scottish veteran of the Napoleonic Wars who had joined Venezuelan revolutionaries in 1811 and had participated in Bolívar's failed 1816 expedition, made the first move. In June 1817, McGregor occupied Amelia Island. Although McGregor hurried to establish the Republic of the Floridas, his material resources to defend this new polity were scarce. With Spanish forces planning a counterattack from Saint Augustine, McGregor left in early September.[2]

Gual, McGregor, and their allies, however, had already issued their call for anti-Spanish revolution—and privateering—from Amelia Island. Aury was on his way from the Gulf Coast. Loaded with supplies and accompanied by newly recruited men from Haiti, Aury arrived on September 17, in time to defend the island from Spanish attack. Along with the Frenchman came other revolutionaries and adventurers from France, the United States, and South America. Amelia Island seemed poised to continue the cosmopolitan and privateering legacies of independent Cartagena.[3]

The new Republic of the Floridas, with the port town of Fernandina as its center, both differed from and resembled Cartagena. Like Cartagena, Fernandina had long attracted contraband traders and privateers from the United States, Europe, and the Antilles. A community of free people of color resided there, but over the early 1800s Anglo-American slaveholders arrived from the US South, strengthening slavery on the island. With the Florida Peninsula still a matter of dispute between the United States, Spain, and Great Britain, the US public paid close attention to the events transpiring on Amelia Island during the summer and fall of 1817. For those interested in grabbing Florida for plantation agriculture, the Haitian seafarers seemed to be on the verge of bringing the complicated forces of the masterless Caribbean onto the very doorstep of the expanding Anglo-American master class.[4]

Anti-Spanish operations in the Floridas thus unfolded amid a complicated set of circumstances, offering new possibilities and challenges. First, privateering could be easily accomplished out of Fernandina. As the new state began to issue letters of marque, Aury obtained command of the privateer brig *Congreso*.[5] Along with the leaders of other armed vessels like the *Patriota*, Aury set out to target Spanish shipping between Havana and Cádiz. Transatlantic ships leaving Cuba bound for Spain had to sail northward and coast along the shores of Florida in order to ride the Gulf current and eventually catch the westerlies, which propelled them across the vast expanse of the ocean. These ships were the perfect prey. During the first two months of Aury's operations, captured merchandise worth half a million dollars passed through Amelia Island. The Floridas' privateers also attacked ships coming in from Africa and bound for Cuba. The privateer *Morgiana*, for example, took a ship carrying African captives in the fall of 1817.[6]

Second, privateering attracted people of color and former slaves, who operated as sailors and officers and aspired to citizenship and political standing. The Republic of the Floridas extended full rights to some of those men. Gual, who arrived in October, was put in charge of drafting a constitution for the Floridas. The constitution would be partially modeled on the US Constitution. With the participation of people from Charleston, Baltimore, Connecticut, Haiti, and several places in South America, the constitution was finished and ratified. The charter made no reference to ethnic background or color, but it enfranchised only free men who had lived on the island for at least fifteen days. All new citizens had to give up their allegiance to other polities, especially those who were not actively fighting for the liberation of Spanish America.[7]

Finally, the palpable tensions between slavery and freedom characteristic of privateering enclaves were present in the Floridas. Unlike Haiti's Pétion, the leaders of Amelia Island had no intention of fighting the slave trade. When they came into possession of African captives, privateers from the Floridas usually tried to smuggle them into the US South, especially Georgia. Because access to the transatlantic slave trade was now forbidden by the US government, Anglo-American slave traders paid high prices for captives. But these slave-trading practices out of Amelia Island coexisted with the presence of over one hundred Haitian free people of color, all of them working for Aury and eligible for citizenship. This variegated combination of slave smuggling, potential political equality, and revolutionary plans soon sparked fear and resentment, both locally and abroad. Many Anglo-Americans on the island, much like others in Georgia and elsewhere in the United States, balked at the idea of enfranchised free people of color, and Haitians in particular, living so close to the slave states and acting as citizens, soldiers, and privateers.[8]

Anxiety, disdain, and conflicts of interest among its residents led Fernandina to experience a serious internal struggle. Two parties began to take shape. On one side, Aury led a coalition of French, Italians, Britons, people of European descent born in the Americas, people of African ancestry, and individuals of mixed African and European ancestry. Members of Aury's coalition tended to support free people of color, who were vocal about obtaining equal rights and privileges. On the other side, the "Americans" were mostly European-descended people from the United States. There were fewer of them at first, but their numbers grew with reinforcements from Georgia (some were veteran soldiers who had served under Andrew Jackson during the War of 1812). The "Americans" opposed ideas of equality and resented having to work or participate in politics alongside free people of color, especially those Aury had recruited in Haiti.[9]

The two factions on Amelia Island had divergent goals. The anti-Spanish republicans affirmed legal equality but tapped into the slave trade in order to make money for themselves and their cause. They conceived of the Floridas as part of the larger Spanish American world they had set out to liberate. By contrast, the "Americans" openly expressed their support of legal discrimination and sympathized with the idea of US expansion into Florida and its potential annexation as a territory. While both sides rejected Spain, they disagreed on what type of sovereignty should emerge after the end of the Spanish regime. These differences became increasingly pronounced. On November 5, 1817, with the "Americans" gaining the upper hand, Aury accused his rivals of seeking to start a civil war on the island. He gathered enough support among his coalition to declare himself supreme leader of the troubled polity.[10]

As he transformed himself from privateering officer into political leader of a small sovereignty, Aury seems to have adapted his political thinking to the new circumstances. He announced martial law, declared war on Spain, and insisted that the republic think of this war as its foremost priority. Much like Bolívar in Tierra Firme, Aury responded to internal conflict and threats from abroad by planning to concentrate political power, build a centralized and belligerent military, and depict Spain as the one true enemy.[11]

We can surmise Aury's evolving political thinking from a speech he gave after taking power, which was later reproduced by the Baltimore press. According to the Baltimore text, Aury spoke of his goal to "wage war against the tyrant of Spain, the oppressor of America and enemy to the rights of man." Aury assured his audience that "when the heat of the passions shall be no more," a provisional government suited to the common interest and the advancement of "our glorious cause" would be established. In the meantime, he asked soldiers and sailors to give "our brethren of the state of the Floridas" sufficient proof of "our military discipline, and of our respect for the properties of its inhabitants."[12] While the property to be respected presumably included slaves, Aury's supporters seemed interested in managing slavery on their own terms, without Anglo-American participation.

Although Aury and his allies had prevailed, the lurking threat from the United States remained intact. The events of the last few months had led US authorities to seriously consider the possibility of intervening.[13] Given the Floridas' proximity to the slave states, any intervention authorized by Washington would most likely close all political space for free people of color, bringing them closer to rightlessness and perhaps even enslavement. When Aury declared martial law and war on Spain, news of this development quickly circulated in US newspapers. One of the reports depicted the situation with grave misgivings. It argued that Aury, now holding "supreme authority," had "put down the Americans" with the help of his "St. Domingo [Haiti] Brigands." It could only be expected, the report continued, that the island would now become a safe haven for runaway slaves from Georgia and other slave states.[14]

Moreover, the connections between the events on Amelia Island

and the larger project of Spanish American liberation were not lost on Anglo-American observers with strong views against people of color. According to the same press report that referred to Haitians as "brigands," some Americans saw the recent developments on Amelia Island positively. But they were wrong to do so, it asserted. Those who regarded what had transpired there as part of the evolution of the "Venezuelan Republic" (a generic name for South American independence) were ignoring a crucial aspect of the process: the insurgents were poised to triumph and the new government "will be in the hands of *Black or Coloured people.*" To drive the point home, the report made the connection with insurgent armies from Tierra Firme more specific. It mentioned that "General Paez, who is said to command 10,000 cavalry in the province of Varinas, is a BLACK MAN."[15] José Antonio Páez had indeed achieved military power in the Venezuelan backcountry, leading an army of plainsmen who joined the struggle against Spain. Páez and most of his men were of mixed African, European, and Native American ancestry.[16]

Words soon led to action. On Christmas Eve 1817, US forces under orders from President James Monroe occupied Amelia Island. Outnumbered and cut off from a reliable supply line, Aury and his comrades realized that resistance would be futile and escaped. The United States thus came into possession of a fragment of Spanish territory, and along with this change in sovereignty came social change as well.[17] As slavery and discrimination against people of African descent became even more entrenched in the US South, laws rejecting seafarers of color and their aspirations to freedom and citizenship began to appear in 1822. First in South Carolina, and later in Georgia, Florida, Alabama, and Louisiana, legislators passed "Negro Seamen Acts." These laws required the imprisonment of free sailors of color arriving in southern port towns, many of them American citizens from the North, as well as foreign nationals from the Caribbean and even Europe.[18]

Following his experience in the Floridas, Aury still hoped to become part of a larger project to defeat Spain in the Americas. His seafaring associates, however, were skeptical of becoming entangled with land operations, so they kept Aury engaged in privateering. After a few months, he was again cruising against Spain. This time he had chosen to operate out of the small island of Old Providence, where privateer William Mitchell had undermined Spanish sovereignty a few years earlier.[19] There, Aury stayed relatively well informed about the political and military developments in Tierra Firme, which he would later call his "adoptive fatherland."[20] His Cartagena experience had made him sympathetic to the cause of Venezuela and New Granada. In a letter to his relatives, he had referred to himself as a Cartagena "patriot," describing Cartagena as "our state" in the "Republic of New Granada."[21] Although at Les Cayes he had hesitated between following Bolívar to the continent or continuing to ply his maritime trade, Aury now seemed finally determined to participate in land warfare. By the end of 1819, the idea of going back to Tierra Firme seemed even more desirable.[22]

The balance of power in Tierra Firme shifted in important ways between 1816 and 1819. After his failed 1816 expedition, Bolívar had turned his gaze upon the Venezuelan backcountry. On the plains of the Orinoco and in the foothills of the Andes, guerrilla fighters—including Páez and his "black men"—had kept their own struggle going, in spite of Morillo's successful reoccupation campaign. Entering the continent through the Orinoco River, Bolívar and his allies took over the city of Angostura. They made contact with guerrilla forces, developing a plan to take over New Granada from its unguarded eastern flank. As the armies marched toward Santa Fe, common people who had endured the recent excesses of the Spanish military began to throw their weight behind the patriots. On August 7, 1819, Bolívar's forces defeated the last military detachment protecting the old viceregal capital. A real military triumph had at last arrived, and the Republic of Colombia was founded in December 1819. Aury anxiously waited for his call to serve this new polity in Tierra Firme, but it was not forthcoming.[23]

Aury's opposition to Bolívar back at Les Cayes and his disagreements with Pedro Luis Brión, a fervent Bolivarian, had not been forgotten. Moreover, Bolívar and his allies conceived of Colombia as a strong unitary state rather than a federation of provincial states, with a centralized political and military elite leading its affairs. For maritime defense, the republic was to rely not on privateering fleets but a regular navy. This would deflect accusations of piracy from other polities and help the emerging country achieve its goals of fending off foreign attacks and gaining international recognition of its independence. The need to build this force would be a fitting excuse to dismiss Aury and disown Afro-Caribbean privateers.[24]

Despite clear signs that such changes were underway, Aury sailed for Tierra Firme. Although he had long ago told his relatives that there was nothing wrong with privateering, he now seemed determined to abandon its ephemeral triumphs for lasting fame on the battlefield.[25] He arrived near Cartagena on November 18, 1820, but he and his men were denied incorporation into the Colombian forces. Aury then set out to plead his case before the central authorities. He undertook the long overland trip from the Caribbean shore to Santa Fe, now renamed Bogotá by the patriots. In Bogotá, Aury met with Bolívar in early 1821. The effort was in vain. Bolívar, president of the new republic, reiterated to Aury the new political reality in a short and harshly worded note: "Against your own efforts to the contrary and without the need for your services, the Republic of Colombia has raised itself to the state of no longer needing any more privateers who degrade its flag in all the seas of the world. Therefore, you may turn back to your ships and take them away from Colombian waters."[26] In Bolívar's eyes, Aury would forever be a mercenary.

Disappointed, Aury descended the Andes and set sail for Old Providence. There, he tried to resume his privateering endeavors. Some of his sailors, however, had already started looking for new horizons. By mid-1821, the seamen on one of his ships had deserted him. Hoping to obtain amnesty from Spanish authorities, they left for Cuba. Increasingly desperate and isolated, Aury wrote an indictment of the Tierra Firme leaders who had blocked his path to conti-

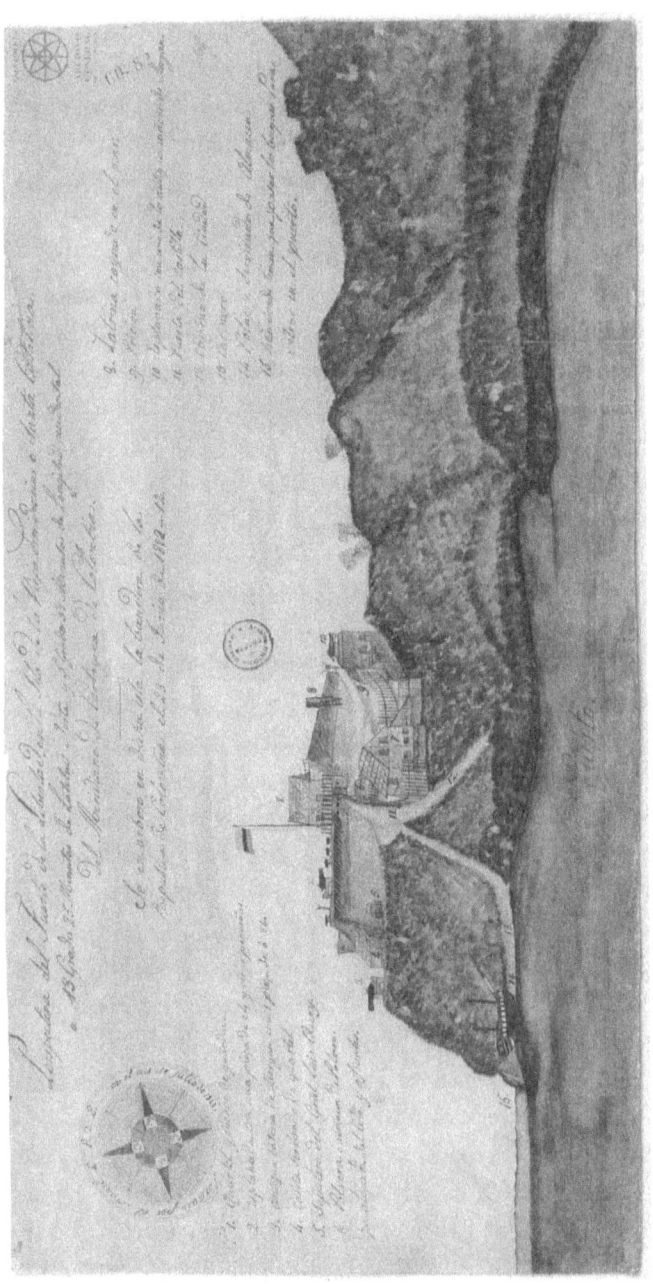

Figure 8. Fuerte de La Libertad, Old Providence Island, 1822. The tomb of Louis-Michel Aury is listed as item 5. By Luis Perú de Lacroix. Courtesy of Archivo General de la Nación (Bogotá).

nental glory (Bolívar and his men had already set out to liberate the rest of South America). But the document, neither finished nor published, became instead a truncated appendix to Aury's truncated life. Aury, "the sailor who would be a soldier, the commodore who would be a general, was thrown from the back of his horse."[27] On August 30, 1821, Aury succumbed to injuries sustained in the accident.[28]

ALTHOUGH THE COLOMBIAN government feared that sponsoring privateers could elicit accusations of piracy, the new republic issued letters of marque from 1822 to 1827. A regular navy could not be built overnight. Once again, irregular maritime warfare supported both the defense and the budget of a country. The potential revenue from privateering was high enough to risk "degrading" the Colombian flag abroad, so the tactical approach first tried by Cartagena could not be discarded altogether. Colombia's privateers operated in the Caribbean, and some even reached the Mediterranean.[29] Bolívar's answer to Aury's petition thus seems to be both an insincere excuse influenced by past disagreements and the declaration of a change in policy that would be slow in the making. Colombia was already bent on disavowing not only Aury and his men, but all maritime and political connections between Tierra Firme and Haiti.

Haiti had remained in vibrant connection with different Atlantic societies after its revolution (including the State of Cartagena), but diplomatic recognition of that country's independence remained partial and complicated.[30] Colombian officials also faced the challenge of diplomatic recognition, the final step in any successful revolution for independence. In spite of the analogous circumstances, the geographic proximity, and the preexisting maritime and political relationships between both countries, foreign affairs officials in Bogotá considered friendship with Haiti a liability for Colombia's diplomatic agenda. By breaking ties with Haiti, Colombia stood a better chance of having its own independence recognized by countries such as France, Great Britain, and the United States, where hostility against Haiti continued to exist. In light of Pétion's support of privateering and anti-Spanish activism in places like Les Cayes and Port-au-Prince, some Haitians perceived Colombia's approach as political ingratitude.[31]

Colombia's about-face followed Haiti's offer for diplomatic and commercial contact between the two republics. Gual, Colombia's secretary of foreign affairs since 1821, rejected Haiti's 1824 proposal to establish an alliance of friendship, defense, and trade. Since no other sovereignty had recognized Haitian independence, argued Gual, Colombia should exercise extreme caution and refrain from defying powerful countries. Haiti, he continued, had "no relationships whatsoever with the civilized world."[32] Unfair and simplistic, this perception was meant to elicit goodwill from French monarchists and former slaveholders who would not so readily recognize the standing of Haiti, a country founded by "enslaved people who overthrew their masters and freed themselves."[33]

As interested as they were in not offending France, Colombian leaders had their own misgivings about the Haitian people. France recognized Haiti in exchange for monetary compensation and trade privileges in 1825. The United States had recognized Colombia in 1822, and Great Britain did so in 1825.[34] Yet Colombia continued to reject the idea of establishing diplomacy and trade with Haiti. Moreover, Colombian officials orchestrated careful efforts in maritime policy and historical narrative to effectuate this rejection. On both fronts, they took steps to expurgate the presence of Haiti and to cover the traces of Colombia's important connections with Afro-Caribbean seagoing people. This was part of Colombia's founding elites' larger effort to "shun the stigma of blackness, barbarism, and obscurantism associated with the Caribbean," presenting the country to the world as "white, civilized, and enlightened."[35]

In maritime policy, Colombia's ongoing privateering had to be carried out without relying on Haitian personnel. While little is known about the social composition of Colombian privateering crews in the 1820s, evidence suggests that Colombian officers and political agents made efforts to recruit foreign sailors with no connections to the revolutionary world of Haiti and no enslaved ancestry. Rather than recruiting French Caribbean sailors to man their privateering ships, Colombian authorities tried to recruit their sailors in Colombia itself or in countries other than Haiti.[36]

At the same time, Colombian politicians were determined to paint the independence of Tierra Firme and the history of the Republic of Colombia in opposition to the Haitian Revolution, seen by many as an unnatural and illegitimate process. In Europe and the United States, Colombian agents depicted the revolutions of Tierra Firme in sharp contrast with other, more radical revolutions, including those in France and Haiti. Colombia, according to this narrative, had achieved independence because of its moral and physical growth, not the sudden turbulence unleashed by slave uprisings or the irresponsible application of abstract ideas of liberty.[37] The early connections with Haiti, embodied mainly by privateers operating out of Cartagena, did not fit into this narrative. As a consequence, those connections had to be portrayed as a misstep.

In 1827, José Manuel Restrepo, the official historian of the Republic, formalized this version of Colombia's founding by expurgating Haiti and Haitians from the historical account of independence. Originally published in Paris, Restrepo's *History of the Revolution of the Republic of Colombia* barely mentioned the participation of Caribbean privateering forces in the revolutionary movements. As a high-ranking member of Colombia's centralist government, Restrepo portrayed the policies and the federalist aspirations of the early provincial states, especially those of Cartagena, as infantile political missteps—foolish developments based on political models not suitable for Tierra Firme.[38] The same year Restrepo's book appeared, Bolívar decided to call off all ongoing privateering operations under Colombian colors. Both in narrative and policy, little room now existed for the motley, rowdy, and irreverent privateering crews of the masterless Caribbean.[39]

Nevertheless, Cartagena's early revolution, its privateering agents, and its cosmopolitan experiences invite us to question the limits of national history, as well as to adjust our own vision of the Age of Revolutions. By bringing back into focus the border-crossers, the amphibious agents, the maritime heralds, and the many who straddled slavery and freedom, the rejected hemispheric and maritime aspects of Spanish American independence come into full relief. Ignacio the Younger, Louis-Michel Aury, the *Bellona*, and other privateers compel us to reimagine Tierra Firme, the Antilles, the Gulf Coast, and South America as spaces of linked social experiences. Together, they can be viewed as the stage of a common history, connected not just by sea but by "the peoples of the sea."[40]

Acknowledgments

I WAS BORN and raised at 8,300 feet above sea level. It was not without risk that I tried my luck at writing a book about seafarers. Over the course of this experiment, I relied on the generous help of colleagues, friends, and family. I want to acknowledge the exemplary mentoring provided by Rebecca J. Scott, Julius S. Scott, Richard L. Turits, Jean M. Hébrard, and Susan Juster. Rebecca generously read the manuscript, providing much-needed scrutiny during the early stages of the book. For their invaluable help and warm collegiality, I thank Oscar Almario García, Juliana Álvarez Olivares, Ernesto Bassi, Guillermo Bustos, Adriana Chira, Luis Miguel Córdoba Ochoa, Natalie Zemon Davis, Marcela Echeverri, Ada Ferrer, Sybille Fischer, Reinaldo Funes Monzote, Orlando García Martínez, Rebecca Goetz, Juan Sebastián Gómez González, Daniel Gutiérrez Ardila, Marial Iglesias Utset, Roberto Luis Jaramillo, Orián Jiménez Meneses, Peter Linebaugh, Peter Mancall, Armando Martínez Garnica, Graham Nessler, Ángela Pérez Villa, Nathan Perl-Rosenthal, Javier Sanjinés, Jean-Frédérique Schaub, Ibrahima Thioub, Sinclair Thomson, Isidro Vanegas Useche, and Michael Zeuske. For constantly sharing his erudition and resources, as well as his home in Bogotá, Daniel deserves a special thank-you.

Many thanks to Ben Cronin, born by the sea and initiated in the waters of Kingston Bay, Massachusetts, for introducing me to the world of the North Atlantic. For the ongoing adventure of the Great Lakes, a heartfelt thanks to Ben and the rest of the crew: Valentine Edgar, Katie Rosenblatt, Anthony Ross, Eric Schewe, and David Schlitt. Eric's help with the manuscript and the illustrations was crucial. Special thanks to Ryan Gordon and Naomi Kirk-Lawlor in Maine, and to Michael Leese and Amy Warhaft in New Hampshire.

My immense gratitude goes to my families north and south: Carly Steinberger, who provides the fairest wind, along with constant help with my prose; my mother, for the gift of life and books; the Steinberger, Love, and Moed families in Michigan and New York; and the Morales Suárez and Arias Morales families in Colombia and Spain.

Thanks to those who listened to and commented on some of the stories told here, especially at the "Getting the Documents to Speak" Atlantic research practicum (Havana, 2011), the "Getting the Documents to Speak" seminar (Ann Arbor, 2012), the "Comparative Thalassologies" workshop at the Eisenberg Institute for Historical Studies (Ann Arbor, 2012), the Third Conference on Afro-Latin American Studies (San Juan, 2012), the History Department Seminar at Johns Hopkins University (Baltimore, 2013), the Louisiana Historical Society (New Orleans, 2014), the "Gathering Piracies" panel at the Latin American Studies Association Meeting (San Juan, 2015), and the New York University Atlantic World Workshop (New York, 2015).

Institutional and economic support for researching and writing this book was granted by the University of Michigan, New York University, Universidad Industrial de Santander (Colombia), Universidad Nacional de Colombia, Instituto Colombiano de Antropología e Historia, Archivo General de la Nación (Bogotá), Biblioteca Luis Ángel Arango (Bogotá), Archivo Nacional de Cuba (Havana), the Jamaica Archives (Spanish Town), the National Library of Jamaica (Kingston), Archives nationales d'outre mer (Aix-en-Provence), Archivo General de Indias (Seville), the New York Public Library, the William L. Clements Library (Ann Arbor), the New Orleans Public Library, the New Orleans Notarial Archives Research Center, and the Dolph Briscoe Center for American History (Austin). For subventions for the production and publication of this book, special thanks to the Office of the Dean, Dana and David Dornsife College of Letters, Arts and Sciences at the University of Southern California, and the USC-Huntington Early Modern Studies Institute. At Vanderbilt University Press, the staff was enormously helpful, especially Beth Kressel Itkin, who provided excellent editorial guidance. To the anonymous readers and Jane Landers at Vanderbilt, thanks for all the suggestions and engagement with the manuscript.

Abbreviations

AA I	Archivo Anexo I, in AGN
AGI	Archivo General de Indias (Seville)
AGN	Archivo General de la Nación (Bogotá)
AGS	Archivo General de Simancas
AHA	Archivo Histórico de Antioquia (Medellín)
AHC	Archivo Histórico de Cartagena de Indias
AHN	Archivo Histórico Nacional (Madrid)
ANC	Archivo Nacional de Cuba (Havana)
ANOM	Archives nationales d'outre mer (Aix-en-Provence)
AP	Asuntos Politicos, in ANC
CCG	Correspondencia de los Capitanes Generales, in ANC
CM	Colección Morillo, Real Academia de la Historia (Madrid)
DBC	Dolph Briscoe Center for American History, University of Texas at Austin
GSC	Gobierno Superior Civil, in ANC
HCVA	High Court of Vice-Admiralty Records, in JA
JA	Jamaica Archives (Spanish Town)
NLJ	National Library of Jamaica (Kingston)
NONARC	New Orleans Notarial Archives Research Center
NYPL	New York Public Library
WCL	William L. Clements Library, University of Michigan (Ann Arbor)

Primary Sources
Cartagena-Flagged Privateers, 1812–1816

1. **Cartagena (George Washington)**
   Federal Gazette (Baltimore), February 1, 1813; *Postscript to the Royal Gazette* (Kingston), November 27–December 4 and December 11–18, 1813; George Little, *Life on the Ocean; Or, Thirty Years at Sea: Being the Personal Adventures of the Author* (1843; Boston: Waite, Peirce, 1845), 196–201, 210–11. (Active 1812–1813.)

2. **Carthagenera**
   Carthagenera formerly *Caroline* to HMS *Sappho*, 1813, JA, HCVA, box 250; *Supplement to the Royal Gazette* (Kingston), January 2–9, 1813.

3. **Lady Madison**
   Democratic Press (Philadelphia), January 2, 1813; *City Gazette and Commercial Daily Advertiser* (Charleston), January 22, 1813; *Postscript to the Royal Gazette* (Kingston), February 20–27 and April 10–17, 1813; *American and Commercial Daily Advertiser* (Charleston), April 20, 1813.

4. **Kingston Packet**
   Postscript to the Royal Gazette (Kingston), April 10–17 and July 17–24, 1813.

5. **Dos Amigos**
   Postscript to the Royal Gazette (Kingston), July 3–10, 1813.

6. **Défenseur de la Patrie (Patriota, Caballo Blanco)**
   Suplemento a la Gazeta de Cartagena, July 15, 1813; AGN, AA I, Historia, 18, no. 24; *Défenseur de la Patrie* als. *Caballo*

Blanco to HMS *Onyx*, 1814, JA, HCVA, box 260; *Union* to HMS *Variable*, 1814, JA, HCVA, box 262; NLJ, Ms. 1735; *Supplement to the Royal Gazette* (Kingston), July 30–August 6, 1814; *Postscript to the Royal Gazette* (Kingston), August 27–September 3, 1814, and September 16–23, 1815; John Lynd, September 28, 1814, NONARC, Acts, 11:399–401.

7. **Providencia**
   Postscript to the Royal Gazette (Kingston), July 25–31, 1813.

8. **Presidente**
   Postscript to the Royal Gazette (Kingston), July 31–August 7, 1813, and February 5–12, 1814.

9. **Veloz**
   Gazeta de Cartagena de Indias, September 2, 1813.

10. **Filantrópico**
    Gazeta de Cartagena de Indias, September 9, 1813; Charles Machin memoir, WCL, Manuscript Division.

11. **Nueva Granada**
    Gazeta de Cartagena de Indias, September 9, 1813; *Postscript to the Royal Gazette* (Kingston), February 5–12, 1814.

12. **Piñeres**
    Postscript to the Royal Gazette (Kingston), September 25–October 2, 1813; AGN, República, Hojas de Servicios, 23:2r–3v.

13. **Atrevido Patriota**
    John Lynd, October 2, 1813, NONARC, Acts, 10:469–70; *Postscript to the Royal Gazette* (Kingston), March 12–19, 1814.

14. **San Francisco de Paula**
    Postscript to the Royal Gazette (Kingston), October 23–30 and November 13–20, 1813; *La Ciencia* to *Sapphire*, 1815, JA, HCVA, box 267; Hallet v. Novion, 1817, William Johnson, *Reports of Cases Argued and Determined in the Supreme Court of Judicature, and in the Court for the Trial of Impeachments and the Correction of Errors, in the State of New-York* (New York:

Banks & Brothers, 1883), 13:272–93; AHN, Consejos, 20272, exp. 2; AGN, República, Hojas de Servicios, 23:21r–3v.

15. **Enterprise**
    Postscript to the Royal Gazette (Kingston), November 20–27, 1813.

16. **Législateur**
    Postscript to the Royal Gazette (Kingston), November 20-27, 1813.

17. **Name unknown, Captain Vincent**
    Postscript to the Royal Gazette (Kingston), November 20–27, 1813.

18. **Once de Noviembre**
    Gazeta de Cartagena de Indias, December 30, 1813.

19. **Nuestra Señora de la Popa**
    Défenseur de la Patrie als. *Caballo Blanco* to HMS *Onyx*, 1814, JA, HCVA, box 260. (Active 1813.)

20. **Congreso de la Nueva Granada**
    AGN, AA I, Guerra y Marina, 122, no. 7, and Solicitudes, 3:568–623. (Active 1813–1814.)

21. **Venganza**
    Gazeta de Cartagena de Indias, January 6, 1814.

22. **Merced**
    Postscript to the Royal Gazette (Kingston), February 5–12, 1814.

23. **Name unknown, Captain Pedro La Maison**
    Postscript to the Royal Gazette (Kingston), March 5–12, 1814.

24. **Carmen**
    Postscript to the Royal Gazette (Kingston), March 5–12, 1814.

25. **Le Chasseur (El Nariño)**
    NLJ, Ms. 1735. (Active 1814.)

26. **General Bolívar**
    John Lynd, April 15, 1814, NONARC, Acts, 11:155–57, and September 29, 1814, 11:404–5.

27. Ejecutivo
Doc. 199, 1814, Manuel Ezequiel Corrales, ed., *Documentos para la historia de la provincia de Cartagena de Indias, hoy Estado Soberano de Bolívar en la Unión Colombiana* (Bogotá: Imprenta de Medardo Rivas, 1883), 663.

28. Bellona
El Mensajero de Cartagena de Indias, August 19, 1814; DBC, Louis-Michel Aury Papers, 1808–1821, box 2J112; AGN, AA I, Guerra y Marina, 131:395–482; ANC, AP, leg. 123, no. 2, and, leg. 109, no. 36; *Postscript to the Royal Gazette* (Kingston), December 9–16, 1815; *Baltimore Patriot and Evening Advertiser*, November 11, 1816.

29. Name unknown, Captain Fleuri
Postscript to the Royal Gazette (Kingston), October 1–8, 1814.

30. Isalovo
John Lynd, February 27, 1815, NONARC, Acts, 12:7–8.

31. Comet
Baltimore Patriot and Evening Advertiser, May 15, 1815; NYPL, Manuscripts & Archives, MssCol 1801; *Postscript to the Royal Gazette* (Kingston), March 16–23, 1816.

32. Colombiana
AGN, AA I, Historia, 18, no. 24. (Active 1815.)

33. General Castillo
Postscript to the Royal Gazette (Kingston), September 16–23, and November 25–December 2, 1815.

34. Augustus
Postscript to the Royal Gazette (Kingston), October 21–28, 1815.

35. Frederico (Frederica)
Postscript to the Royal Gazette (Kingston), November 18–25, and November 25–December 2, 1815.

36. Júpiter
Postscript to the Royal Gazette (Kingston), November 18–25, 1815; ANC, AP, leg. 123, no. 2.

37. Constitución
 Postscript to the Royal Gazette (Kingston), December 16–23, 1815; *Baltimore Patriot and Evening Advertiser*, November 15, 1816.

38. Gran Sultán
 Postscript to the Royal Gazette (Kingston), December 16–23, 1815; ANC, AP, leg. 109, no. 36.

39. Popa de Cartagena
 ANC, AP, leg. 123, no. 2, 3, and leg. 124, no. 39. (Active 1815–1816.)

40. Criolla
 AGN, AA I, Guerra y Marina, 131:403r; ANC, AP, leg. 109, no. 36; *Baltimore Patriot and Evening Advertiser*, November 11, 1816; AGN, República, Hojas de Servicios, 23:2r–3v. (Active 1815–1816.)

Notes

KEY FIGURES

1. Deposition of Ignacio, March 6, 1815, "Autos seguidos en el gobierno de esta capital de Santiago de Veragua contra los individuos que sirvieron de corsarios con . . . Nación leal, en la goleta nombrada la Belona, y la suerte les condujo a varar en el Escudo de Veragua, en la goleta apresada por aquella nombrada Alta Gracia," AA I, Guerra y Marina, 131:403r–v. Translations of primary sources in this book are mine.

INTRODUCTION

1. Louis-Michel Aury to Maignet, Samaná de Saint-Domingue, September 6, 1808, in DBC, Louis-Michel Aury Papers, box 2J112 [hereafter "Aury Papers"]; Stanley Faye, "Commodore Aury," *Louisiana Historical Quarterly* 24.3 (July 1941): 611–12. Because his father had passed away and his sister was not yet married, Aury was head of the household and responsible for his sister's honor and well-being. As a privateer, Aury would eventually earn enough money to comfortably provide his sister Victoire with a dowry.
2. Privateers were expected to carry a document attesting to their official commission, known as a *letter of marque* or *bill of marque* in English, *patente de corso* in Spanish, *carta de corso* in Portuguese, *lettre de course* in French, and *kaperbrief* in Dutch. Possession of letters of marque could protect seamen from accusations of piracy, potentially saving them from the gallows (Joaquín Escriche, *Diccionario razonado de legislación y jurisprudencia* [Paris: Librería de Rosa, Bouret & Ca., 1851], s.v. *corsario* and *patente*). On the legal ambiguities of privateering during the Spanish American Wars of Independence, see Matthew McCarthy, *Privateering, Piracy and British Policy in Spanish America,*

[171]

1810–1830 (Woodbridge, UK: Boydell Press, 2013). In the words of French historian Fernand Braudel, "Privateering was an ancient form of piracy native to the Mediterranean, with its own familiar customs, agreements and negotiations" (*The Mediterranean and the Mediterranean World in the Age of Philip II* [New York: Harper and Row, 1973], 2:867). Europeans brought privateering to the Caribbean beginning in the late 1500s. On the history of Mediterranean privateering, see Braudel, *Mediterranean*, 2:865–997; Salvatore Bono, *Corsari nel Mediterraneo: Christiani e musulmani far guerra, schiavittù e commerce* (Milan: Arnoldo Mondadori Editore, 1993); Michel Vergé-Franceschi and Antoine-Marie Graziani, eds., *La guerre de course en Méditerranée (1515–1830)* (Paris: Université de Paris IV-Sorbonne; Ajaccio, France: Editions Alain Piazzola, 2000); Susan Rose, *Medieval Naval Warfare, 1000–1500* (London: Routledge, 2002).

3. Louis-Michel Aury to Maignet, Samaná de Saint-Domingue, September 6, 1808, Aury Papers; Louis-Michel Aury to Victoire Aury, and Louis-Michel Aury to Maignet, Cartagena de Indias, October 24, 1814, Aury Papers; Maurice Persat, *Mémoires du commandant Persat, 1806 à 1844: Publiés avec une introduction et des notes par Gustave Schlumberger* (Paris: Plon, 1910), 32–33; Faye, "Commodore Aury."

4. For primary sources on Atlantic privateering prior to the Age of Revolutions, see J. Franklin Jameson, *Privateering and Piracy in the Colonial Period: Illustrative Documents* (New York: Macmillan, 1923).

5. Louis-Michel Aury to his mother, Saint-Pierre de la Martinique, March 6, 1803, Aury Papers; Faye, "Commodore Aury," 612. On French revolutionary privateering in the Caribbean, see Laurent Dubois, *A Colony of Citizens: Revolution and Slave Emancipation in the French Caribbean, 1787–1804* (Chapel Hill: University of North Carolina Press, Omohundro Institute of Early American History and Culture, 2004), 241–46; Michel Rodigneaux, *La guerre de course en Guadeloupe, XVIIIe–XIXe siècles: Ou Alger sous les tropiques* (Paris: L'Harmattan, 2006); Nathan Perl-Rosenthal, *Citizen Sailors: Becoming American in the Age of Revolution* (Cambridge, MA: Harvard University Press, 2015), 153–71; Han Jordaan, "Patriots, Privateers and International Politics: The Myth of the Conspiracy of Jean Baptiste Tierce Cadet," in *Curaçao in the Age of Revolutions, 1795–1800*, edited by Wim Klooster and Gert Oostindie (Leiden, Netherlands: KITLV Press, 2011), 141–69.

6. Julius S. Scott, "The Common Wind: Currents of Afro-American Communication in the Era of the Haitian Revolution" (PhD diss., Duke University, 1986); Dubois, *Colony*, 241–46; Rodigneaux, *La guerre*; Laurent Dubois, *Avengers of the New World: The Story of the Haitian Revolution* (Cambridge, MA: Harvard University Press, 2004).

7. Louis-Michel Aury to his mother, Saint-Pierre de la Martinique, March 6, 1803, Aury Papers; Louis-Michel Aury to Maignet, Baltimore, October 10, 1812, Aury Papers; Persat, *Mémoires*, 32–33; Faye, "Commodore Aury," 612.

8. *National Intelligencer* (Washington City), November 30, 1811; Faye, "Commodore Aury," 612–13; David Head, *Privateers of the Americas: Spanish American Privateering from the United States in the Early Republic* (Athens, GA: University of Georgia Press, 2015), 13–37, 42–50, 63–91.

9. On Tierra Firme and South American Independence, see Clément Thibaud, *Repúblicas en armas: Los ejércitos bolivarianos en la guerra de independencia en Colombia y Venezuela* (Bogotá: Planeta, 2003); Matthew Brown, *Adventuring through Spanish Colonies: Simón Bolívar, Foreign Mercenaries and the Birth of New Nations* (Liverpool, UK: Liverpool University Press, 2006); Jaime E. Rodríguez O., *La revolución política durante la época de la independencia: El Reino de Quito, 1808–1822* (Quito, Ecuador: Universidad Andina Simón Bolívar, Corporación Editora Nacional, 2006); Peter Blanchard, *Under the Flags of Freedom: Slave Soldiers and the Wars of Independence in Spanish South America* (Pittsburgh: University of Pittsburgh Press, 2008); Matthew Brown, *The Struggle for Power in Post-Independence Colombia and Venezuela* (New York: Palgrave Macmillan, 2012).

10. On Cartagena and Caribbean Colombia during the Age of Revolutions, see Adelaida Sourdis de De la Vega, *Cartagena de Indias durante la primera república, 1810–1815* (Bogotá: Banco de la República, 1988); Gustavo Bell Lemus, *Cartagena de Indias: De la colonia a la república* (Bogotá: Fundación Simón y Lola Guberek, 1991); Alfonso Múnera, *El fracaso de la nación: Región, clase y raza en el Caribe colombiano (1717–1821)* (Bogotá: Banco de la República, 1998); Aline Helg, *Liberty and Equality in Caribbean Colombia, 1770–1835* (Chapel Hill: University of North Carolina Press, 2004); María Teresa Ripoll, *La elite de Cartagena y su tránsito a la República: Revolución política sin renovación social* (Bogotá: Universidad de los Andes, 2006); Marixa Lasso, *Myths*

of Harmony: Race and Republicanism during the Age of Revolution, Colombia, 1795–1831 (Pittsburgh: University of Pittsburgh Press, 2007); Justo Cuño, *El retorno del Rey: El restablecimiento del régimen colonial en Cartagena de Indias (1815–1821)* (Castellón de la Plana, Spain: Universitat Jaume I, 2008); Armando Martínez Garnica and Daniel Gutiérrez Ardila, eds., *La contrarevolución de los pueblos de las Sabanas de Tolú y el Sinú (1812)* (Bucaramanga, Colombia: Universidad Industrial de Santander, 2010); Haroldo Calvo Stevenson and Adolfo Meisel Roca, eds., *Cartagena de Indias en la Independencia* (Cartagena: Banco de la República, 2011).

11. The only book-length study on Cartagena's privateers during the revolutionary period is Edgardo Pérez Morales's *El gran diablo hecho barco: Corsarios, esclavos y revolución en Cartagena y el Gran Caribe, 1791–1817* (Bucaramanga, Colombia: Universidad Industrial de Santander, 2012). In the present book, I have relied on the sources and narrative of my previous work in Spanish, incorporating new evidence and perspectives. On Spanish American privateering from the vantage point of US port towns and US citizens, see Head, *Privateers*. For British perspectives, see McCarthy, *Privateering*. On the flag of Cartagena (three concentric rectangles—red, yellow, and green—with a white star in the center), see Daniel Gutiérrez Ardila, "La heráldica revolucionaria durante el interregno neogranadino (1810–1815)," *Revista de Santander* 5 (2010): 36–47.

12. Johanna von Grafenstein Gareis, "Corso y piratería en el Golfo-Caribe durante las guerras de independencia hispanoamericanas," in *La violence et la mer dans l'espace atlantique (XIIe–XIXe siècle)*, edited by Mickaël Augeron and Mathias Tranchant (Rennes, France: Presses Universitaires de Rennes, 2004), 269–82; McCarthy, *Privateering*; Head, *Privateers*; Nicolas Terrien, *"Des patriotes sans patrie": Histoire des corsaires insurgés de l'Amérique espagnole (1810–1825)* (Mordelles, France: Les Perséides, 2015).

13. Deposition of Pierre Yolet, *Carthagenera* formerly *Caroline* to HMS *Sappho*, 1813, HCVA, box 250; depositions of Jean Baptiste Pemerlé and José Joaquín, *Défenseur de la Patrie* als. *Caballo Blanco* to HMS *Onyx*, 1814, HCVA, box 260; *Postscript to the Royal Gazette* (Kingston), September 23–30, 1815; deposition of Antonio Suárez, June 14, 1816, "Minutas de los oficios del gobernador de Santiago de Cuba, fecha

24 junio 1816, sobre haberse retirado los corsarios piratas que se hallaban en la bahía de Naranjo al norte de la Isla, en la jurisdicción de Holguín, y de sus designios de seguir las hostilidades sobre las costas del reino de México," AP, leg. 109, no. 36. See also Charles Machin memoir, WCL, Manuscripts Division; "Journal du corsaire *Le Chasseur* (a) *el Nariño*. Capitaine Jacques Cyran parti de Cartagène de Indias le 21 mars 1814 en croisière," NLJ, Ms. 1735.

14. Faye, "Commodore Aury," 613–15; Harold A. Bierck Jr., *Vida pública de don Pedro Gual* (Caracas: Ministerio de Educación Nacional, 1947), 70–71; Carlos A. Ferro, *Vida de Luis Aury: Corsario de Buenos Aires en las luchas por la independencia de Venezuela, Colombia y Centroamérica* (Buenos Aires: Cuarto Poder, 1976), 19–20; Daniel Gutiérrez Ardila, *Un Nuevo Reino: Geografía política, pactismo y diplomacia durante el interregno en Nueva Granada (1808–1816)* (Bogotá: Universidad Externado de Colombia, 2010), 522–33; Jane Landers, *Atlantic Creoles in the Age of Revolutions* (Cambridge, MA: Harvard University Press, 2010), 129–36.

15. Joseph Conrad, a master of sea tales in the English language and a seaman himself, once wrote that a ship was "alive with the lives of those beings who trod her decks" (*The Nigger of the Narcissus* [1897; Garden City: Doubleday, 1914], 46).

16. Deposition of Pierre Maller, June 4, 1805, ANOM, Dépôt des papiers publics des colonies, Agence des prises de la Guadeloupe, 6SUPSDOM/4, vol. 4, 1804–1808, Registre des déclarations; J. Coghlan to James Richard Dacres, Port Royal Harbour, November 21, 1805, The National Archives (Kew), Admiralty, and Ministry of Defence, Navy Department: Correspondence and Papers, 1/255 (document courtesy of Rebecca J. Scott).

17. Deposition of Ignacio, March 6, 1815, "Autos seguidos en el gobierno de esta capital de Santiago de Veragua contra los individuos que sirvieron de corsarios con . . . Nación leal, en la goleta nombrada la Belona, y la suerte les condujo a varar en el Escudo de Veragua, en la goleta apresada por aquella nombrada Alta Gracia," AA I, Guerra y Marina, 131:403r–v.

18. Deposition of Antonio Suárez, June 14, 1816, "Minutas," AP, leg. 109, no. 36.

19. Persat, *Mémoires*, 32–33; Faye, "Commodore Aury," 611–13.

20. Deposition of Hilario, February 24, 1815, "Autos," AA I, Guerra y Marina, 131:397r; deposition of Ignacio, March 6, 1815, "Autos," AA I, Guerra y Marina, 131:403r–v.
21. Deposition of Ignacio, March 6, 1815, "Autos," AA I, Guerra y Marina, 131:403r–407r. On the mobility of sailors from or with connections to Tierra Firme, see Ernesto Bassi, *An Aqueous Territory: Sailor Geographies and New Granada's Transimperial Greater Caribbean World* (Durham, NC: Duke University Press, 2016), 55–82.
22. Louis-Michel Aury, "Diario del corsario la *Belona* presentado a S. E. el Excmo. Sr. Presidente del Estado," *El Mensajero de Cartagena de Indias*, August 19, 1814; Louis-Michel Aury to Victoire Aury, and Louis-Michel Aury to Maignet, Cartagena de Indias, October 24, 1814, Aury Papers.
23. The notion of the "masterless Caribbean" was developed by Julius S. Scott, in "Common Wind," 6–58. See also W. Jeffrey Bolster, *Black Jacks: African American Seamen in the Age of Sail* (Cambridge, MA: Harvard University Press, 1997); Peter Linebaugh and Marcus Rediker, *The Many-Headed Hydra: Sailors, Slaves, Commoners, and the Hidden History of the Revolutionary Atlantic* (Boston: Beacon Press, 2000), 211–47; Neville A. T. Hall, "Maritime Maroons: *Grand Marronage* from the Danish West Indies," in *Origins of the Black Atlantic*, edited by Laurent Dubois and Julius S. Scott (New York: Routledge, 2010), 47–68.
24. *The Interesting Narrative of the Life of Olaudah Equiano written by Himself, with Related Documents* (1789; Boston: Bedford/St. Martin's, 2007); Julius S. Scott, "Common Wind," 60, 107–8; Julius S. Scott, "Afro-American Sailors and the International Communication Network: The Case of Newport Bowers," in *African Americans and the Haitian Revolution: Selected Essays and Historical Documents*, edited by Maurice Jackson and Jacqueline Bacon (New York: Routledge, 2010), 25–28; Bolster, *Black Jacks*.
25. Scott, "Common Wind"; Julius S. Scott, "Crisscrossing Empires: Ships, Sailors, and Resistance in the Lesser Antilles in the Eighteenth Century," in *The Lesser Antilles in the Age of European Expansion*, edited by Robert Paquette and Stanley Engerman (Gainesville: University Press of Florida, 1998), 128–43; Ada Ferrer, "Speaking of Haiti: Slavery, Revolution, and Freedom in Cuban Slave Testimony,"

in *The World of the Haitian Revolution*, edited by David Patrick Geggus and Norman Fiering (Bloomington: Indiana University Press, 2009), 223–47; Ada Ferrer, *Freedom's Mirror: Cuba and Haiti in the Age of Revolution* (New York: Cambridge University Press, 2014), 44–82. The Atlantic turn in the study of free people of color is deployed in the international contributions to the special issue "I liberi di colore nello spazio atlantico," edited by Federica Morelli and Clément Thibaud, *Quaderni Storici* 50.1 (April 2015).

26. Marcus Rediker, *Between the Devil and the Deep Blue Sea: Merchant Seamen, Pirates, and the Anglo-American Maritime World, 1700–1750* (New York: Cambridge University Press, 1987), 153–253.

27. Daniel Gutiérrez Ardila, *El reconocimiento de Colombia: Diplomacia y propaganda en la coyuntura de las restauraciones (1819–1831)* (Bogotá: Universidad Externado de Colombia, 2012), 237–70; Daniel Gutiérrez Ardila, "La Colombie et Haïti, histoire d'un rendez-vous manqué entre 1819 et 1830," *Bulletin de l'Institut Pierre Renouvin* 32 (2010): 111–28; Bassi, *Aqueous Territory*, 172–203.

28. The "Atlantic world" is a notion that too often "serves as shorthand for the history of the *British* Atlantic." See Allan Greer, "National, Transnational, and Hypernational Historiographies: New France Meets Early American History," *Canadian Historical Review* 91.4 (2010): 717–18. The Atlantic world was more than a collection of separate entities—Spanish, British, Portuguese, French, and Dutch Atlantic societies. However, historians tend to approach these societies in a compartmentalized fashion, from historiographical canons that seldom intersect. Scholars in the United States often fail to recognize the relevance of works by French-, Spanish-, and Italian-speaking colleagues. In *Atlantic History: A Critical Appraisal* (New York: Oxford University Press, 2009), edited by Jack P. Greene and Philip D. Morgan, most contributing authors broadly approach the Atlantic world as a group of separate entities. Walter Mignolo, Serge Gruzinski, and Jean-Frédéric Schaub raise important issues around the epistemological and historiographical implications of linguistic and academic ethnocentrisms. See Walter D. Mignolo, *Local Histories/ Global Designs: Coloniality, Subaltern Knowledges and Border Thinking* (Princeton, NJ: Princeton University Press, 2000); Serge Gruzinski, *Las cuatro partes del mundo: Historia de una mundialización* (Mexico

City: Fondo de Cultura Económica, 2010); and Jean-Frédéric Schaub, *Pour une histoire politique de la race* (Paris: Éditions du Seuil, 2015). For a critical perspective on traditional divisions of the Atlantic, see Ernesto Bassi, "Beyond Compartmentalized Atlantics: A Case for Embracing the Atlantic from Spanish American Shores," *History Compass* 12.9 (2014): 704–16, and Bassi, *Aqueous Territory*.

29. On connected and entangled histories, see Sanjay Subrahmanyam, "Connected Histories: Notes towards a Reconfiguration of Early Modern Eurasia," in *Beyond Binary Histories: Re-Imagining Eurasia to c. 1830*, edited by Victor B. Lieberman (Ann Arbor: University of Michigan Press, 1999), 297–302; Sanjay Subrahmanyam, *Explorations in Connected History: From the Tagus to the Ganges* (New Delhi: Oxford University Press, 2005); David Armitage and Sanjay Subrahmanyam, eds., *The Age of Revolutions in Global Context, c. 1760–1840* (London: Palgrave Macmillan, 2010); Serge Gruzinski, "Les mondes mêlés de la monarchie catholique et autres 'connected histories,'" *Annales* 56.1 (2001): 85–117; and Eliga H. Gould, "Entangled Histories, Entangled Worlds: The English-Speaking Atlantic as Spanish Periphery," *American Historical Review* 112.3 (June 2007): 764–86. On interdependent Caribbean societies, see Scott, "Common Wind"; Rebecca J. Scott, *Degrees of Freedom: Louisiana and Cuba after Slavery* (Cambridge, MA: Harvard University Press, 2005); Rebecca J. Scott and Jean M. Hébrard, *Freedom Papers: An Atlantic Odyssey in the Age of Emancipation* (Cambridge, MA: Harvard University Press, 2012); and Bassi, *Aqueous Territory*. See also Lara Putnam, "To Study the Fragments/Whole: Microhistory and the Atlantic World," *Journal of Social History* 39.3 (Spring 2006): 615–30, and Laurent Dubois, "An Enslaved Enlightenment: Rethinking the Intellectual History of the French Atlantic," *Social History* 31.1 (February 2006): 1–14. On social interdependencies, see the works of Norbert Elias, especially *On the Process of Civilization: Sociogenetic and Psychogenetic Investigations* (1939; Dublin: University College Dublin Press, 2012), *The Court Society* (1969; Dublin: University College Dublin Press, 2006), *What Is Sociology?* (1970; Dublin: University College Dublin Press, 2012), *The Society of Individuals* (1987; Dublin: University College Dublin Press, 2010) and *The Genesis of the Naval Profession* (Dublin: University College Dublin Press, 2007).

30. Peggy K. Liss, *Atlantic Empires: The Network of Trade and Revolution, 1713–1826* (Baltimore: Johns Hopkins University Press, 1983); Johanna von Grafenstein Gareis, *Nueva España en el circuncaribe, 1779–1808: Revolución, competencia imperial y vínculos intercoloniales* (Mexico City: Universidad Nacional Autónoma de México, 1997); Jeremy Adelman, *Sovereignty and Revolution in the Iberian Atlantic* (Princeton, NJ: Princeton University Press, 2006).
31. Rediker, *Between the Devil*, 7–8.
32. Von Grafenstein Gareis, "Corso"; María Elena Capriles P., "Bolívar y la actuación de Venezuela en el Caribe a través de sus corsarios: Santo Domingo, Puerto Rico, Cuba y México," *Boletín de la Academia Nacional de Historia* 89.355 (July–September 2006): 149–59; McCarthy, *Privateering*; Head, *Privateers*; Terrien, "*Des patriotes sans patrie*."
33. On privateering from Cartagena as an "act of sovereignty," see "Paralelo de los corsarios de Panamá con los de Cartagena," *Suplemento a la Gazeta de Cartagena* (Cartagena de Indias), July 15, 1813 (reference courtesy of Isidro Vanegas Useche and Daniel Gutiérrez Ardila).
34. For a systematic approach to these "alternative communities," see Bassi, *Aqueous Territory*. The most comprehensive recent studies on the early revolutionary process and the first polities to form in Tierra Firme between 1808 and 1815 are Daniel Gutiérrez Ardila's *Un Nuevo Reino* and Isidro Vanegas Useche's *La Revolución Neogranadina* (Bogotá: Ediciones Plural, 2013). On national history and the disavowing of early protagonists and polities, see Sergio Mejía, *La revolución en letras: La historia de la Revolución en Colombia de José Manuel Restrepo (1781–1863)* (Bogotá: Universidad de los Andes, 2007).
35. See Kris E. Lane, *Pillaging the Empire: Piracy in the Americas, 1500–1750* (Armonk, NY: M. E. Sharpe, 1998), and Markus Rediker, *Villains of All Nations: Atlantic Pirates in the Golden Age* (Boston: Beacon Press, 2004).
36. "Comunicación del capitán general al intendente general, fecha Habana 20 septiembre 1816 relacionado con la captura del bergantín *San Andrés*, por corsarios insurgentes," AP, leg. 108, no. 45.
37. "Autos," AA I, Guerra y Marina, 131:465r–466r, 470r–v, 473r.
38. Conventional understandings of the Caribbean, limited to the Antilles, "tend to create an artificial barrier between the continent's coast and the Caribbean islands" (Bassi, *Aqueous Territory*, 9).

CHAPTER 1

1. Olaudah Equiano, *The Interesting Narrative of the Life of Olaudah Equiano Written by Himself, with Related Documents* (1789; Boston: Bedford, 2007), 42–103; W. Jeffrey Bolster, *Black Jacks: African American Seamen in the Age of Sail* (Cambridge, MA: Harvard University Press, 1997); Ray Costello, *Black Salt: Seafarers of African Descent on British Ships* (Liverpool, UK: Liverpool University Press, 2012); Nathan Perl-Rosenthal, *Citizen Sailors: Becoming American in the Age of Revolution* (Cambridge, MA: Harvard University Press, 2015).
2. Equiano, *Interesting Narrative*.
3. Equiano, *Interesting Narrative*, 116–28; Julius S. Scott, "The Common Wind: Currents of Afro-American Communication in the Era of the Haitian Revolution" (PhD diss., Duke University, 1986), 59–113; Marcus Rediker, *Between the Devil and the Deep Blue Sea: Merchant Seamen, Pirates, and the Anglo-American Maritime World, 1700–1750* (New York: Cambridge University Press, 1987), 116–152; Bolster, *Black Jacks*, 131–57.
4. Scott, "Common Wind," 59.
5. Equiano, *Interesting Narrative*, 119, 122. See also Julius S. Scott, "Afro-American Sailors and the International Communication Network: The Case of Newport Bowers," in *African Americans and the Haitian Revolution: Selected Essays and Historical Documents*, edited by Maurice Jackson and Jacqueline Bacon (New York: Routledge, 2010), 25–28.
6. Phillip J. Curtin, *The Rise and Fall of the Plantation Complex: Essays in Atlantic History* (New York: Cambridge University Press, 1998); John K. Thornton, *Africa and African in the Making of the Atlantic World, 1400–1800* (New York: Cambridge University Press, 1998).
7. Scott, "Common Wind"; Neville A. T. Hall, "Maritime Maroons: Grand Marronage from the Danish West Indies," in *Origins of the Black Atlantic*, edited by Laurent Dubois and Julius S. Scott (New York: Routledge, 2010), 47–68.
8. For border-crossing from the shores of Tierra Firme, see Ernesto Bassi, *An Aqueous Territory: Sailor Geographies and New Granada's Transimperial Greater Caribbean World* (Durham, NC: Duke University Press, 2016), 55–82.
9. On cultural border-crossers and cultural mediators, see Berta Ares Queija and Serge Gruzinski, eds., *Entre dos mundos: Fronteras cultura-*

les y agentes mediadores (Seville, Spain: Escuela de Estudios Hispano-Americanos, Consejo Superior de Investigaciones Científicas, 1997); Rui Manuel Loureiro and Serge Gruzinski, eds., *Passar as fronteiras: Actas do II Colóquio Internacional Sobre Mediadores Culturais, séculos XV a XVIII* (Lagos, Portugal: Centro de Estudos Gil Eanes, 1999); Clara García Ayluardo and Manuel Ramos Medina, eds., *Ciudades mestizas: Intercambios y continuidades en la expansión occidental, siglos XVI a XIX: Actas del 3er. Congreso Internacional Mediadores Culturales* (Mexico City: Centro de Estudios de Historia de México Condumex, Instituto Nacional de Antropología e Historia, 2001); Scarlett O'Phelan Godoy and Carmen Salazar-Soler, eds., *Passeurs, mediadores culturales y agentes de la primera globalización en el mundo ibérico, siglos XVI–XIX* (Lima: Pontificia Universidad Católica del Perú, Instituto Francés de Estudios Andinos, 2005).

10. *Affiches Américaines* (Saint-Domingue), June 25, 1785. All references to the *Affiches Américaines* are from *Marronage in Saint-Domingue (Haïti): History, Memory, Technology*, Université de Sherbrooke, www.marronnage.info.

11. "Autos seguidos en el gobierno de esta capital de Santiago de Veragua contra los individuos que sirvieron de corsarios con . . . Nación leal, en la goleta nombrada la Belona, y la suerte les condujo a varar en el Escudo de Veragua, en la goleta apresada por aquella nombrada Alta Gracia," AA I, Guerra y Marina, 131:402v. See also David Head, *Privateers of the Americas: Spanish American Privateering from the United States in the Early Republic* (Athens: University of Georgia Press, 2015), 139.

12. Equiano, *Interesting Narrative*, 103.

13. *Kingston Daily Advertiser*, February 4, 1791. Quoted by Julius S. Scott, "'Negroes in Foreign Bottoms': Sailors, Slaves and Communication," in Dubois and Scott, *Origins*, 69.

14. Frederick Douglass, who had worked as a caulker in Maryland shipyards, escaped from Baltimore to New York in 1838 by impersonating a sailor. Writing about the day he escaped to freedom, Douglass said: "In my clothing I was rigged out in sailor style. I had on a red shirt and a tarpaulin hat and black cravat, tied in sailor fashion, carelessly and loosely about my neck. My knowledge of ships and sailor's talk came much to my assistance, for I knew a ship from stem to stern, and from keelson to cross-trees, and could talk sailor like an 'old salt'"

(*Life and Times of Frederick Douglass, Written by Himself* [Boston: De Wolfe & Fiske, 1892], 247).

15. Laurent Dubois, *Avengers of the New World: The Story of the Haitian Revolution* (Cambridge, MA: Harvard University Press, 2004), 1–45; Laurent Dubois, "Avenging America: The Politics of Violence in the Haitian Revolution," in *The World of the Haitian Revolution*, edited by David Patrick Geggus and Norman Fiering (Bloomington: Indiana University Press, 2009), 111–24; Malick W. Ghachem, "Prosecuting Torture: The Strategic Ethics of Slavery in Pre-Revolutionary Saint-Domingue (Haiti)," *Law and History Review* 29.4 (2011): 985–1029.

16. *Marronage in Saint-Domingue (Haïti): History, Memory, Technology*, Université de Sherbrooke, www.marronnage.info.

17. *Affiches Américaines* (Saint-Domingue), July 8, 1767.

18. *Affiches Américaines* (Saint-Domingue), February 22, 1783

19. *Affiches Américaines* (Saint-Domingue), March 20, 1784; *Affiches Américaines* (Saint-Domingue), June 25, 1785; *Affiches Américaines* (Saint-Domingue), July 20, 1785.

20. Equiano, *Interesting Narrative*, 130–52.

21. *Postscript to the Royal Gazette* (Kingston), September 23–30, 1815.

22. *Supplement to the Royal Gazette* (Kingston), May 6–18, 1815; Diana Paton, *No Bond but the Law: Punishment, Race, and Gender in Jamaican State Formation, 1780–1870* (Durham, NC: Duke University Press, 2004), 22–23.

23. Scott, "Common Wind," 255. See also Scott, "Case," 27–36.

24. Kris E. Lane, *Pillaging the Empire: Piracy in the Americas, 1500–1750* (Armonk, New York: M. E. Sharpe, 1998), 62–129.

25. Rediker, *Between the Devil*, 156; Marcus Rediker, *Villains of All Nations: Atlantic Pirates in the Golden Age* (Boston: Beacon Press, 2004), 50–59.

26. Carla Rahn Phillips, "The Labor Market for Sailors in Spain, 1570–1870," in *"Those Emblems of Hell"? European Sailors and the Maritime Labour Market, 1570–1870*, edited by Paul van Royen, Jaap Bruijn, and Jan Lucassen (St. John's, Newfoundland: International Maritime Economic History Association, 1997), 338–39. The internationalization of navies seems to have led to an increase in mutinies, desertions, and betrayals, especially during the 1790s (Niklas Frykman, "Seamen on Late Eighteenth-Century European Warships," *International Review of Social History* 54 [2009]: 67–68, 73).

27. Deposition of Ignacio, March 6, 1815, "Autos," AA I, Guerra y Marina, 131:403r–v.
28. *Postscript to the Royal Gazette* (Kingston), December 9–16, 1815. See also *Postscript to the St. Jago Gazette* (Spanish Town), December 9–16, 1815.
29. Emma Christopher, *Slave Ship Sailors and Their Captive Cargoes, 1730–1807* (New York: Cambridge University Press, 2006), 51–90.
30. On the adoption of "rolls" in US merchant shipping and related political implications, see Perl-Rosenthal, *Citizen Sailors*, 162–67, 200–203, 219–21.
31. "Expediente sobre el apresamiento por un corsario francés *La Venganza de la Perla* del corsario americano *Gobernador Brook*, en Santo Domingo...26 Marzo de 1806," AP, leg. 135, no. 23.
32. *La Rosa* to HMS *Algerine*, 1812, HCVA, box 253.
33. *Blanche* als. *General Monteverde* to HMS *Sappho*, 1812, HCVA, box 248.
34. Michael Duffy, *Soldiers, Sugar, and Power: The British Expeditions to the West Indies and the War against Revolutionary France* (Oxford: Clarendon Press, 1987), 326–67; Laurent Dubois, *A Colony of Citizens: Revolution and Slave Emancipation in the French Caribbean, 1787–1804* (Chapel Hill: University of North Carolina Press, Omohundro Institute of Early American History and Culture, 2004), 224; Frykman, "Seamen," 70.
35. J. Franklin Jameson, *Privateering and Piracy in the Colonial Period: Illustrative Documents* (New York: Macmillan, 1923).
36. William Falconer, *An Universal Dictionary of the Marine: Or, a Copious Explanation of the Technical Terms and Phrases Employed in the Construction Equipment, Furniture, Machinery, Movements, and Military Operations of a Ship* (London: T. Cadell, 1769), s.v. "schooner." See also *Diccionario marítimo español, que además de las definiciones de las voces con sus equivalentes en francés, inglés e italiano, contiene tres vocabularios de estos idiomas con las correspondencias castellanas: Redactado por orden del Rey Nuestro Señor* (Madrid: Imprenta Real, 1831), 298. For an inventory and description of a French schooner, see AGN, Colonia, Aduanas, vol. 22, no. 25: 952r–953r, 958r–v.
37. In the words of Cuban novelist Alejo Carpentier, "From the point of view of naval strategy, only privateering—privateering in the grand, authentic, classical manner—had given results in Caribbean waters,

by using light, mobile ships, which could easily take refuge in shallow inlets and maneuver in places bristling with coral reefs. This had always worked against the heavy Spanish galleons of the old days, and it would work today, against the over-heavily armed British ships" (*Explosion in a Cathedral*, translated by John Sturrock [1962; New York: Harper and Row, 1979], 168).
38. Dubois, *Colony*, 50–51.
39. Dubois, *Colony*. On the Haitian Revolution, see C. L. R. James, *The Black Jacobins: Toussaint L'Ouverture and the San Domingo Revolution* (1938; New York: Vintage, 1989); Caroline Fick, *The Making of Haiti: The Saint Domingue Revolution from Below* (Knoxville: University of Tennessee Press, 1990); David Patrick Geggus, *Haitian Revolutionary Studies* (Bloomington: Indiana University Press, 2002); Dubois, *Avengers*; José Luciano Franco, *Historia de la Revolución de Haití* (Santo Domingo: Sociedad Dominicana de Bibliófilos, 2008); and Malick W. Ghachem, *The Old Regime and the Haitian Revolution* (New York: Cambridge University Press, 2012).
40. Still remembered by some people in Guadeloupe and other places in the Caribbean in the mid-twentieth century, Hugues inspired Alejo Carpentier's acclaimed novel *Explosion in a Cathedral*.
41. José Luciano Franco, *La batalla por el dominio del Caribe y el Golfo de México, tomo 1: Política continental americana de España en Cuba, 1812–1830* (Havana: Instituto de Historia, Academia de Ciencias, 1964), 119–20; Dubois, *Colony*, 241–46; Michel Rodigneaux, *La guerre de course en Guadeloupe, XVIIIe–XIXe siècles: Ou Alger sous les tropiques* (Paris: L'Harmattan, 2006), 71–96.

CHAPTER 2

1. *Papel Periódico de la Ciudad de Santafé de Bogotá, 1791–1797*, facsimile edition (Bogotá: Banco de la República, 1978). On the French Revolution in the *Papel Periódico* and the intersections with the local political context, see Renán Silva, *Prensa y revolución a finales del siglo XVIII: Contribución a un análisis de la formación de la ideología de independencia nacional* (Bogotá: Banco de la República, 1988).
2. Julius S. Scott, "The Common Wind: Currents of Afro-American Communication in the Era of the Haitian Revolution" (PhD diss.,

Duke University, 1986); Ada Ferrer, *Freedom's Mirror: Cuba and Haiti in the Age of Revolution* (New York: Cambridge University Press, 2014).

3. *Tratado de alianza ofensiva y defensiva entre el Rey Nuestro Señor y la República Francesa, concluido y firmado en S. Ildefonso á 18 de agosto de 1796* (Madrid: Imprenta Real, 1796); César García del Pino, *Corsarios, piratas y Santiago de Cuba* (Havana: Editorial de Ciencias Sociales, 2009), 112–15. On the British presence in Tierra Firme, see Ernesto Bassi, *An Aqueous Territory: Sailor Geographies and New Granada's Transimperial Greater Caribbean World* (Durham, NC: Duke University Press, 2016).
4. Ferrer, *Freedom's Mirror*, 56–82, 164–73.
5. Anastasio Cejudo to the viceroy, Cartagena de Indias, April 9, 1799, and Anastasio Cejudo to Francisco de Saavedra, Cartagena de Indias, April 30, 1799, AGI, Estado, 53, N. 77(1) and (1a).
6. "Comunicación de Vicente de Liston al gobernador de Santiago de Cuba dando cuenta de la llegada de una goleta con bandera francesa en busca del capitán corsario Labarrière," CCG, leg. 30 A, no. 7.
7. "Comunicación de Joseph Nicolás Pérez Garvey a don Juan Nepomuceno de Quintana dando cuenta de la entrada del corsario *El Derecho del Hombre*," CCG, leg. 30 A, no. 10.
8. "Escrito del ciudadano francés Antoine Labarrière, capitán de un corsario, al gobernador, pidiendo se ordene su libertad," Santiago de Cuba, March 17, 1796, CCG, leg. 30 A, no. 12.
9. Manuel Moreno Fraginals, *El ingenio: Complejo económico social cubano del azúcar*, 3 vols. (Havana: Editorial de Ciencias Sociales, 1978); Sherry Johnson, *The Social Transformation of Eighteenth-Century Cuba* (Gainesville: University Press of Florida, 2001); Mercedes García Rodríguez, *Entre haciendas y plantaciones: Orígenes de la manufactura azucarera en La Habana* (Havana: Editorial de Ciencias Sociales, 2007); Reinaldo Funes Monzote, *From Rainforest to Cane Field in Cuba: An Environmental History since 1492* (Chapel Hill: University of North Carolina Press, 2008); William C. Van Norman, *Shade-Grown Slavery: The Lives of Slaves on Coffee Plantations in Cuba* (Nashville: Vanderbilt University Press, 2013); Ferrer, *Freedom's Mirror*.
10. Francisco de Arango y Parreño, "Representación manifestando las ventajas de una absoluta libertad en la introducción de negros, y

solicitando se amplíe a ocho la prórroga concedida por dos años," Aranjuez, May 10, 1791, in *Obras de D. Francisco de Arango y Parreño* (Havana: Ministerio de Educación, 1952), 1:97–102. Up-to-date information on the dimensions of the slave trade can be found at *The Trans-Atlantic Slave Trade Database*, www.slavevoyages.org.

11. Francisco de Arango y Parreño, "Representación hecha a Su Majestad con motivo de la sublevación de esclavos en los dominios franceses de la isla de Santo Domingo," San Lorenzo, November 22, 1791, in *Obras*, 1:111–12. See also "Observaciones de la Compañía de Cuesta Manzanal y Hermano, referentes al Comercio de Negros," Havana, November 23, 1809, ANC, Junta de Fomento de la Isla de Cuba, leg. 74, no. 2836, 16r–22r, and Ferrer, *Freedom's Mirror*, 17–43.

12. Ferrer, *Freedom's Mirror*, 1–10, 44–82.

13. Ferrer, *Freedom's Mirror*, 56–82, 164–73.

14. Dépôt des papiers publics des colonies, Agence de prises de la Guadeloupe, ANOM, 6 SUPSDOM/4; Agnès Renault, *D'une île rebelle à une fidèle: Les Français de Santiago de Cuba (1791–1825)* (Mont-Saint-Aignan, France: Universités de Rouen et du Havre, 2012); Rebecca J. Scott and Jean M. Hébrard, *Freedom Papers: An Atlantic Odyssey in the Age of Emancipation* (Cambridge, MA: Harvard University Press, 2012), 49–82; Rebecca J. Scott, "Paper Thin: Freedom and Re-enslavement in the Diaspora of the Haitian Revolution," *Law and History Review* 29.4 (November 2011): 1061–87; Marial Iglesias Utset, "Los Despaigne en Saint-Domingue y Cuba: Narrativa microhistórica de una experiencia Atlántica," *Revista de Indias* 71.251 (2011): 77–108; Michel Rodigneaux, *La guerre de course en Guadeloupe, XVIIIe–XIXe siècles: Ou Alger sous les tropiques* (Paris: L'Harmattan, 2006), 164–67.

15. Ferrer, *Freedom's Mirror*, 11, 45–82. See also Ada Ferrer, "Speaking of Haiti: Slavery, Revolution, and Freedom in Cuban Slave Testimony," in *The World of the Haitian Revolution*, edited by David Patrick Geggus and Norman Fiering (Bloomington: Indiana University Press, 2009), 223–47; Laurent Dubois, "An Enslaved Enlightenment: Rethinking the Intellectual History of the French Atlantic," *Social History* 31.1 (February 2006): 1–14.

16. On documentation aboard, see the papers on the French schooner *Aimable Margueritte*, "Papeles sobre la goleta francesa nombrada *La Amable o Hermosa Margarita*, apresada, o detenida en la costa

firme por los Buques Guarda Costas de Su Majestad del mando de don Domingo de Jáuregui. Su cargazón 400 barriles de harina," AGN, Colonia, Aduanas, vol. 2, no. 23; for a US example, see the papers on board the ship *Governor Brooks*, "Expediente sobre el apresamiento por un corsario francés *La Venganza de la Perla* del corsario americano *Gobernador Brook*, en Santo Domingo, 26 Marzo de 1806," AP, leg. 135, no. 23; for a British and a Spanish example, see the papers on board the *Ottawa* and the *San Bernardo*: *Ottawa* to HMS *Moselle* and *Anaconda*, 1815, HCVA, box 268, and *San Bernardo* als. *Las Cortes de España* to HMS *Garland*, 1812, HCVA, box 247. See also *Postscript to the Royal Gazette* (Kingston), March 7–14 and May 16–23, 1812; Louis-Michel Aury, "Diario del corsario la *Belona* presentado a S. E. el Excmo. Sr. Presidente del Estado de Cartagena de Indias," *El Mensajero de Cartagena de Indias*, August 19, 1814; deposition of Antonio Suárez, June 14, 1816, "Minutas de los oficios del gobernador de Santiago de Cuba, fecha 24 junio 1816, sobre haberse retirado los corsarios piratas que se hallaban en la bahía de Naranjo al norte de la Isla, en la jurisdicción de Holguín, y de sus designios de seguir las hostilidades sobre las costas del Reino de México," AP, leg. 109, no. 36.

17. "An Act for Enforcing the Instructions Given to All Captains or Commanding Officers of Ships and Vessels, Having Letters of Marque and Reprisals against the Enemy," *Royal Gazette* (Kingston), August 5–12, 1797; minutes of August 12 and 13, 1811, JA, Jamaica Minutes of the Council, 1B/5/3/22.
18. José de Ezpeleta to Príncipe de la Paz, Santa Fe, December 6, 1796, AGI, Estado, 52, N. 38.
19. Scott, "Common Wind," 244–45, 256–58.
20. Anastasio Cejudo to the viceroy, Cartagena de Indias, April 9, 1799, and Anastasio Cejudo to Francisco de Saavedra, Cartagena de Indias, April 30, 1799, AGI, Estado, 53, N. 77(1) and (1a). See also David Patrick Geggus, ed., *The Impact of the Haitian Revolution in the Atlantic World* (Columbia: University of South Carolina Press, 2001).
21. Anastasio Cejudo to Francisco de Saavedra, Cartagena de Indias, April 30, 1799, AGI, Estado, 53, N. 77(1).
22. On the complexities of the label "French Negroes," see Ashli White, *Encountering Revolution: Haiti and the Making of the Early American*

Republic (Baltimore: Johns Hopkins University Press, 2010); Ferrer, *Freedom's Mirror*, 60–82.

23. Anastasio Cejudo to the viceroy, Cartagena de Indias, April 9, 1799, AGI, Estado, 53, N. 77(1). See also Pedro de Mendinueta to Francisco de Saavedra, Santa Fe, May 19, 1799, AGI, Estado, 52, N. 76 (1).
24. Anastasio Cejudo to Francisco de Saavedra, Cartagena de Indias, April 30, 1799, AGI, Estado, 53, N. 77(1).
25. Pedro de Mendinueta to Pedro Cevallos, Santa Fe, April 19, 1803, AGI, Estado, 52, N. 137; Laurent Dubois, *A Colony of Citizens: Revolution and Slave Emancipation in the French Caribbean, 1787–1804* (Chapel Hill: University of North Carolina Press, Omohundro Institute of Early American History and Culture, 2004), 388–422.
26. Pedro de Mendinueta to Pedro Cevallos, Santa Fe, April 19, 1803, AGI, Estado, 52, N. 137.
27. See, for example, the article "Santa Marta" in *Gazeta Ministerial de Cundinamarca* (Santafé de Bogotá), May 13, 1813 (reference courtesy of Daniel Gutiérrez Ardila).
28. *Postscript to the Royal Gazette* (Kingston), December 21–28, 1811 (italics in the original).
29. Julia Gaffield, *Haitian Connections in the Atlantic World: Recognition after Revolution* (Chapel Hill: University of North Carolina Press, 2015).
30. *Postscript to the Royal Gazette* (Kingston), February 8–15, 1812.
31. Bartolomé and Lucille Bennassar, *Los cristianos de Alá: La fascinante aventura de los renegados* (Madrid: Nerea, 1989).
32. *Postscript to the Royal Gazette* (Kingston), February 8–15, 1812.
33. *Postscript to the Royal Gazette* (Kingston), May 16–23, 1812.
34. *Supplement to the Royal Gazette* (Kingston), January 2–9, 1813; Richard Paul Jodrell, *Philology on the English Language* (London: Cox & Baylis, 1920), s.v. "marauder."
35. *Postscript to the Royal Gazette* (Kingston), April 10–17, 1813.
36. Samuel Johnson, *A Dictionary of the English Language* (London: Longman, Hurst, Rees, Orme, and Brown, 1818), s.v. "desperado."
37. José Ignacio de Pombo, "Memoria sobre el contrabando en el virreinato de Santa Fe," Cartagena de Indias, March 12, 1804, in *Comercio y contrabando en Cartagena de Indias* (Bogotá: Nueva

Biblioteca Colombiana de Cultura, 1986), 88 (reference courtesy of Juan Sebastián Gómez González).
38. Pombo, "Memoria," 89–90.

CHAPTER 3

1. On the history of Spanish Cartagena de Indias (1533–1811), see Juan Marchena Fernández, *La institución militar en Cartagena de Indias en el siglo XVIII* (Seville, Spain: Escuela de Estudios Hispano-Americanos, 1982); Eduardo Lemaitre, *Historia general de Cartagena* (Bogotá: Banco de la República, 1983), vols. 1–2; Fermina Álvarez Alonso, *La Inquisición en Cartagena de Indias durante el siglo XVII* (Madrid: Fundación Universitaria Española, 1999); Haroldo Calvo Stevenson, ed., *Cartagena de Indias en el siglo XVIII* (Bogotá: Banco de la República, 2005); Adolfo Meisel Roca and Haroldo Calvo Stevenson, eds., *Cartagena de Indias en el siglo XVII* (Cartagena: Banco de la República, 2007); Haroldo Calvo Stevenson and Adolfo Meisel Roca, eds., *Cartagena de Indias en el siglo XVI* (Cartagena: Banco de la República, 2009); and Nicole von Germeten, *Violent Delights, Violent Ends: Sex, Race and Honor in Colonial Cartagena de Indias* (Albuquerque: University of New Mexico Press, 2013).
2. Royal ceremonies took place in Cartagena right up to the critical year of 1808. See "Descripción de las honras fúnebres de María Antonia de Borbón realizadas en Cartagena y Popayán, 1807," "Noticia de la celebración realizada en Cartagena de la abdicación de Carlos 40 en su hijo Fernando 70, 1808," "Noticia dada por el Cabildo de Cartagena a las autoridades eclesiásticas respecto la jura de Fernando 70 en esa ciudad, 1808," and "Documentos relativos al reconocimiento de Fernando 70 en la Provincia de Cartagena, y particularmente en Simití, 1808," in *Plenitud y disolución del poder monárquico en la Nueva Granada: Documentos, 1807–1819*, edited by Isidro Vanegas Useche (Bucaramanga, Colombia: Universidad Industrial de Santander, 2010), 1:44–48, 57–62, 151–65.
3. Allan J. Kuethe, *Military Reform and Society in New Granada, 1773–1808* (Gainesville: University Press of Florida, 1978); Lance Grahn, *The Political Economy of Smuggling: Regional Informal Economies in Early Bourbon New Granada* (Boulder, CO: Westview Press,

1997); Alfonso Múnera, *El fracaso de la nación: Región, clase y raza en el Caribe Colombiano (1717–1821)* (Bogotá: Planeta, 2008); Ernesto Bassi, *An Aqueous Territory: Sailor Geographies and New Granada's Transimperial Greater Caribbean World* (Durham, NC: Duke University Press, 2016).

4. Múnera, *El fracaso*; Alfonso Múnera, "Pedro Romero: El rostro impreciso de los mulatos libres," in *Fronteras imaginadas: La construcción de las razas y de la geografía en el siglo XIX colombiano* (Bogotá: Planeta, 2005), 153–74; Armando Martínez Garnica, "Prejuicio moral e instrucción: Dos obstáculos para la incorporación de los pardos a la nación," *Revista Colombiana de Educación* 59 (2010): 14–32; Aline Helg, *Liberty and Equality in Caribbean Colombia, 1770–1835* (Chapel Hill: University of North Carolina Press, 2004), 100–105; Marixa Lasso, *Myths of Harmony: Race and Republicanism during the Age of Revolution, Colombia 1795–1831* (Pittsburgh: University of Pittsburgh Press, 2007), 16–33.

5. Aline Helg, "A Fragmented Majority: Free 'Of All Colors,' Indians and Slaves in Caribbean Colombia during the Haitian Revolution," in *The Impact of the Haitian Revolution in the Atlantic World*, edited by David Patrick Geggus (Columbia: University of South Carolina, 2001), 157–75.

6. "El Consulado de Cartagena: Sobre las medidas que han tomado a exhortar y a estimular a los individuos hacendados y negociantes de aquel distrito a donativos gratuitos a favor de la Metrópoli," Cartagena de Indias, November 10, 1808, AGN, Consulados, 1, doc. 19, 505v.

7. "Acta de independencia de la provincia de Cartagena en la Nueva Granada," Cartagena de Indias, November 11, 1811, in *Documentos para la historia de la provincia de Cartagena de Indias, hoy Estado Soberano de Bolívar en la Unión Colombiana*, edited by Manuel Ezequiel Corrales (Bogotá: Imprenta de Medardo Rivas, 1883), doc. 108, 351–56

8. "Constitución del Estado de Cartagena de Indias, expedida el 14 de junio de 1812," Cartagena de Indias, June 14, 1812, in Corrales, *Documentos*, 485–546.

9. Manuel Chust, ed., *1808: La eclosión juntera en el mundo hispano* (Mexico City: Fondo de Cultura Económica, El Colegio de México, 2007).

10. José Gregorio Gutiérrez Moreno to Agustín Gutiérrez Moreno, Maracaibo, July 21, 1808, in *Dos vidas una revolución: Epistolario de*

José Gregorio y Agustín Gutiérrez Moreno (1808–1816), edited by Isidro Vanegas Useche (Bogotá: Universidad del Rosario, 2011), 33–34; "Nota del gobernador de la plaza de Cartagena, por la cual da parte al virrey de Santafé de haber adoptado medidas para impedir la introducción de papeles subversivos al orden," Cartagena de Indias, November 19, 1808, in Corrales, *Documentos*, doc. 4, 15–16.

11. Daniel Gutiérrez Ardila, ed., *Las vacilaciones de Cartagena: Polémicas neogranadinas en torno a la creación del Consejo de Regencia* (Bogotá: Academia Colombiana de la Historia, 2012).

12. Múnera, *El fracaso*, 91–151; María Teresa Ripoll, *La elite en Cartagena y su tránsito a la república: Revolución política sin renovación social* (Bogotá: Universidad de los Andes, 2006), 46–60; Bassi, *Aqueous Territory*, 23–54.

13. "El Consulado de Cartagena," AGN, Consulados, vol. 1, doc. 19, 512r; Múnera, *El fracaso*, 47–68, 125–51.

14. "Sobre el cumplimiento del término de la contrata de Don Bernardo Ruiz de Noriega," 1751, AGI, Santa Fe, 1167; Múnera, *El fracaso*, 78–89, 125–56; Ripoll, *La elite*, 59; Gustavo Bell Lemus, *Cartagena de Indias: De la colonia a la república* (Bogotá: Fundación Simón y Lola Guberek, 1991), 16–23; María Aguilera Díaz and Adolfo Meisel Roca, *Tres siglos de historia demográfica de Cartagena de Indias* (Cartagena de Indias: Banco de la República, 2009), 16–43.

15. Múnera, *El fracaso*, 155; Adolfo Meisel Roca, "Entre Cádiz y Cartagena de Indias: La red familiar de los Amador, del comercio a la lucha por la independencia americana," *Cuadernos de historia económica y empresarial* 12 (July 2004): 1–29. On McFadon, an active transatlantic businessman, see the *Baltimore Evening Post*, March 2, 1793; *Federal Intelligencer and Baltimore Daily*, January 10, 1795, and July 21, 1795; *Federal Gazette and Baltimore Daily Advertiser*, January 28, 1796, and June 3, 1797; *Poulson's American Daily Advertiser* (Philadelphia), June 2, 1811; Crowell and Others v. M'Fadon, 12 U.S. 94, February 16, 1814; Robert Walsh, "Case of the Schooner *Exchange*," in *The American Review of History and Politics, and General Repository of Literature and State Papers* (Philadelphia: Farrand and Nicholas, 1812), 3:159–75.

16. Juan de Dios Amador, passenger file, 1793, AGI, Arribadas, 517, N. 70; "Sobre la llegada a este puerto de un bergantín americano nombrado la Esperanza en lastre, a conducir a Don Mauricio Martín García, Don Juan de Dios, y Don Martín Amador vecinos de esta ciudad y

solicitud del pago de su pasaje," AGN, Colonia, Policía, vol. 7, doc. 22. See also Meisel Roca, "Entre Cádiz."
17. Múnera, *El fracaso*, 135–36.
18. Múnera, *El fracaso*, 153–60.
19. "Acta del cabildo de Cartagena del 16 de mayo de 1810," in Gutiérrez Ardila, *Las vacilaciones*, 64–70; Daniel Gutiérrez Ardila, *Un Nuevo Reino: Geografía política, pactismo y diplomacia durante el interregno en Nueva Granada (1808–1816)* (Bogotá: Universidad Externado de Colombia, 2010).
20. Bell Lemus, *Cartagena*, 26; Ripoll, *La elite*, 21–29, 63–98.
21. "Oficios cambiados entre los señores gobernador de Cartagena y Alcaldes ordinarios, sobre los temores de una subversión del orden," Cartagena de Indias, May 15, 1810, in Corrales, *Documentos*, doc. 26, 65–66; "Acta de la sesión del Cabildo de Cartagena tenida el 14 de junio de 1810, en que, por los graves motivos que se expresan, dicha Corporación tuvo por conveniente separar, y separó, al Gobernador Don Francisco de Montes del ejercicio de su empleo," in Corrales, *Documentos*, doc. 37, 81–90; José María García de Toledo to Antonio Amar y Borbón, Cartagena de Indias, July 10, 1810, in Corrales, *Documentos*, doc. 52, 116–18; *A todos los estantes y habitantes de esta plaza y su provincia* (Cartagena de Indias: November 9, 1810); Múnera, *El fracaso*, 164–72; Gutiérrez Ardila, *Un Nuevo Reino*, 194–98.
22. Múnera, *El fracaso*, 170–71.
23. Gutiérrez Ardila, *Un Nuevo Reino*, 41–233; Armando Martínez Garnica, "Las juntas neogranadinas de 1810," in *La Independencia en los países andinos: Nuevas perspectivas; Memorias del primer módulo itinerante de la Cátedra de Historia de Iberoamerica, Quito, December 9 al 12 de 2003*, edited by Armando Martínez Garnica and Guillermo Bustos (Bucaramanga, Colombia: Universidad Andina Simón Bolívar-Ecuador, Organización de los Estados Iberoamericanos para la Educación, la Ciencia y la Cultura, 2004), 112–34.
24. Armando Martínez Garnica, *El legado de la "Patria Boba"* (Bucaramanga, Colombia: Universidad Industrial de Santander, 1998); Jaime E. Rodríguez O., *La revolución política durante la época de la independencia: El Reino de Quito, 1808–1822* (Quito: Universidad Andina Simón Bolívar, Corporación Editora Nacional, 2006); Gutiérrez Ardila, *Un Nuevo Reino*; Martínez Garnica, "Las juntas."
25. Adolfo Meisel Roca, "La crisis fiscal de Cartagena en la era de la

independencia, 1808–1821," in *Cartagena de Indias en la Independencia*, edited by Haroldo Calvo Stevenson and Adolfo Meisel Roca (Cartagena: Banco de la República, 2011), 371–403.
26. Aguilera Díaz and Meisel Roca, *Tres siglos*, 39–43; Marchena Fernández, *La institución militar*, 437–52; Helg, *Liberty*, 100–105; Lasso, *Myths*, 16–33; Martínez Garnica, "Prejuicio"; Sergio Paolo Solano D., "Pedro Romero, el artesano: Trabajo, raza y diferenciación social en Cartagena de Indias a finales del dominio colonial," *Historia Crítica* 61 (2016): 151–70.
27. "Edicto por el cual el Cabildo de Cartagena excita a los habitantes de las ciudad a procurar la unión, a que respeten y obedezcan a las Autoridades, y ordena la formación de dos batallones," Cartagena de Indias, June 19, 1810, in Corrales, *Documentos*, doc. 40, 94; Manuel Marcelino Núñez, "Exposición de los acontecimientos memorables relacionados con mi vida política, que tuvieron lugar en este país desde 1810 en adelante," Cartagena de Indias, February 22, 1864, in Corrales, *Documentos*, doc. 114, 411; Múnera, *El fracaso*, 186–89, 208. On Pedro Romero, see Múnera, "Pedro Romero," and Solano D., "Pedro Romero."
28. Gutiérrez Ardila, *Un Nuevo Reino*, 198–207; Armando Martínez Garnica and Daniel Gutiérrez Ardila, eds., *La contrarevolución de los pueblos de las Sabanas de Tolú y el Sinú (1812)* (Bucaramanga, Colombia: Universidad Industrial de Santander, 2010), 9–11, 14.
29. Cartagena Junta to the Secretary of State and Universal Ministry, Cartagena de Indias, February 7, 1811, AGI, Santa Fe, 1011; "Insurrección del Regimiento 'Fijo,' en Cartagena de Indias," Cartagena de Indias, February 4, 1811, and "Alocución de la Junta de Cartagena con motivo de la Insurrección del Regimiento 'Fijo,' verificada el 4 de febrero de 1811," Cartagena de Indias, February 6, 1811, in Corrales, *Documentos*, docs. 79 and 80, 238–39; Múnera, *El fracaso*, 190–93.
30. Múnera, *El fracaso*, 194–96; Jorge Conde Calderón, "Ciudadanos *de color* y revolución de independencia o el itinerario de la pardocracia en el Caribe colombiano," *Historia Caribe* 14 (2009): 113–14.
31. Múnera, *El fracaso*, 200–203; Martínez Garnica, "Prejuicio."
32. Núñez, "Exposición," 410–13; *Súplica a los hombres de bien: Los ciudadanos Gabriel Gutiérrez de Piñeres e Ignacio Muñoz al pueblo libre de Cartagena* (Cartagena: Imprenta del Consulado, 1811); José Manuel Restrepo, *Historia de la revolución de la república de Colombia*

en la América meridional (1827; Medellín, Colombia: Universidad de Antioquia, 2009), 1:157–68; Múnera, *El fracaso*, 204–8.
33. Núñez, "Exposición," 410–12; "Acta de independencia," in Corrales, *Documentos*, doc. 108, 351–56; Restrepo, *Historia*, 1:157–68; Múnera, *El fracaso*, 204–8.
34. Múnera, *El fracaso*, 209–10.
35. "Constitución," in Corrales, *Documentos*, 485–546.
36. Fourteen constitutional texts were written across the old viceroyalty between 1810 and 1815. See Isidro Vanegas Useche, *El constitucionalismo fundacional* (Bogotá: Ediciones Plural, 2014).
37. "Constitución," title 13, art. 1, in Corrales, *Documentos*, 540–41.
38. Anna María Splendiani, ed., *Cincuenta años de Inquisición en el tribunal de Cartagena de Indias, 1610–1660* (Bogotá: Pontificia Universidad Javeriana, Instituto Colombiano de Cultura Hispánica, 1997).
39. Defying Spanish policy, however, in 1809 local merchants had printed the first Cartagenan newspaper, titled *Noticias Públicas*. J. T. Medina, *La imprenta en Cartagena de Indias (1809–1820): Notas bibliográficas* (Santiago de Chile: Imprenta Elzeviriana, 1904), v–xviii and docs. 29–49; María Teresa Ripoll, "*El Argos Americano*: Crónica de una desilusión," in Calvo Stevenson and Meisel Roca, *Cartagena de Indias en la Independencia*, 529–69. Newspapers in independent Cartagena included *El Argos Americano*, *Gazeta de Cartagena de Indias*, *El Efímero de Cartagena*, *Década: Miscelánea de Cartagena*, *El Mensajero de Cartagena de Indias*, and *Boletín de Cartagena*.
40. "Constitución," title 13, art. 9, in Corrales, *Documentos*, 541; "Constitución," Apéndice, in Corrales, *Documentos*, 549–50.
41. In the 1600s, foreigners were active in Cartagena. In 1630, 184 foreigners resided in the city, most of them Portuguese—technically Spanish subjects at the time—but also some Italians, French, Flemish, one Polish, one Scot, and even someone from Tangiers. After independence, however, almost two hundred years later, the foreign presence seems to have exploded, possibly numbering in the thousands. Enriqueta Vila Vilar, *Aspectos sociales en América colonial: De extranjeros, contrabando y esclavos* (Bogotá: Instituto Caro y Cuervo, Universidad de Bogotá Jorge Tadeo Lozano, 2001), 1–40; María Cristina Navarrete Peláez, *La diáspora judeoconversa en Colombia, siglos XVI y XVII: Incertidumbres de su arribo, establecimiento y persecución* (Cali, Colombia: Universidad del Valle, 2010), 68, 169–70; "Alocución

del vice-gobernador del Estado de Cartagena, con motivo de la derrota que sufrieron las fuerzas republicanas en 'Papáres,'" Cartagena de Indias, May 14, 1813, in Corrales, *Documentos*, doc. 177, 595–96; *El mensajero de Cartagena de Indias*, April 22, 1814; *Carthagenera* formerly *Caroline* to HMS *Sappho*, 1813, JA, HCVA, box 250; Jorge Conde Calderón, "Ciudadanos," 119; Rodrigo García Estrada, "Los extranjeros y su participación en el primer período de la independencia en la Nueva Granada, 1808–1816," *Historia Caribe* 16 (2010): 71.

42. *El mensajero de Cartagena de Indias*, December 31, 1813. See also "Decreto reglamentando el comercio dictado por el gobierno del Estado de Cartagena de Indias," Cartagena de Indias, December 30, 1813, AHA, Independencia, Comercio, vol. 887, doc. 13800.

43. On connections with Jamaica, see *El Argos Americano* (Cartagena de Indias), May 27, 1811; Juan Francisco Infanzón and Paula Pérez, marriage registry, Kingston, September 23, 1813, Francisco Martín Salcedo de Bustamante, burial note, Kingston, October 8, 1814, and Athanazio de la Masa, burial note, Kingston, November 17, 1815, Roman Catholic Archives (Kingston), Roman Catholic Marriages 1802–1827, 63–64, Roman Catholic Burials, book 4, 217, 245, references available through www.jamaicanfamilysearch.com. Meisel Roca, "La crisis," 377; Bell Lemus, *Cartagena*, 27–33; Bassi, *Aqueous Territory*, 23–141.

44. *American and Commercial Daily Advertiser* (Baltimore), March 30, 1812; *Baltimore Weekly Price Current*, December 5, 1812; *Federal Gazette* (Baltimore), December 7, 1812; *Courrier de la Louisiane* (New Orleans), April 5, 1813; and the following acts of John Lynd housed at NONARC: October 18, 1813, 10:93–94; November 19, 1813, 10:543–44; August 4, 1814, 11:321–22; August 11, 1814, 11:337–38; and September 29, 1814, 11:401–4.

CHAPTER 4

1. *American and Commercial Daily Advertiser* (Baltimore), March 30, 1812; *Baltimore Weekly Price Current*, December 5, 1812; *Federal Gazette* (Baltimore), December 7, 1812; Daniel Gutiérrez Ardila, *Un Nuevo Reino: Geografía política, pactismo y diplomacia durante el interregno en Nueva Granada (1808–1816)* (Bogotá: Universidad Externado de Colombia, 2010), 524.

2. Juan de Dios Amador to Miguel Pombo, Cartagena de Indias, July 30,

1811, in *Colección de documentos para la historia de Colombia (Época de la Independencia): Tercera serie*, edited by Sergio Elías Ortíz (Bogotá: Academia Colombiana de Historia, 1966), 212–13.
3. On the role of the American Revolution and the early United States in the Spanish American revolutions, see the special issue "La referencia estadounidense en los inicios de las naciones de la América española," *Co-herencia* 13.25 (July–December 2016).
4. Gutiérrez Ardila, *Un Nuevo Reino*, 525.
5. Stanley Faye, "Commodore Aury," *Louisiana Historical Quarterly* 24.3 (July 1941): 612–14.
6. On sailors of color and US citizenship, see Nathan Perl-Rosenthal, *Citizen Sailors: Becoming American in the Age of Revolution* (Cambridge, MA: Harvard University Press, 2015).
7. José Ignacio de Pombo, "Informe de Don José Ignacio de Pombo del Consulado de Cartagena sobre asuntos económicos y fiscales," Cartagena de Indias, April 18, 1807, in *Escritos de dos economistas coloniales: Don Antonio de Narváez y la Torre y don José Ignacio de Pombo*, edited by Sergio Elías Ortíz (Bogotá: Banco de la República, 1965), 121–34.
8. John Lynd, June 29, 1815, NONARC, Acts, 12:260–61.
9. Amador to Pombo, 212.
10. Amador to Pombo, 213; Gutiérrez Ardila, *Un Nuevo Reino*, 96–102.
11. Amador to Pombo, 212–13. See also Isidro Vanegas Useche, "La revolución angloamericana como herramienta: Nueva Granada, 1808–1816," *Co-herencia* 13.25 (July–December 2016): 89–118.
12. "Exposición que la Junta de la Provincia de Cartagena de Indias hace a las demás de la Nueva Granada, relativa al lugar en que convendría se reuniese el Congreso General," Cartagena de Indias, September 19, 1810, in *Documentos para la historia de la provincia de Cartagena de Indias, hoy Estado Soberano de Bolívar en la Unión Colombiana*, edited by Manuel Ezequiel Corrales (Bogotá: Imprenta de Medardo Rivas, 1883), doc. 64, 153–63; *Acta de Federación de las Provincias-Unidas de la Nueva Granada* (Santafé de Bogotá: D. Bruno Espinosa, 1812); Gutiérrez Ardila, *Un Nuevo Reino*, 216–22.
13. *Gazeta de Cartagena de Indias*, July 16, 1812.
14. US citizens continued to travel to and reside in Cartagena for a few more years. José Manuel Restrepo, *Historia de la revolución de*

la república de Colombia en la América meridional (1827; Medellín, Colombia: Universidad de Antioquia, 2009), 1:388; *Postscript to the Royal Gazette* (Kingston), January 13–20, 1816; *City Gazette and Daily Advertiser* (Charleston), February 22, 1816.

15. Ernesto Bassi, "Turning South before Swinging East: Geopolitics and Geopolitical Imagination in the Southwestern Caribbean after the American Revolution," *Itineratio* 36.3 (2012): 107–32; George Little, *Life on the Ocean; Or, Thirty Years at Sea: Being the Personal Adventures of the Author* (1843; Boston: Waite, Peirce , 1845), 197, 199. See also Ernesto Bassi, *An Aqueous Territory: Sailor Geographies and New Granada's Transimperial Greater Caribbean World* (Durham, NC: Duke University Press, 2016), and Matthew McCarthy, *Privateering, Piracy and British Policy in Spanish America, 1810–1830* (Woodbridge, UK: The Boydell Press, 2013).

16. *Supplement to the Royal Gazette* (Kingston), January 2–9, 1813; *Postscript to the Royal Gazette* (Kingston), February 20–27, 1813.

17. Adelaida Sourdis de De la Vega, *Cartagena de Indias durante l a primera república, 1810–1815* (Bogotá: Banco de la República, 1988), 47–50.

18. Marina Alfonso Mola and Carlos Martínez Shaw, "La introducción de la matrícula de mar en Indias," in *El sistema atlántico español (siglos XVII–XIX)*, edited by Carlos Martínez Shaw and José María Oliva Melgar (Madrid: Marcial Pons, 2005), 271–84. More generally, the maritime labor market in the Spanish world was somewhat restricted, and authorities found it difficult to recruit individuals with maritime skills. See Cesáreo Fernández Duro, *Armada Española desde la unión de los reinos de Castilla y Aragón* (Madrid: Museo Naval, 1973), vol. 7; Carla Rahn Phillips, "The Labor Market for Sailors in Spain, 1570–1870," in *"Those Emblems of Hell"? European Sailors and the Maritime Labour Market, 1570–1870*, edited by Paul van Royen, Jaap Bruijn, and Jan Lucassen (St. John's, Newfoundland: International Maritime Economic History Association, 1997), 345–47; Norbert Elias, *The Genesis of the Naval Profession* (Dublin: University College Dublin Press, 2007); and Manuel-Reyes García Hurtado, ed., *La Armada Española en el siglo XVIII: Ciencia, hombres y barcos* (Madrid: Sílex, 2012).

19. "El Consulado de Cartagena sobre las medidas que han tomado

para exhortar y estimular a los individuos hacendados y negociantes de aquel Distrito a donativos gratuitos en favor de la Metrópoli," Cartagena de Indias, November 10, 1808, AGN, Consulados, vol. 1, doc. 19, 511r–v.

20. Bassi, *Aqueous Territory*, 23–54.
21. Steinar A. Saether, *Identidades e independencia en Santa Marta y Riohacha, 1750–1850* (Bogotá: Instituto Colombiano de Antropología e Historia, 2005), 149–81.
22. "Instrucción sobre el Estado en que deja el Nuevo Reino de Granada el Excelentísimo señor Virrey don Francisco de Montalvo, en 30 de Enero de 1818, a su sucesor el Excelentísimo señor don Juan de Sámano," in *Relaciones e informes de los gobernantes de la Nueva Granada*, edited by Germán Colmenares (Bogotá: Biblioteca Banco Popular, 1989), 3:193–249.
23. Corrales, *Documentos*, esp. 217–630; Saether, *Identidades*, 177–96; Steinar A. Saether, "La relación entre Cartagena y Santa Marta, 1810–1813," in *Cartagena de Indias en la Independencia*, edited by Haroldo Calvo Stevenson and Adolfo Meisel Roca (Cartagena: Banco de la República, 2011), 181–214; Anthony McFarlane, "La 'revolución de las sabanas': Rebelión popular y contrarrevolución en el estado de Cartagena 1812," in Calvo Stevenson and Meisel Roca, *Cartagena de Indias*, 215–47; Armando Martínez Garnica and Daniel Gutiérrez Ardila, eds., *La contrarevolución de los pueblos de las Sabanas de Tolú y el Sinú (1812)* (Bucaramanga, Colombia: Universidad Industrial de Santander, 2010), 30–71.
24. *Discurso del Exmo. Señor presidente gobernador del Estado independiente de Cartagena, en la apertura de las sesiones de la Cámara de Representantes de aquel Estado* (Santa Fe de Bogotá: Imprenta de D. Bruno Espinoza, 1823).
25. Gutiérrez Ardila, *Un Nuevo Reino*, 525. Very few out of possibly hundreds of letters of marque issued by Cartagena seem to have survived. For an original document, see Manuel Rodríguez Torices and Antonio Leleux (Pierre Antoine Leleux), letter of marque, Cartagena de Indias, August 14, 1814, in "Autos obrados sobre la entrada del corsario insurgente titulado el *Congreso* a Cartagena y el bergantín español *La Esperanza*," AA I, Guerra y Marina, 122:41r (reference courtesy of Daniel Gutiérrez Ardila). For an English translation of

one of these documents, see *Carthagenera* formerly *Caroline* to HMS *Sappho*, 1813, HCVA, box 250. See also the transcription of a letter of marque in "Paralelo de los corsarios de Panamá con los de Cartagena," *Suplemento a la Gazeta de Cartagena* (Cartagena de Indias), July 15, 1813 (reference courtesy of Isidro Vanegas Useche and Daniel Gutiérrez Ardila).

26. "Juicio imparcial sobre los corsarios de Cartagena," *Gazeta de Cartagena de Indias*, September 2 and September 9, 1813; José Luciano Franco, *La batalla por el dominio del Caribe y el Golfo de México, tomo 1: Política continental americana de España en Cuba, 1812–1830* (Havana: Instituto de Historia, Academia de Ciencias, 1964), 121.
27. Little, *Life*, 197–99.
28. Little, *Life*, 200–201, 210–11. It remains difficult to corroborate the details of Little's account with other sources.
29. Sourdis de De la Vega, *Cartagena*, 48–49; Gutiérrez Ardila, *Un Nuevo Reino*, 522–33.
30. Gutiérrez Ardila, *Un Nuevo Reino*, 522–33.
31. *National Intelligencer* (Washington City), November 30, 1811; Faye, "Commodore Aury," 612–13; David Head, *Privateers of the Americas: Spanish American Privateering from the United States in the Early Republic* (Athens, GA: University of Georgia Press, 2015), 1–11, 63–91.
32. Hallet v. Novion, 1817, in William Johnson, *Reports of Cases Argued and Determined in the Supreme Court of Judicature, and in the Court for the Trial of Impeachments and the Correction of Errors, in the State of New-York* (New York: Banks and Brothers, 1883), 13:272–93; Faye, "Commodore Aury," 613–14; Carlos A. Ferro, *Vida de Luis Aury: Corsario de Buenos Aires en las luchas por la independencia de Venezuela, Colombia y Centroamérica* (Buenos Aires: Editorial Cuarto Poder, 1976), 18–20.
33. Louis-Michel Aury to Monsieur Maignet, Cartagena de Indias, October 24, 1814, DBC, Louis-Michel Aury Papers, 1808–1821, box 2J112.
34. *Democratic Press* (Philadelphia), January 2, 1813; *City Gazette and Commercial Daily Advertiser* (Charleston), January 22, 1813; *Postscript to the Royal Gazette* (Kingston), February 20–27 and April 10–17, 1813; *American and Commercial Daily Advertiser* (Charleston), April 20, 1813.

35. *Postscript to the Royal Gazette* (Kingston), April 10–17, 1813.
36. *Postscript to the Royal Gazette* (Kingston), July 17–24, 1813.
37. *Democratic Press* (Philadelphia), January 2, 1813; *City Gazette and Commercial Daily Advertiser* (Charleston), January 22, 1813; *American and Commercial Daily Advertiser* (Charleston), April 20, 1813.
38. *Postscript to the Royal Gazette* (Kingston), July 17–24, 1813.
39. *Postscript to the Royal Gazette* (Kingston), July 24–31, 1813.
40. "Comunicación al almirante de las fuerzas navales en Jamaica, fecha Cuba y noviembre 1812, con el fin de que impida la salida de dos mil franceses que parece pretenden proteger a los insurgentes de Cartagena de Indias," AP, leg. 13, no. 37; "Comunicación, fecha Madrid 4 Febrero 1814, acusando recibo de la que dio cuenta del apresamiento de la goleta española El Tigre por tres corsarios de Cartagena," AP, leg. 15, no. 5. See also *Postscript to the Royal Gazette* (Kingston), July 31–August 7, 1813.
41. Sergio Elias Ortíz, *Franceses en la independencia de Colombia* (Bogotá: Academia Colombiana de Historia, 1971); Matthew Brown, *Adventuring through Spanish Colonies: Simón Bolívar, Foreign Mercenaries and the Birth of New Nations* (Liverpool, UK: Liverpool University Press, 2006); Rodrigo García Estrada, "Los extranjeros y su participación en el primer período de la independencia en la Nueva Granada, 1808–1816," *Historia Caribe* 16 (2010): 53–74.
42. Deposition of Ignacio, March 6, 1815, "Autos seguidos en el gobierno de esta capital de Santiago de Veragua contra los individuos que sirvieron de corsarios con . . . Nación leal, en la goleta nombrada la Belona, y la suerte les condujo a varar en el Escudo de Veragua, en la goleta apresada por aquella nombrada Alta Gracia," AA I, Guerra y Marina, 131:403r–v; "Minutas de los oficios del gobernador de Santiago de Cuba, fecha 24 junio 1816," AP, leg. 109, no. 36 "Declaración dada por don Pedro Bruno y otros en 24 enero 1816, sobre las circunstancias ocurridas en el apresamiento por el corsario insurgente la *Popa de Cartagena* y observaciones que hicieron sobre el asilo que reciben del gobierno del General Alejandro Pétion," AP, leg. 123, no. 2.
43. Deposition of Ignacio, March 6, 1815, "Autos," AA I, Guerra y Marina, 131:403r–v; *Postscript to the Royal Gazette* (Kingston), December 9–16, 1815; *Postscript to the St. Jago Gazette* (Spanish Town), December 9–16, 1815; deposition of Antonio Suárez, June 14, 1816, "Minutas de

los oficios del gobernador de Santiago de cuba, fecha 24 junio 1816, sobre haberse retirado los corsarios piratas que se hallaban en la bahía de Naranjo al norte de la Isla, en la jurisdicción de Holguín, y de sus designios de seguir las hostilidades sobre las costas del Reino de México," AP, leg. 109, no. 36; *Baltimore Patriot and Evening Advertiser*, November 11, 1816.

44. "Constitución del Estado de Cartagena de Indias, expedida el 14 de junio de 1812," Cartagena de Indias, June 14, 1812, in Corrales, *Documentos*, 485–546.
45. "Autos obrados sobre la entrada del corsario insurgente titulado el *Congreso* a Cartagena y el bergantín español La Esperanza," AA I, Guerra y Marina, 122:741r–746v; "Paralelo."
46. Depositions of Pierre Yolet and Juan Francisco Pérez, *Carthagenera* formerly *Caroline* to HMS *Sappho*, 1813, HCVA, box 250. The use of the word "subject" instead of "citizen" of Cartagena further reveals the pragmatic, fragile, and volatile processes by which people obtained political belonging in newly independent polities. Citizenship as a form of political identification and as a claim on rights guaranteed by a sovereign state had only begun to take shape at this point. As historian Nathan Perl-Rosenthal has suggested, mariners occupied a central place in the development of ideas and practices of citizenship based on political allegiance, and therefore subject to change, rather than on birth and cultural background, and perhaps immutable. Some officials and private individuals continued to think of political allegiance in the old way, employing the notion of subject when others would have said citizen. See Nathan Perl-Rosenthal, *Citizen Sailors*.
47. Depositions of André Ranché, Jean Baptiste Pemerlé and José Joaquín, *Défenseur de la Patrie* als. *Caballo Blanco* to HMS *Onyx*, 1814, HCVA, box 260; *Supplement to the Royal Gazette* (Kingston), July 30–August 6, 1814. Ranché seems to have later settled on Hispaniola. See José Pierret, *Índice del Archivo de notarios y alcaldes en función de notarios desde el año de 1823 hasta el año de 1886* (Puerto Plata, 1913), series 1823–1838, year 1837, nos. 14 and 20.
48. José Ignacio de Pombo, "Memoria sobre el contrabando en el virreinato de Santa Fe," Cartagena de Indias, March 12, 1804, in *Comercio y contrabando en Cartagena de Indias* (Bogotá: Nueva Biblioteca Colombiana de Cultura, 1986), 89–90.

CHAPTER 5

1. "Journal du Corsaire *Le Chasseur* (a) *el Nariño*: Capitaine Jacques Cyran Parti de Cartagène de Indias le 21 mars 1814 en Croisière," entries of May 9–10, 10–11, NLJ, Ms. 1735.
2. Herman Melville, who worked for years aboard sailing ships, described the bad time some landsmen had when they found themselves on a seagoing ship: "Nobody is so heartily despised as a pusillanimous, lazy, good-for-nothing land-lubber; a sailor has no bowels of compassion for him. . . . He is set about all the vilest work. Is there a heavy job at tarring to be done, he is pitched neck and shoulders into a tar-barrel, and set to work at it. Moreover, he is made to fetch and carry like a dog" (*Omoo: A Narrative of Adventures in the South Seas* [1847; Boston: Dana Estes, 1892], 57.
3. Marcus Rediker, *Between the Devil and the Deep Blue Sea: Merchant Seamen, Pirates, and the Anglo-American Maritime World, 1700–1750* (New York: Cambridge University Press, 1987), 153–253.
4. Nathan Perl-Rosenthal, *Citizen Sailors: Becoming American in the Age of Revolution* (Cambridge, MA: Harvard University Press, 2015); Ernesto Bassi, *An Aqueous Territory: Sailor Geographies and New Granada's Transimperial Greater Caribbean World* (Durham, NC: Duke University Press, 2016).
5. *Gazeta de Cartagena de Indias*, April 22, May 6, September 2, and September 9, 1813.
6. Norbert Elias, *The Genesis of the Naval Profession* (Dublin: University College Dublin Press, 2007), 30. In a novel by James Fenimore Cooper, who began his sailing career at age seventeen in 1806, the mate of the *John* is surprised to see a young would-be sailor named Wallingford, who with no previous experience aboard, ably completes difficult tasks aloft. The aspiring sailor had gained his basic knowledge by studying under his father, a former sailor, with the help of a "large, full-rigged model." The mate calls Wallingford the "ripest piece of green stuff" he had ever seen (*Afloat and Ashore: A Sea Tale* [1844; New York: D. Appleton, 1873], 50–55).
7. Deposition of John Syerr, October 26, 1812, to HMS *Ringdove*, 1814, HCVA, box 261.
8. *La Rosa* to HMS *Algerine*, 1812, HCVA, box 253.
9. Tamar Herzog, *Defining Nations: Immigrants and Citizens in Early*

Modern Spain and Spanish America (New Haven, CT: Yale University Press, 2003); Peter Sahlins, *Unnaturally French: Foreign Citizens in the Old Regime and After* (Ithaca, NY: Cornell University Press, 2004); Perl-Rosenthal, *Citizen Sailors*; Bassi, *Aqueous Territory*.

10. Quoted by Marcus Rediker, in *Villains of All Nations: Atlantic Pirates in the Golden Age* (Boston: Beacon Press, 2004), 53.
11. Quoted by David Head, in *Privateers of the Americas: Spanish American Privateering from the United States in the Early Republic* (Athens: University of Georgia Press, 2015), 139.
12. Deposition of Francisco Díaz, April 17, 1815, "Autos seguidos en el gobierno de esta capital de Santiago de Veragua contra los individuos que sirvieron de corsarios con . . . Nación leal, en la goleta nombrada la *Belona*, y la suerte les condujo a varar en el Escudo de Veragua, en la goleta apresada por aquella nombrada Alta Gracia," AA I, Guerra y Marina, 131:449r. See also Ernesto Bassi, *Aqueous Territory*, 65–74.
13. See Elias, *Genesis*, and Rediker, *Between the Devil*.
14. Marcus Rediker, *Between the Devil*, 116–52, 167–69. Joseph Conrad referred to merchant ships as spaces where "discipline is not ceremonious," "the sense of hierarchy is weak," and "all feel themselves equal before the unconcerned immensity of the sea and the exacting appeal of the work" (*The Nigger of the Narcissus*, [1897; Garden City, NY: Doubleday, 1914]), 30.
15. Margaret S. Creighton and Lisa Norling, eds., *Iron Men, Wooden Women: Gender and Seafaring in the Atlantic World, 1700–1920* (Baltimore: Johns Hopkins University Press, 1996).
16. *Postscript to the Royal Gazette* (Kingston), September 10–17, 1814.
17. Deposition of Ignacio, March 6, 1815, "Autos," AA I, Guerra y Marina, 131:403v.
18. W. Jeffrey Bolster, *Black Jacks: African American Seamen in the Age of Sail* (Cambridge, MA: Harvard University Press, 1997), 44–67.
19. There is a place in northwest Haiti called Grand Diable, but this does not seem to be the main lead.
20. Philibert-Joseph Le Roux, *Dictionnaire comique, satyrique, critique, burlesque, libre et proverbial: Avec une explication tres-fidèle de toutes les manières de parler burlesques, comiques, libres, satyriques, critiques & proverbiales, qui peuvent se rencontrer dans les meilleurs auteurs, tant anciens que modernes; Le tout pour faciliter aux étrangers, & aux François mêmes, l'intelligente de toutes sortes des livres* (Lyon, France:

Chez Les Héritiers de Beringos Fratres, 1752), 1:201; Rif Winfield, *British Warships in the Age of Sail, 1793–1817: Design, Construction, Careers and Fates* (Barnsley, UK: Seaforth, 2008), 263; Juan de Santa Gertrudis, *Maravillas de la naturaleza* (ca. 1775; Bogotá: Biblioteca Banco Popular, 1970), 1:101.

21. Marcus Rediker, *Between the Devil*, 173–79.
22. See Carmen Bernand and Serge Gruzinski, *De la idolatría: Una arqueología de las ciencias religiosas* (1988; Mexico City: Fondo de Cultura Económica, 1992), and David D. Hall, *Worlds of Wonder, Days of Judgment: Popular Religious Belief in Early New England* (Cambridge, MA: Harvard University Press, 1989).
23. Rediker, *Villains*. For other approaches to the criminalization of cultural practices and beliefs, see Carlo Ginzburg, *Ecstasies: Deciphering the Witches' Sabbath* (Chicago: University of Chicago Press, 1991), and Stuart B. Schwartz, *All Can Be Saved: Religious Tolerance and Salvation in the Iberian Atlantic World* (New Haven, CT: Yale University Press, 2008).
24. Niklas Frykman, "Seamen on Late Eighteenth-Century European Warships," *International Review of Social History* 54 (2009): 67–93.
25. "Comunicación del capitán general al gobernador militar interino de Santiago de Cuba, fecha Habana 31 agosto 1815, sobre los tripulantes de una polacra española y fragata *Neptuno* apresados por los corsarios de Cartagena," AP, leg. 109, no. 13.
26. Deposition of José Vigre, June 23, 1816, "Minutas de los oficios del gobernador de Santiago de Cuba, fecha 24 junio 1816, sobre haberse retirado los corsarios piratas que se hallaban en la bahía de Naranjo al norte de la Isla, en la jurisdicción de Holguín, y de sus designios de seguir las hostilidades sobre las costas del Reino de México," AP, leg. 109, no. 36.
27. Deposition of José Vigre, June 23, 1816, "Minutas," AP, leg. 109, no. 36. See also "Journal du corsaire," NLJ, Ms. 1735.
28. October 26, 1812, to HMS *Ringdove*, 1814, HCVA, box 261; *Postscript to the Royal Gazette* (Kingston), July 18–25, 1812. On the flag of Cartagena and the heraldry of the different revolutionary states in Tierra Firme, see Daniel Gutiérrez Ardila, "La heráldica revolucionaria durante el interregno neogranadino (1810–1815)," *Revista de Santander* 5 (2010): 36–47.
29. *Supplement to the Royal Gazette* (Kingston), July 30–August 6, 1814.

30. *Blanche* als. *General Monteverde* to HMS *Sappho*, 1812, HCVA, box 248. See also John Lynd, November 26, 1812, NONARC, Acts, 9:387–88.
31. *Postscript to the Royal Gazette* (Kingston), September 23–30, 1815.
32. Deposition of Ignacio, March 6, 1815, "Autos," AA I, Guerra y Marina, 131:403v; Louis-Michel Aury, "Diario del corsario la *Belona* presentado a S. E. el Excmo. Sr. Presidente del Estado," *El Mensajero de Cartagena de Indias*, August 19, 1814.
33. *Union* to HMS *Variable*, 1814, HCVA, box 262.
34. Confession of Ignacio, March 29, 1815, "Autos," AA I, Guerra y Marina, 131:403v.
35. Confession of Ignacio, March 29, 1815, "Autos," AA I, Guerra y Marina, 131:403v.
36. Ignacio's fate is described in more detail in Chapter 6.
37. Confession of Hilario, March 22, 1815, "Autos," AA I, Guerra y Marina, 131:425r.
38. Charles Machin memoir WCL, Manuscripts Division; "Paralelo de los corsarios de Panamá con los de Cartagena," *Suplemento a la Gazeta de Cartagena de Indias*, July 15, 1813; *El Mensajero de Cartagena de Indias*, February 25, 1814; "Decretos del supremo poder ejecutivo del Estado de Cartagena de Indias," Estableciendo un derecho de patente, Cartagena de Indias, November 18, 1814, in *Documentos para la historia de la provincia de Cartagena de Indias, hoy Estado Soberano de Bolívar en la Unión Colombiana*, edited by Manuel Ezequiel Corrales (Bogotá: Imprenta de Medardo Rivas, 1883), doc. 200, 664–65; Stanley Faye, "Commodore Aury," *Louisiana Historical Quarterly* 24.3 (July 1941): 613–15; Antonio Cacua Prada, *El corsario Luis Aury: Intimidades de la Independencia* (Bogotá: Academia Colombiana de Historia, 2001), 10–11.
39. "Autos obrados sobre la entrada del corsario insurgente titulado el *Congreso* a Cartagena y el bergantín español *La Esperanza*," AA I, Guerra y Marina, 122:741r–746v; Charles Machin memoir; "Paralelo"; Cacua Prada, *El corsario*, 10–11.
40. "Paralelo."
41. Charles Machin memoir.
42. Charles Machin memoir, 134.
43. Depositions by Pierre Yolet and Juan Francisco Pérez, *Carthagenera* formerly *Caroline* to HMS *Sappho*, 1813, HCVA, box 250; John Lynd, April 15, 1814, NONARC, Acts, 11:155–57.

44. Depositions by André Ranché and Jean Baptiste Pemerlé, *Défenseur de la Patrie* als. *Caballo Blanco* to HMS *Onyx*, 1814, HCVA, box 260.
45. See "Allegation" and "Claim and affidavit," *Défenseur de la Patrie* als. *Caballo Blanco* to HMS *Onyx*, 1814, HCVA, box 260.
46. *Postscript to the Royal Gazette* (Kingston), March 23–April 4, 1812.

CHAPTER 6

1. Louis-Michel Aury, "Diario del corsario la *Belona* presentado a S. E. el Excmo. Sr. Presidente del Estado de Cartagena de Indias," *El Mensajero de Cartagena de Indias*, August 19, 1814.
2. Aury, "Diario."
3. Aury, "Diario."
4. Aury, "Diario."
5. Aury, "Diario."
6. Louis-Michel Aury to Maignet, Samaná de Saint-Domingue, September 6, 1808, and Louis-Michel Aury to Monsieur Maignet, Cartagena de Indias, October 24, 1814, DBC, Louis-Michel Aury Papers, 1808–1821, box 2J112.
7. *Postscript to the Royal Gazette* (Kingston), May 29–June 5, 1813.
8. *Postscript to the Royal Gazette* (Kingston), July 3–10, 1813.
9. *Postscript to the Royal Gazette* (Kingston), July–August 7, 1813.
10. *Postscript to the Royal Gazette* (Kingston), November 27–December 4, 1813. Besides the already cited issues, see July 10–17, August 7–14, and September 4–11, 1813.
11. *Gazeta de Cartagena de Indias*, September 9, 1813.
12. *Gazeta de Cartagena de Indias*, December 30, 1813.
13. "Real Consulado de la Habana," 1r–v, 3v, 11v, in *La Ciencia* to *Sapphire*, 1815, HCVA, box 267. See also "Recurso de injusticia notoria introducido por Don Fernando Gargollo, vecino y del comercio de la Ciudad de Cádiz, de las providencias dadas por el tribunal del Consulado de la misma ciudad, y su Juez de Alzadas en los autos seguidos con Don Joaquín de la Vega del propio comercio y vecindad sobre pago de cierto seguro,"AHN, Consejos, 20272, exp. 2, 1817. Cuesta Manzanal & Hermano had already been targeted by privateers. The French *General Morlot*, captained by Pierre Brugman, had intercepted the company's slave ship *Ciudad de Zaragoza*,

carrying 323 captives directly from Africa. See *Postscript to the Royal Gazette* (Kingston), June 27–July 4, 1812. On Cuesta Manzanal & Hermano, see Edgardo Pérez Morales, "Tricks of the Slave Trade: Cuba and the Small-Scale Dynamics of the Spanish Transatlantic Trade in Human Beings," *New West Indian Guide* 91 (2017): 1–29.

14. Information on the ships operating in 1816 (*Centinela, Republicano, Estrella, Plancha*, and *Arrogante Guallanés*, as well as a schooner commanded by Luis Brión) remains elusive. See "Declaración dada por don Pedro Bruno y otros en 24 enero 1816, sobre las circunstancias ocurridas en el apresamiento por el corsario insurgente la *Popa de Cartagena* y observaciones que hicieron sobre el asilo que reciben del gobierno del General Alejandro Pétion," AP, leg. 123, no. 2, and "Minutas de los oficios del gobernador de Santiago de Cuba, fecha 24 junio 1816, sobre haberse retirado los corsarios piratas que se hallaban en la bahía de Naranjo al norte de la Isla, en la jurisdicción de Holguín, y de sus designios de seguir las hostilidades sobre las costas del Reino de México," AP, leg. 109, no. 36. For sources on the main forty Cartagenan privateers, see Primary Sources in this volume.

15. Marcus Rediker, *Between the Devil and the Deep Blue Sea: Merchant Seamen, Pirates, and the Anglo-American Maritime World, 1700–1750* (New York: Cambridge University Press, 1987), 259; Niklas Frykman, "Seamen on Late Eighteenth-Century European Warships," *International Review of Social History* 54 (2009): 74, 78.

16. Deposition of Pierre Yolet, *Carthagenera* formerly *Caroline* to HMS *Sappho*, 1813, HCVA, box 250; depositions of Jean Baptiste Pemerlé and José Joaquín, *Défenseur de la Patrie* als. *Caballo Blanco* to HMS *Onyx*, 1814, HCVA, box 260; Charles Machin memoir, WCL, Manuscripts Division, 131; "Declaración dada por don Pedro Bruno y otros en 24 enero 1816, sobre las circunstancias ocurridas en el apresamiento por el corsario insurgente la *Popa de Cartagena* y observaciones que hicieron sobre el asilo que reciben del gobierno del General Alejandro Pétion," AP, leg. 123, no. 2; deposition of Antonio Suárez, June 14, 1816, "Minutas de los oficios del gobernador de Santiago de Cuba, fecha 24 junio 1816, sobre haberse retirado los corsarios piratas que se hallaban en la bahía de Naranjo al norte de la Isla, en la jurisdicción de Holguín, y de sus designios de seguir las hostilidades sobre las costas del Reino de México," AP, leg. 109, no. 36.

17. Manuel Moreno Fraginals, *El ingenio: Complejo económico social*

cubano del azúcar (Havana: Editorial de Ciencias Sociales, 1978), 3 vols.; Sherry Johnson, *The Social Transformation of Eighteenth-Century Cuba* (Gainesville: University Press of Florida, 2001); Mercedes García Rodríguez, *Entre haciendas y plantaciones: Orígenes de la manufactura azucarera en La Habana* (Havana: Editorial de Ciencias Sociales, 2007); Reinaldo Funes Monzote, *From Rainforest to Cane Field in Cuba: An Environmental History since 1492* (Chapel Hill: University of North Carolina Press, 2008); William C. Van Norman, *Shade-Grown Slavery: The Lives of Slaves on Coffee Plantations in Cuba* (Nashville: Vanderbilt University Press, 2013); Ada Ferrer, *Freedom's Mirror: Cuba and Haiti in the Age of Revolution* (New York: Cambridge University Press, 2014).

18. Adolfo Meisel Roca, "Puertos vibrantes y sector rural vacío: El Caribe neogranadino a fines del período colonial," in, *¿Por qué perdió la costa Caribe el siglo XX?* (Cartagena: Banco de la República, 2009), 113–31. See also Alberto Abello Vives, ed., *Un Caribe sin plantación: Memorias de la cátedra del Caribe colombiano* (San Andrés: Universidad Nacional de Colombia, 2006).

19. Alfonso Múnera, *Fronteras imaginadas: La construcción de las razas y de la geografía en el siglo XIX colombiano* (Bogotá: Planeta, 2005), 45–88; Armando Martínez Garnica and Daniel Gutiérrez Ardila, eds., *Quién es quién en 1810: Guía de forasteros del Virreinato de Santafé* (Bogotá: Universidad del Rosario, 2010), 69.

20. José Ignacio de Pombo, "Memoria sobre el contrabando en el virreinato de Santa Fe," Cartagena de Indias, March 12, 1804, in *Comercio y contrabando en Cartagena de Indias* (Bogotá: Nueva Biblioteca Colombiana de Cultura, 1986), 87–90.

21. Pombo, "Memoria," 88–90.
22. Ferrer, *Freedom's Mirror*, 17–43.
23. Pombo, "Memoria," 88–89.
24. Pombo, "Memoria," 90.
25. Ferrer, *Freedom's Mirror*, 17–82, 146–88.
26. *El Mensajero de Cartagena de Indias*, February 25, 1814.
27. *Gazeta de la Regencia de las Españas* (Madrid), January 24, 1814.
28. "Comunicación, fecha Madrid 26 marzo 1814, acusando el recibo de la que participaba las presas hechas por corsarios del gobierno revolucionario de Cartagena que han intentado un desembarco en Baracoa," AP, leg. 15, no. 14.

29. "Documento que se refiere a la correspondencia del capitán general al gobernador de Santiago de Cuba, fecha Habana 20 de noviembre de 1813, aprobando lo realizado por el teniente gobernador de Baracoa ante la amenaza de los corsarios de Cartagena," AP, leg. 215, no. 11.
30. Deposition of José Vigre, June 23, 1816, "Minutas," AP, leg. 109, no. 36.
31. "Documento que se refiere a la correspondencia del capitán general al gobernador de Santiago de Cuba, fecha Habana 24 de noviembre de 1813, relativa a que por la marina se han habilitado buques para perseguir los corsarios de Cartagena," AP, leg. 215, no. 18.
32. *Postscript to the Royal Gazette* (Kingston), December 25, 1813–January 1, 1814.
33. "Documento que se refiere a la correspondencia del capitán general al gobernador de Santiago de Cuba, fecha Habana 30 de diciembre de 1813, sobre los pliegos de servicios llegados a Baracoa y de un combate con los corsarios de Cartagena," AP, leg. 215, no. 30.
34. "Real orden, fecha Madrid 18 abril 1814, para que la Diputación Provincial proporcione al comandante general de marina los arbitrios necesarios para perseguir y exterminar los corsarios," AP, leg. 15, no. 16.
35. "Real orden, fecha Madrid 21 de febrero de 1814 'contestando a la carta No. 304 sobre armamento de tres buques para perseguir los corsarios de Cartagena previene que no debe descuidarse en todos los puntos de la isla del armamento de buques particulares, con aquel fin,'" AP, leg. 15, no. 9.
36. "Documento sobre el armamento de buques que persigan hasta exterminar con los piratas que infestan nuestros mares," GSC, leg. 700, no. 23077.
37. "Documento sobre el armamento." With anti-Spanish privateers operating mainly near small port towns, especially in the northern and eastern areas of the island, authorities ordered that the taxes, originally planned for Havana, should apply to other districts as well.
38. Johanna von Grafenstein Gareis, "Corso y piratería en el Golfo-Caribe durante las guerras de independencia hispanoamericanas," in *La violence et la mer dans l'espace atlantique (XIIe–XIXe siècle)*, edited by Mickaël Augeron and Mathias Tranchant (Rennes, France: Presses Universitaires de Rennes, 2004), 269–82; María Elena Capriles P., "Bolívar y la actuación de Venezuela en el Caribe a través de sus

corsarios: Santo Domingo, Puerto Rico, Cuba y México," *Boletín de la Academia Nacional de Historia* 89.355 (July–September 2006): 149–59; David Head, *Privateers of the Americas: Spanish American Privateering from the United States in the Early Republic* (Athens: University of Georgia Press, 2015).

39. "Constitución del Estado de Cartagena de Indias, expedida el 14 de junio de 1812," Cartagena de Indias, June 14, 1812, in *Documentos para la historia de la provincia de Cartagena de Indias, hoy Estado Soberano de Bolívar en la Unión Colombiana*, edited by Manuel Ezequiel Corrales (Bogotá: Imprenta de Medardo Rivas, 1883), 540.

40. "Autos seguidos en el gobierno de esta capital de Santiago de Veragua contra los individuos que sirvieron de corsarios con . . . Nación leal, en la goleta nombrada la Belona, y la suerte les condujo a varar en el Escudo de Veragua, en la goleta apresada por aquella nombrada *Alta Gracia*," AA I, Guerra y Marina, 131.

41. Inventario, March 6, 1815, vista fiscal, March 9, 1815, and deposition of Francisco Díaz, April 17, 1815, "Autos," AGN, AA I, Guerra y Marina, 131:407r, 421r, and 449r–v.

42. "Minuta de comunicación dirigida 'al Sr Baldey comandante del bergantín de SMB El Variable en camino libre esta costa,' fecha Cuba 17 de agosto 1814, acerca de la gratitud del gobierno por los oficios de libertador que ejerce sobre nuestras costas contra la abominable y ruinosa persecución que los piratas bajo el salvo conducto del gobierno ilegítimo de Cartagena ocasiona al comercio español, etc," AP, leg. 15, no. 26.

43. Head, *Privateers*, 46; David Head, "Slave Smuggling by Foreign Privateers: The Illegal Slave Trade and the Geopolitics of the Early Republic," *Journal of the Early Republic* 33.3 (2013): 433–62. See also John T. Noonan, Jr., *The Antelope: The Ordeal of the Recaptured Africans in the Administrations of James Monroe and John Quincy Adams* (Berkeley: University of California Press, 1977).

44. Rebecca J. Scott, "Freedom and Re-enslavement in the Diaspora of the Haitian Revolution," *Law and History Review* 29.4 (November 2011): 1061–87; Ada Ferrer, "Haiti, Free Soil, and Anti-Slavery in the Revolutionary Atlantic," *American Historical Review* 117.1 (February 2012): 40–66.

45. Michael Zeuske, *Amistad: A Hidden Network of Slavers and Merchants*

(Princeton, NJ: Markus Wiener, 2015), 83–94. See also Noonan, *Antelope*.
46. "Documento que se refiere a la correspondencia del Comandante de la Fortaleza al gobernador de Santiago de Cuba, fecha Castillo del Morro 17 de noviembre de 1813, dando cuenta de la entrada del bergantín español *Ana María* saqueado por los corsarios insurgentes," AP, leg. 215, no. 7.
47. "Autos," AGN, AA I, Guerra y Marina, 131.
48. "Autos," AGN, AA I, Guerra y Marina, 131:465r–466r, 470r–v, 473r.
49. "Autos," AGN, AA I, Guerra y Marina, 131:474r–481v.
50. Aury, "Diario."

CHAPTER 7

1. On the interruption of travel and communication after 1811, see pension claim by Bárbara Ortíz y Palacio, Santa Fe, November 10, 1813, AA I, Solicitudes, 3:176–88 (document courtesy of Daniel Gutiérrez Ardila).
2. Ada Ferrer, *Freedom's Mirror: Cuba and Haiti in the Age of Revolution* (New York: Cambridge University Press, 2014); Ada Ferrer, "Haiti, Free Soil, and Anti-Slavery in the Revolutionary Atlantic," *American Historical Review* 117.1 (February 2012): 40–66; Ernesto Bassi, *An Aqueous Territory: Sailor Geographies and New Granada's Transimperial Greater Caribbean World* (Durham, NC: Duke University Press, 2016), 142–71.
3. Conde de Castro-Terreño to Señor 1er. Secretario de Estado, Badajoz, November 17, 1818, AGI, Estado, 101, N. 105, 1r; Paul Verna, "Les Français dans l'histoire du Venezuela," *Cahiers du monde hispanique et luso-brésilien* 32 (1979): 178–79; Karen Racine, *Francisco de Miranda: A Transatlantic Life in the Age of Revolution* (Wilmington, DE: Scholarly Resources, 2003), 206; John Lynch, *Simón Bolívar: A Life* (New Haven, CT: Yale University Press, 2006), 48–54; Daniel Gutiérrez Ardila, *Un Nuevo Reino: Geografía política, pactismo y diplomacia durante el interregno en Nueva Granada (1808–1816)* (Bogotá: Universidad Externado de Colombia, 2010), 580–84.
4. Alexandre Pétion to J. Marion, Port-au-Prince, January 4 and February 25, 1816, in *Memorias del General Daniel Francisco O'Leary*

(Caracas: Ministerio de la Defensa, 1981), 15:46 and 49; Gutiérrez Ardila, *Un Nuevo Reino*, 580–84.
5. *El Mensajero de Cartagena de Indias*, October 14, 1814.
6. *Postscript to the Royal Gazette* (Kingston), July 31–August 7, 1813.
7. Laurent Dubois, *Avengers of the New World: The Story of the Haitian Revolution* (Cambridge, MA: Harvard University Press, 2004), 27–28; John D. Garrigus, *Before Haiti: Citizenship in French Saint-Domingue* (New York: Palgrave Macmillan, 2006).
8. M. L. E. Moreau de Saint-Méry, *Description topographique, physique, civile, politique et historique de la partie française de l'isle Saint-Domingue: Avec des observations généales sur sa population, sur le caractère & les moeurs de ses divers habitans; sur son climat, sa culture, ses productions, son administration, &c. &c.* (Philadelphia: 1797–1798), 2:696–98.
9. Moreau de Saint-Méry, *Description*, 2:703, 708.
10. Moreau de Saint-Méry, *Description*, 2:705, 712.
11. Julius S. Scott, "The Common Wind: Currents of Afro-American Communication in the Era of the Haitian Revolution" (PhD diss., Duke University, 1986), 31–32, 69, 73; Garrigus, *Before Haiti*, 174–75.
12. *Postscript to the Royal Gazette* (Kingston), January 5–12, 1811.
13. "Comunicación al almirante de las fuerzas navales en Jamaica, fecha Cuba y noviembre 1812, con el fin de que impida la salida de dos mil franceses que parece pretenden proteger a los insurgentes de Cartagena de Indias," AP, leg. 13, no. 37; "Real orden, fecha Madrid 18 abril 1814, para que la Diputación Provincial proporcione al comandante general de marina los arbitrios necesarios para perseguir y exterminar los corsarios," AP, leg. 15, no. 16; "Comunicación, fecha Madrid 4 febrero 1814, acusando recibo de la que dio cuenta del apresamiento de la goleta española *El Tigre* por tres corsarios de Cartagena," AP, leg. 15, no. 5.
14. Deposition of Ignacio, March 6, 1815, "Autos seguidos en el gobierno de esta capital de Santiago de Veragua contra los individuos que sirvieron de corsarios con . . . Nación leal, en la goleta nombrada la *Belona*, y la suerte les condujo a varar en el Escudo de Veragua, en la goleta apresada por aquella nombrada Alta Gracia," AA I, Guerra y Marina, 131:402r–407r.
15. *City Gazette and Commercial Daily Advertiser* (Charleston), January

22, 1813; *Democratic Press* (Philadelphia), January 2, 1813; *American and Commercial Daily Advertiser* (Charleston), April 20, 1813.

16. "Declaración dada por Don Pedro Bruno y otros en 24 enero 1816, sobre las circunstancias ocurridas en el apresamiento por el corsario insurgente la *Popa de Cartagena* y observaciones que hicieron sobre el asilo que reciben del gobierno del General Alejandro Pétion," AP, leg. 123, no. 2.
17. "Declaración dada por Don Pedro Bruno."
18. "Declaración dada por Don Pedro Bruno."
19. *Carthagenera* formerly *Caroline* to HMS *Sappho*, 1813, HCVA, box 250. Names of ships sometimes expressed the interests, political convictions, or particular experiences of their owners. On May 5, 1813, André Ranché bought a schooner from José María Guerra y Posada in Cartagena. Ranché named it the *Défenseur de la Patrie* (Defender of the Fatherland). This ship would operate under privateering commissions on behalf of the State of Cartagena. The ship's new name was a far cry from her previous, traditional Spanish name, *Nuestra Señora del Carmen*. See "Translation of Bill of Sale," fols. 1–5, *Défenseur de la Patrie* als. *Caballo Blanco* to HMS *Onyx*, 1814, HCVA, box 260. In a fictional passage inspired by Victor Hugues's French revolutionary privateering regime in 1790s Guadeloupe, the Cuban novelist Alejo Carpentier suggests how the small gesture of changing a name could be charged with not-so-small political implications. The novel describes activities aboard and around several ships on shore:

> Carpenters, caulkers and men with paint-brushes, saw and hammer were toiling in rowdy concert. . . . One of their lesser tasks was to change the names of the vessels. *La Calypso* had suddenly turned into *La Tyrannicide*; *La Sémillante* into *La Carmagnole*; *L'Hirondelle* into *La Marie-Tapage*; *Le Lutin* into *Le Vengeur*. Other new names were coming to light, painted in very visible letters against the old timbers which had served the King for so long: *La Tintamarre, La Cruelle, Ça-ira, La Sans-jupe, L'Athénienne, La Pignard, La Guillotine, L'ami du Peuple, Le Terroriste, La Bande Joyeuse*. (Alejo Carpentier, *Explosion in a Cathedral*, trans. by John Sturrock [1962; New York: Harper and Row, 1979], 166).

20. *El Mensajero de Cartagena de Indias*, October 14, 1814.

21. Manuel Rodríguez Torices and Antonio Leleux, letter of marque, Cartagena de Indias, August 14, 1814, "Autos obrados sobre la entrada del corsario insurgente titulado el *Congreso* a Cartagena y el bergantín español *La Esperanza*," AA I, Guerra y Marina, 122:41r; Pierre Antoine Leleux to Conde de Castro Terreño, Calais, September 29, 1818, Conde de Castro-Terreño to Señor 1er. Secretario de Estado, Badajoz, November 17, 1818, AGI, Estado, 101, N. 105, 1r; Agustín Gutiérrez Moreno to his mother, London, September 22, 1822, in *Dos vidas, una revolución: Epistolario de José Gregorio y Agustín Gutiérrez Moreno*, edited by Isidro Vanegas Useche (Bogotá: Universidad del Rosario, 2011), 488; Verna, "Les Français," 178–79; Racine, *Francisco*, 200–206; Lynch, *Simón Bolívar*, 48–54; Gutiérrez Ardila, *Un Nuevo Reino*, 580–81; Inés Quintero, "Venezolanos en Cartagena, 1812–1815," in *Cartagena de Indias en la Independencia*, edited by Haroldo Calvo Stevenson and Adolfo Meisel Roca (Cartagena: Banco de la República, 2011), 268–71.
22. José Manuel Restrepo, *Historia de la revolución de la República de Colombia en la América meridional* (1827; Medellín, Colombia: Universidad de Antioquia, 2009), 1:603–47; Racine, *Francisco*, 211–41; Gutiérrez Ardila, *Un Nuevo Reino*, 580–81; Clément Thibaud, *Repúblicas en armas: Los ejércitos bolivarianos en la guerra de independencia en Colombia y Venezuela* (Bogotá: IFEA, Planeta, 2003), 91–92.
23. Quintero, "Venezolanos," 265–67.
24. Simón Bolívar and Vicente Tejera to Congreso de la Nueva Granada, Cartagena de Indias, November 27, 1812, and Simón Bolívar to Ciudadanos de la Nueva Granada, Cartagena de Indias, December 15, 1812, in *Memorias del General Daniel Francisco O'Leary* (Caracas: Imprenta Nacional, 1956), 13:57–60 and 27:86–96; Restrepo, *Historia*, 1:204–10, 223–28; Steinar A. Saether, *Identidades e independencia en Santa Marta y Riohacha, 1750–1850* (Bogotá: Instituto Colombiano de Antropología e Historia, 2005), 189–96. On the principles of "armed revolution" and the interdependencies of military and political change, see Jean-Paul Bertaud, *La revolution armée: Les soldats citoyens de la Révolution Française* (Paris: Robert Laffont, 1979), and Thibaud, *Repúblicas*, 39–105.
25. Restrepo, *Historia*, 1:662–98.
26. Restrepo, *Historia*, 1:204–312; Lynch, *Simón Bolívar*, 65–89.
27. Restrepo, *Historia*, 1:326–33; Lynch, *Simón Bolívar*, 88–90; Quintero,

"Venezolanos," 265–80; Stanley Faye, "Commodore Aury," *Louisiana Historical Quarterly* 24.3 (July 1941): 622.
28. *Boletín de Cartagena*, March 29, 1815; Restrepo, *Historia*, 1:334–40; Lynch, *Simón Bolívar*, 88–90; Quintero, "Venezolanos," 265–80.
29. Restrepo, *Historia*, 1:341–42; Lynch, *Simón Bolívar*, 88–90; Quintero, "Venezolanos," 265–80.
30. Restrepo, *Historia*, 1:343–45; Lynch, *Simón Bolívar*, 88–90.
31. Lynch, *Simón Bolívar*, 96.

CHAPTER 8

1. José Manuel Serrano Álvarez, "El Ejército Expedicionario de Tierra Firme en Nueva Granada," in *Cartagena de Indias en la independencia*, edited by Haroldo Calvo Stevenson and Adolfo Meisel Roca (Cartagena: Banco de la República, 2011), 337–70.
2. John Lynd, June 29, 1815, NONARC, Acts, 12:260–61; "Bloqueo, y rendición de la Plaza de Cartagena de Indias, con las operaciones ejecutadas en su Provincia," 1816, CM, sig. 9/7651, leg. 8, 335r–337v; "Acta de la legislatura de la provincia de Cartagena," Cartagena de Indias, October 13, 1815, Gustavo Bell Lemus, *Cartagena de Indias: De la colonia a la república* (Bogotá: Fundación Simón y Lola Guberek, 1991), 70.
3. José Manuel Restrepo, *Historia de la revolución de la República de Colombia en la América meridional* (1827; Medellín, Colombia: Universidad de Antioquia, 2009), 1:384–85.
4. Paul Verna, *Robert Sutherland: Un amigo de Bolívar en Haití; Contribución al estudio de los destierros del Libertador en Haití, y de sus Expediciones de Los Cayos y de Jacmel* (Caracas: Fundación John Boulton, 1966); Paul Verna, *Pétion y Bolívar: Cuarenta años (1790–1830) de relaciones haitiano-venezolanas y su aporte a la emancipación de Hispanoamérica* (Caracas: Oficina Central de Información, 1969); Sibylle Fischer, "Bolívar in Haiti: Republicanism in the Revolutionary Atlantic," in *Haiti and the Americas*, edited by Carla Calargé et al. (Jackson: University Press of Mississippi, 2013), 25–53; Ernesto Bassi, *An Aqueous Territory: Sailor Geographies and New Granada's Transimperial Greater Caribbean World* (Durham, NC: Duke University Press, 2016), 142–71.
5. "Bloqueo," 331r–v.

6. "Bloqueo," 332r–333r, 345r.
7. Restrepo, *Historia*, 1:364.
8. "Bloqueo," 335r–337v.
9. "Bloqueo," 335r–337v; Julián Bayer to Pablo Morillo, Chimá, September 21, 1815, in José P. Urueta, *Los mártires de Cartagena* (Cartagena: Tip. de Antonio Araújo, a cargo de O'Byrne, 1886), 33–37.
10. Restrepo, *Historia*, 1:365–72, 380–90. See also Adelaida Sourdis de De la Vega, *Cartagena de Indias durante la primera república, 1810–1815* (Bogotá: Banco de la República, 1988), 113–52, and Justo Cuño Bonito, *El retorno del Rey: El restablecimiento del régimen colonial en Cartagena de Indias (1815–1821)* (Castellón de la Plana, Spain: Universitat Jaume I, 2008), 75–88.
11. "Acta de la legislatura," Cartagena de Indias, October 13, 1815, in Bell Lemus, *Cartagena*, 70.
12. Restrepo, *Historia*, 1:381; Bell Lemus, *Cartagena*, 32, 39–67.
13. Louis-Michel Aury to his relatives, Port-au-Prince, March 15, 1816, in DBC, Louis-Michel Aury Papers, 1808–1821, box 2J112.
14. Restrepo, *Historia*, 1:383.
15. John Lynd, June 29, 1815, NONARC, Acts, 12:260–61. See also power of attorney by Juan de Dios Amador, Cartagena de Indias, February 21, 1815, AHC, Protocolos notariales, 1815, 36v–37r (T1 P24).
16. John Lynd, April 23, 1816, NONARC, Acts, 13:216–17.
17. "Bloqueo," 341r.
18. "Bloqueo," 341v–342r.
19. Restrepo, *Historia*, 1:384–85.
20. "Bloqueo," 343; Restrepo, *Historia*, 1:384–85.
21. "Horrors of Cartagena," *City Gazette and Daily Advertiser* (Charleston), April 27, 1816; Restrepo, *Historia*, 1:389. See also Louis-Michel Aury to his relatives, Port-au-Prince, March 15, 1816, in DBC, Louis-Michel Aury Papers, 1808–1821, box 2J112.
22. *Postscript to the Royal Gazette* (Kingston), April 22–29, 1815.
23. Restrepo, *Historia*, 1:399–400; Urueta, *Los mártires*, vii; Alfonso Múnera, *El fracaso de la nación: Región, clase y raza en el Caribe colombiano (1717–1821)* (Bogotá: Planeta, 2008), 220–21.
24. For a fresh interpretation of the Spanish "reconquest" of Tierra Firme, more accurately named a "restoration," see Daniel Gutiérrez Ardila, *La Restauración en la Nueva Granada (1815–1819)* (Bogotá: Universidad Externado de Colombia, 2016).

25. "Declaración dada por Don Pedro Bruno," AP, leg. 123, no. 2; *Postscript to the St. Jago Gazette* (Spanish Town), January 6–13, 1816.
26. *City Gazette and Daily Advertiser* (Charleston), April 27, 1816.
27. Julius S. Scott, "The Common Wind: Currents of Afro-American Communication in the Era of the Haitian Revolution" (PhD diss., Duke University, 1986), 85–86, 213–21; Patrick Bryan, "Émigrés: Conflict and Reconciliation; The French Émigrés in Nineteenth Century Jamaica," *Jamaica Journal* 7.3 (September 1973): 13–19. On migration and exile throughout the revolutionary Caribbean, see Jacques de Cauna-Ladevie, "La diaspora des colons de Saint-Domingue et le monde créole: Le cas de la Jamaïque," *Revue française d'histoire d'outre-mer* 81.304 (1994): 333–59; Johanna von Grafenstein Gareis, *Nueva España en el circuncaribe, 1779–1808: Revolución, competencia imperial y vínculos intercoloniales* (Mexico City: Universidad Nacional Autónoma de México, Centro Coordinador y Difusor de Estudios Latinoamericanos, 1997), 219–57; Susan Branson and Leslie Patrick, "Étrangers dans un pays étrange: Saint-Domingan Refugees of Color in Philadelphia," in *The Impact of the Haitian Revolution in the Atlantic World*, edited by David Patrick Geggus (Columbia: University of South Carolina Press, 2001), 193–208; Paul Lachance, "Repercussions of the Haitian Revolution in Louisiana," in David Patrick Geggus, *Impact*, 209–30; Kit Candlin, "The Empire of Women: Transient Entrepreneurs in the Southern Caribbean, 1790–1820," *Journal of Imperial and Commonwealth History* 38.3 (September 2010): 351–72; Maya Jasanoff, "Revolutionary Exiles: The American Loyalists and French Émigré Diasporas," in *The Age of Revolutions in Global Context, c. 1760–1840*, edited by David Armitage and Sanjay Subrahmanyam (London: Palgrave Macmillan, 2010), 37–58; Rebecca J. Scott and Jean M. Hébrard, *Freedom Papers: An Atlantic Odyssey in the Age of Emancipation* (Cambridge, MA: Harvard University Press, 2012), 20–99; Rebecca J. Scott, *Was Freedom Portable? Wartime Journeys from Saint-Domingue to Jamaica to Cuba to Louisiana* (Kingston: University of the West Indies, Elsa Goveia Memorial Lecture, 2013).
28. Juan Reyna and María de la Cruz Barrera, marriage registry, Kingston, November 10, 1816, Roman Catholic Archives (Kingston), Roman Catholic Marriages 1802–1827, vol. 24; available at *www.jamaicanfamilysearch.com*.
29. Alfonso Múnera, "Pedro Romero: El rostro impreciso de los mulatos

libres," in *Fronteras imaginadas: La construcción de las razas y de la geografía en el siglo XIX colombiano* (Bogotá: Planeta, 2005), 153–74; John Lynch, *Simón Bolívar: A Life* (New Haven, CT: Yale University Press, 2006), 91–97.

30. Lynch, *Simón Bolívar*, 95.
31. "Declaración dada por Don Pedro Bruno," AP, leg. 123, no. 2; Louis-Michel Aury to his relatives, Port-au-Prince, March 15, 1816, in DBC, Louis-Michel Aury Papers, 1808–1821, box 2J112; *Postscript to the Royal Gazette* (Kingston), December 9–16, 1815; *Postscript to the St. Jago Gazette* (Spanish Town), December 9–16, 1815; Stanley Faye, "Commodore Aury," *Louisiana Historical Quarterly* 24.3 (July 1941): 620–28. On Curaçao and its connections to Tierra Firme, see Linda M. Rupert, *Creolization and Contraband: Curaçao in the Early Modern Atlantic World* (Athens: University of Georgia Press, 2012). See also Wim Klooster and Gert Oostindie, eds., *Curaçao in the Age of Revolutions, 1795–1800* (Leiden, Netherlands: KITLV Press, 2011).
32. "Declaración dada por Don Pedro Bruno," AP, leg. 123, no. 2. A printed, undated, and unissued letter of marque with the heading "República de Venezuela. Simón Bolívar" remains extant and may date to the period between early 1816 and early 1819. AGN, Ministerio del Interior y Relaciones Exteriores, 154:113 (reference courtesy of Daniel Gutiérrez Ardila).
33. "Declaración dada por Don Pedro Bruno."
34. "Declaración dada por Don Pedro Bruno.". See also Verna, *Pétion y Bolívar*.
35. "Minutas de cartas dirigidas al capitán general de Santo Domingo, al General del Ejército Expedicionario, fecha Santiago de Cuba 25 de enero de 1816, sobre dos buques procedentes de la Costa-Firme, que fueron apresados en la travesía de Jamaica por el corsario *La Popa de Cartagena*," AP, leg. 123, no. 3.
36. Pablo Morillo to Alexandre Pétion, Cartagena de Indias, December 12, 1815, AGI, Estado, 57, N. 33.
37. Morillo to Pétion; Alexandre Pétion to Pablo Morillo, Port-au-Prince, February 25, 1816, AGI, Estado, 57, N. 33; Simón Bolívar to Alexandre Pétion, Les Cayes, February 8, 1816, and Alexandre Pétion to Simón Bolívar, Les Cayes, February 18, 1816, in *Memorias del General O'Leary* (Caracas: Ministerio de la Defensa, 1981), 29:96, 12:343; Faye, "Com-

modore Aury," 620–29; Daniel Gutiérrez Ardila, *Un Nuevo Reino: Geografía política, pactismo y diplomacia durante el interregno en Nueva Granada (1808–1816)* (Bogotá: Universidad Externado de Colombia, 2010), 583–84.

38. "Comunicación del capitán general, al gobernador de Santiago de Cuba, fecha Habana 24 de febrero de 1816, sobre las noticias de los insurgentes escapados de Cartagena y la protección que les brinda Alexandro Pétion," AP, leg. 123, no. 5.

39. "Comunicación del virrey del Nuevo Reino de Granada, al gobernador de Santiago de Cuba, fecha Cartagena de Indias 14 de marzo de 1816, acusando recibo de las noticias sobre los corsarios reunidos en los Cayos de San Luis," AP, leg. 124, no. 36; "Comunicación del capitán general, al gobernador de Santiago de Cuba, fecha Habana 10 de mayo de 1816, acusando recibo de la declaración de un capitán sueco sobre los corsarios de Cartagena y las comunicaciones cruzadas entre Morillo y Pétion," AP, leg. 124, no. 43.

40. "Comunicación del virrey del Nuevo Reino de Granada, al gobernador de Santiago de Cuba, fecha Cartagena 18 de abril de 1816, sobre los presos del corsario *La Popa* y Expedición de los Cayos," AP, leg. 124, no. 39.

41. Simón Bolívar to Alexandre Pétion, Les Cayes, February 8, 1816, and Alexandre Pétion to Simón Bolívar, Port-au-Prince, February 18, 1816, in *Memorias*, 29:96, 12:343.

42. Faye, "Commodore Aury," 620–29; Verna, *Pétion y Bolívar*; Verna, *Robert Sutherland*; Lynch, *Simón Bolívar*, 97–100.

43. Lynch, *Simón Bolívar*, 99–101. See also Verna, *Pétion y Bolívar*; Verna, *Robert Sutherland*; and Bassi, *Aqueous Territory*, 142–71

44. "Comunicación del gobernador de Santiago de Cuba al comandante de la fragata *Diana*, fecha 30 de abril de 1816, avisándole la división entre los corsarios, que acompañaban la Expedición de Bolívar," AP, leg. 124, no. 41.

45. Louis-Michel Aury to his relatives, Port-au-Prince, March 15, 1816, in DBC, Louis-Michel Aury Papers, 1808–1821, box 2J112.

46. Louis-Michel Aury, "Exposición de los hechos que me han excluido del servicio de Venezuela y oferta de unirme al de Colombia," 1820, in Antonio Cacua Prada, *El corsario Luis Aury: Intimidades de la independencia* (Bogotá: Academia Colombiana de Historia, 2001),

179–86; Faye, "Commodore Aury," 627–39; Carlos A. Ferro, *Vida de Luis Aury: Corsario de Buenos Aires en las luchas por la independencia de Venezuela, Colombia y Centroamérica* (Buenos Aires: Cuarto Poder, 1976), 31–38.

CHAPTER 9

1. "Horrors of Cartagena," *City Gazette and Daily Advertiser* (Charleston), April 27, 1816; José Manuel Restrepo, *Historia de la revolución de la república de Colombia en la América meridional* (1827; Medellín: Universidad de Antioquia, 2009), 1:389. See also Louis-Michel Aury to his relatives, Port-au-Prince, March 15, 1816, DBC, Louis-Michel Aury Papers, 1808–1821, box 2J112.
2. "Horrors."
3. "Horrors."
4. "Horrors."
5. "Horrors."
6. Deposition of Archbeld Mikella, San Andrés, March 4, 1816, AA I, Guerra y Marina, 138:66–69 (document courtesy of Daniel Gutiérrez Ardila); *Postscript to the Royal Gazette* (Kingston), March 16–23, 1816; Restrepo, *Historia*, 1:389.
7. *City Gazette and Daily Advertiser* (Charleston), February 22, 1816.
8. USS *Boxer* logbook, entry of April 7, 1816, NYPL, Manuscripts & Archives, MssCol 1801.
9. Stanley Faye, "Commodore Aury," *Louisiana Historical Quarterly* 24.3 (July 1941): 620–29.
10. Faye, "Commodore Aury," 620-629; Antonio Cacua Prada, *El corsario Luis Aury: Intimidades de la independencia* (Bogotá: Academia Colombiana de Historia, 2001), 40–43.
11. Juan Marimón to J. Marion, Les Cayes, January 27, 1816; Alexandre Pétion to J. Marion, Port-au-Prince, January 30, 1816; and Alexandre Pétion to J. Marion, Port-au-Prince, March 19, 1816, in *Memorias del General O'Leary* (Caracas: Ministerio de la Defensa, 1981), 15:47–48, 51.
12. Deposition of Antonio Suárez, June 14, 1816, "Minutas de los oficios del gobernador de Santiago de Cuba, fecha 24 junio 1816, sobre haberse retirado los corsarios piratas que se hallaban en la bahía de Naranjo al norte de la Isla, en la jurisdicción de Holguín, y de sus

designios de seguir las hostilidades sobre las costas del Reino de México," AP, leg. 109, no. 36.
13. Deposition of José Vigre, June 23, 1816, in "Minutas," AP, leg. 109, no. 36.
14. Eusebio Escudero to Ministro de Estado, June 24, 1816, Francisco de Zayas to Eusebio Escudero, June 16, 1816, Francisco de Zayas to Eusebio Escudero, June 17, 1816, "Minutas," AP, leg. 109, Nos. 5, 27, 28; Faye, "Commodore Aury," 628–29; David Head, *Privateers of the Americas: Spanish American Privateering from the United States in the Early Republic* (Athens: University of Georgia Press, 2015), 92–99.
15. "Comunicación del capitán general al gobernador de Santiago de Cuba, fecha Habana 28 septiembre 1816, recibo de la que le notifica la captura de un corsario en que se hallaba Bolívar," AP, leg. 109, no. 55.
16. The captain was perhaps Joseph Osman, who left Charleston for Amelia Island—a crossroads of privateering, insurgency and smuggling—early that year. See *City Gazette and Daily Advertiser* (Charleston), January 8, 1816.
17. "Circular del gobernador de Santiago de Cuba, fecha 11 octubre 1816, dando cuenta de la captura del corsario pirata *La Margariteña*," AP, leg. 109, no 57.
18. "Circular."
19. Johanna von Grafenstein Gareis, "Corso y piratería en el Golfo-Caribe durante las guerras de independencia hispanoamericanas," in *La violence et la mer dans l'espace atlantique (XIIe-XIXe siècles)*, edited by Mickaël Augeron and Mathias Tranchant (Rennes, France: Presses Universitaires de Rennes, 2004), 269–82; Head, *Privateers*.
20. "Comunicación del capitán general al intendente general, fecha Habana 20 septiembre 1816 relacionado con la captura del bergantín *San Andrés*, por corsarios insurgentes," AP, leg. 108, no. 45.
21. "Comunicación del cónsul de Su Majestad en Baltimore dirigida al intendente general de La Habana, fecha 25 septiembre 1816, dando cuenta de la captura del bergantín *Sereno* por el corsario del capitán Almeida y actividades de Mina," AP, leg. 109, no. 51; *Baltimore Patriot and Evening Advertiser*, July 29, November 5, and November 29, 1816; Head, *Privateers*, 63–91; Juan Ramón de Andrés Martín, "La reacción realista antes los preparativos insurgentes de Javier Mina en los Estados Unidos y Haití (1816–1817)," *Relaciones* 29.114 (Spring 2008): 205–34.

22. "Comunicación del cónsul," *Baltimore Patriot and Evening Advertiser*, September 16, 1816.
23. (5) Eusebio Escudero to Ministro de Estado, June 24, 1816, (27) Francisco de Zayas to Eusebio Escudero, June 16, 1816, (28) Francisco de Zayas to Eusebio Escudero, June 17, 1816, "Minutas," AP, leg. 109, no. 36; "Comunicación del gobernador de Santiago de Cuba al comandante de la fragata *Diana*, fecha 30 de abril de 1816, avisándole la división entre los corsarios, que acompañaban la Expedición de Bolívar," AP, leg. 124, no. 41; Louis-Michel Aury to Victoire Aury, Galveston, January 14, 1817, DBC, Louis-Michel Aury Papers, 1808–1821, box 2J112.
24. See Julius S. Scott, "The Common Wind: Currents of Afro-American Communication in the Era of the Haitian Revolution" (PhD diss., Duke University, 1986); W. Jeffrey Bolster, *Black Jacks: African American Seamen in the Age of Sail* (Cambridge, MA: Harvard University Press, 1997); Neville A. T. Hall, "Maritime Maroons: *Grand Marronage* from the Danish West Indies," in *Origins of the Black Atlantic*, edited by Laurent Dubois and Julius S. Scott (New York: Routledge, 2010), 47–68.
25. *Baltimore Patriot and Evening Advertiser*, November 11, 1816.
26. *Baltimore Patriot and Evening Advertiser*, October 4, 1816.
27. *Baltimore Patriot and Evening Advertiser* October 4, 1816.
28. See Head, *Privateers*.
29. Peña gave his account on September 30, 1816, before the Spanish consul in New Orleans. The consul sent a copy of the deposition to Havana, where it was reproduced in the local official gazette, the *Diario del gobierno de La Habana*. This version, in turn, was transcribed by José Luciano Franco, who published the text in *La batalla por el dominio del Caribe y el Golfo de México, tomo 1: Política continental americana de España en Cuba, 1812–1830* (Havana: Instituto de Historia, Academia de Ciencias, 1964), 128–31.
30. Franco, *La batalla*, 128–31.
31. Franco, *La batalla*, 130; Faye, "Commodore Aury," 632–34; Head, *Privateers*, 97–98.
32. Franco, *La batalla*, 130; Faye, "Commodore Aury," 632–34; Head, *Privateers*, 97–98.
33. Louis-Michel Aury to Victoire Aury, Galveston, January 14, 1817,

DBC, Louis-Michel Aury Papers, 1808–1821, box 2J112; *Baltimore Patriot and Evening Advertiser*, November 11, 1816.
34. L. Aury to V. Aury; *Baltimore Patriot and Evening Advertiser*, November 11, 1816. See also Franco, *La batalla*, 130–31, and Gerald E. Poyo, "La República de las Floridas: The Mexican Connection, 1814–1817," in *La República de las Floridas: Texts and Documents*, edited by David Bushnell (Mexico City: Pan American Institute of Geography and History, 1986), 38.
35. Laurent Dubois, *Avengers of the New World: The Story of the Haitian Revolution* (Cambridge, MA: Harvard University Press, 2004), 91–114; Laurent Dubois, "Avenging America: The Politics of Violence in the Haitian Revolution," in *The World of the Haitian Revolution*, edited by David Patrick Geggus and Norman Fiering (Bloomington: Indiana University Press, 2009), 111–24. Destruction—through fire and otherwise—was common during the Haitian Revolution. Acts of destruction served tactics and specific interests. Some insurgents, instead of destroying sugar-making equipment, sold it to Spanish officers active in Hispaniola in 1794 (Ada Ferrer, *Freedom's Mirror: Cuba and Haiti in the Age of Revolution* [New York: Cambridge University Press, 2014], 102).
36. Aury himself wrote that the mutineers left for Haiti "because all were men of color" (Louis-Michel Aury to Victoire Aury, Galveston, January 14, 1817, DBC, Louis-Michel Aury Papers, 1808–1821, box 2J112). See Ada Ferrer, "Haiti, Free Soil, and Anti-Slavery in the Revolutionary Atlantic," *American Historical Review* 117.1 (February 2012): 40–66. *Baltimore Patriot and Evening Advertiser*, November 15, 1816; *Postscript to the Royal Gazette* (Kingston), December 16–23, 1815.

EPILOGUE

1   Luis de las Casas to Conde del Campo de Alange, Havana, July 1, 1795, AGS, Secretaría de Estado y del Despacho de Guerra, vol. 7243, 34 (188); Juan Ruíz de Apodaca to Primer Secretario de Estado, Mexico, September 30, 1818, AGI, Estado, 32, N. 28 (1); Harold A. Bierck Jr., *Vida pública de don Pedro Gual* (Caracas: Ministerio de Educación Nacional, 1947), 137–50; Carlos A. Ferro, *Vida de Luis Aury: Corsario de Buenos Aires en las luchas por la independencia de*

Venezuela, Colombia y Centroamérica (Buenos Aires: Cuarto Poder, 1976), 39–57; Jane Landers, *Black Society in Spanish Florida* (Urbana: University of Illinois Press, 1999).

2. Agustín Codazzi, *Las memorias* (Caracas: Universidad Central de Venezuela, 1970), 63–65; Bierck, *Vida pública*, 137–50; David Head, *Privateers of the Americas: Spanish American Privateering from the United States in the Early Republic* (Athens: University of Georgia Press, 2015), 102–6.

3. Codazzi, *Las memorias*, 63–65; Bierck, *Vida pública*, 137–50; Stanley Faye, "Commodore Aury," *Louisiana Historical Quarterly* 24.3 (July 1941): 639–48; Head, *Privateers*, 102–6.

4. Luis de las Casas to Conde del Campo de Alange, Havana, July 1, 1795, AGS, Secretaría de Estado y del Despacho de Guerra, vol. 7243, 34 (188); Landers, *Black Society*, 237–44; Head, *Privateers*, 13–37, 92–121.

5. *Baltimore Patriot and Mercantile Advertiser*, September 27, 1817.

6. *Baltimore Patriot and Mercantile Advertiser*, October 9, 1817; Head, *Privateers*, 106.

7. Maurice Persat, *Mémoires du commandant Persat, 1806 à 1844: Publiés avec un introduction et des notes par Gustave Schlumberger* (París: Plon, 1910), 32–35; David Bushnell, ed., *La República de las Floridas: Texts and Documents* (Mexico City: Pan American Institute of Geography and History, 1986); Jane Landers, *Atlantic Creoles in the Age of Revolutions* (Cambridge, MA: Harvard University Press, 2010), 130–33.

8. Landers, *Atlantic Creoles*, 131–36.

9. Persat, *Mémoires*, 27–31; Codazzi, *Las memorias*, 59–70; Head, *Privateers*, 107–8.

10. *Baltimore Patriot and Mercantile Advertiser*, November 21, 1817.

11. *Baltimore Patriot and Mercantile Advertiser*, November 21, 1817.

12. *Baltimore Patriot and Mercantile Advertiser*, November 21, 1817. See also Luis Aury, *Proclama* (Fernandina: F. Maligot, 1817).

13. Head, *Privateers*, 108–14.

14. *Baltimore Patriot and Mercantile Advertiser*, November 24, 1817.

15. *Baltimore Patriot and Mercantile Advertiser*, November 24, 1817 (italics and capitalization in the original).

16. Clément Thibaud, *Repúblicas en armas: Los ejércitos bolivarianos en la guerra de independencia en Colombia y Venezuela* (Bogotá: Planeta, 2003), 276–92; Head, *Privateers*, 129–30.

17. John D. Henley to B. W. Crowninshield, December 24, 1817, and Louis Aury to John D. Henley, December 22, 1817, *Baltimore Patriot and Mercantile Advertiser*, January 16, 1818; Landers, *Atlantic Creoles*, 134–37.
18. W. Jeffrey Bolster, *Black Jacks: African American Seamen in the Age of Sail* (Cambridge, MA: Harvard University Press, 1997), 190–214. See also Nathan Perl-Rosenthal, *Citizen Sailors: Becoming American in the Age of Revolution* (Cambridge, MA: Harvard University Press, 2015).
19. Faye, "Commodore Aury," 654–90.
20. Louis-Michel Aury, "Exposición de los hechos que me han excluido del servicio de Venezuela y oferta de unirme al de Colombia," 1820, in Antonio Cacua Prada, *El corsario Luis Aury: Intimidades de la Independencia* (Bogotá: Academia Colombiana de Historia, 2001), 179–86.
21. Louis-Michel Aury to his relatives, Port-au-Prince, March 15, 1816, DBC, Louis-Michel Aury Papers, 1808–1821, box 2J112.
22. Aury, "Exposición."
23. Faye, "Commodore Aury," 672–90.
24. Thibaud, *Repúblicas*; Daniel Gutiérrez Ardila, *El reconocimiento de Colombia: Diplomacia y propaganda en la coyuntura de las restauraciones (1819–1831)* (Bogotá: Universidad Externado de Colombia, 2012).
25. Louis-Michel Aury to Maignet, Samaná de Saint-Domingue, September 6, 1808, DBC, Louis-Michel Aury Papers, box 2J112.
26. Simón Bolívar to Luis Aury, Bogotá, January 18, 1821, in *Memorias del General O'Leary* (Caracas: El Monitor, 1882), 18:25.
27. Faye, "Commodore Aury," 697.
28. C. to Madame Dupuis (Victoire Aury), New Orleans, November 18, 1818, and death certificate of Louis Aury, Saint Catherine and Old Providence, August 30, 1821, DBC, Louis-Michel Aury Papers, 1808–1821, box 2J112; Faye, "Commodore Aury," 697; Cacua Prada, *El corsario*, 253–56.
29. *Gazeta de Cartagena de Colombia*, October 19, 1822; February 19, 1823; March 12, 1823; March 26, 1823; May 3, 1823; Henri Louis Ducoudray Holstein, *Memoirs of Simón Bolívar and of His Principal Generals, Comprising a Secret History of the Revolution, and the Events Which Preceded It, from 1807 to 1828* (1828; Middletown, MD: Terra Firma, 2010), 353–60; María Elena Capriles P., "Bolívar y la actuación de Venezuela en el Caribe a través de sus corsarios: Santo Domingo,

Puerto Rico, Cuba y México," *Boletín de la Academia Nacional de Historia* 89.355 (July–September 2006): 149–59; Gutiérrez Ardila, *El reconocimiento*, 46–53.

30. Julia Gaffield, *Haitian Connections in the Atlantic World: Recognition after Revolution* (Chapel Hill: University of North Carolina Press, 2015); Ada Ferrer, "Haiti, Free Soil, and Anti-Slavery in the Revolutionary Atlantic," *American Historical Review* 117.1 (February 2012): 40–66; Sibylle Fischer, "Bolívar in Haiti: Republicanism in the Revolutionary Atlantic," in *Haiti and the Americas*, edited by Carla Calargé et al. (Jackson: University Press of Mississippi, 2013), 25–53.
31. Gutiérrez Ardila, *El reconocimiento*, 237–70. See also Daniel Gutiérrez Ardila, "La Colombie et Haïti, histoire d'un rendez-vous manqué entre 1819 et 1830," *Bulletin de l'Institut Pierre Renouvin* 32 (2010): 111–28.
32. Pedro Gual to Manual José Hurtado, Bogotá, July 19, 1824, AGN, Ministerio de Relaciones Exteriores, Delegaciones, Transferencia 2, 300:90v (reference courtesy of Daniel Gutiérrez Ardila). See also Gutiérrez Ardila, *El reconocimiento*, 260. In 1893, American former slave, political leader, and diplomat Frederick Douglass stated that the reason for the "coolness" in relationships between the United States and Haiti was because "Haiti is black, and we have not yet forgiven Haiti for being black or forgiven the Almighty for making her black" ("Lecture on Haiti. The Haitian Pavilion Dedication Ceremonies Delivered at the World's Fair, in Jackson Park, Chicago, Jan. 2d, 1893," in *African Americans and the Haitian Revolution: Selected Essays and Historical Documents*, edited by Maurice Jackson and Jacqueline Bacon (New York: Routledge, 2010), 203.
33. Laurent Dubois, *Haiti: The Aftershocks of History* (New York: Picador, 2013), 4, 52–88. On the complexities of Haiti's Atlantic political standing, see Gaffield, *Haitian Connections*.
34. Gutiérrez Ardila, *El reconocimiento*, 59–63, 237–70.
35. Ernesto Bassi, *An Aqueous Territory: Sailor Geographies and New Granada's Transimperial Greater Caribbean World* (Durham, NC: Duke University Press, 2016), 173.
36. *Gazeta de Cartagena de Colombia*, October 19, 1822; *Suplemento a la Gazeta de Cartagena de Colombia*, January 4, 1823; *Suplemento a la Gazeta de Cartagena de Colombia*, January 18, 1823; Capriles P., "Bolívar," 159–63; Head, *Privateers*, 122, 127, 129.

37. Gutiérrez Ardila, *El reconocimiento*, 260–62.
38. José Manuel Restrepo, *Historia de la revolución de la república de Colombia en la América meridional* (1827; Medellín: Universidad de Antioquia, 2009), 1:183–208, 233–34, 384–86.
39. Capriles, "Bolívar," 159–63; Sergio Mejía, *La revolución en letras: La historia de la Revolución en Colombia de José Manuel Restrepo (1781–1863)* (Bogotá: Universidad de los Andes, 2007), 113–48.
40. Fernand Braudel, *The Mediterranean and the Mediterranean World in the Age of Philip II* (1949; New York: Harper and Row, 1973), 1:276.

Index

Page numbers in *italic* refer to tables and illustrations

Affiches Américaines, 19–20
Africa, 3–4, 6, 13, 15, 80–81
Afro-Caribbeans
  citizenship and rights of, 29–30, 44, 49, 51, 71–72
  as privateers and seamen, 4, 6, 23–24
  and Republic of Colombia, 11, 144, 152, 155–57
  and slavery, 9, 14–15, 32–35
  traditions of, 17, 80–81
  See also free people of color
Age of Revolutions, 1–4, 7, 25–26
Age of Sail, 77, 84–85
Alta Gracia, 104–5
alternative communities, 13, 179n34
Amador, Juan de Dios, xi, 46, 56, 59–60, 117, 122–26, 133–35
Ambroses, Juan, 106
Amelia Island, 144–50. *See also* Florida Peninsula
American Revolution, 2, 12, 25, 55, 58, 126
Amethyste, 37
Ana María, 106
Andrews, John, *42–43*
Aquiles, 96
Arango y Parreño, Francisco de, 31
Arce, Manuel José de, 106
artisans, 41, 49–51

Atlantic world, 7, 11, 22, 25, 177n28
Augustus, 21
Aury, Louis Michel, xi, *153*
  command of *Bellona*, 23, 71
  mutiny against, 141–43, 223n36
  privateering activity of, 1–8, 57–58, 85–87, 93–95, 112, 137–44, 146–54, 171n1
  and slave trade, 104–6
  and Spanish American independence, 11, 68, 118, 120, 127–28, 131

Baltimore, 6, 46, 57–60, 66–68, 138–41. *See also* United States
Barrera, María de la Cruz, 127
Barret, Thomas, 55
Barú, 121
Batigne, Bellegarde, 142
Bellona, xii
  crew diversity, 23, 71, 83–84, 157
  and mutiny, 141–43, 223n36
  records of, 12
  and slave trade, 104–6
  and Spanish shipping, 6–8, 93–95, 112–13, 128, 131, 137–38
Blanche (*General Monteverde*), 24, 85
Bogotá (Santa Fe)
  and political conflicts, 115–19, 122, 151
  and Spanish rule, 40–41, 45–46, 48, 54, 57, 59–60, 64

[229]

Bolívar, Simón, xi, 11, 114, 116–17, 128–31, 136–37, 144, 156
Bonaparte, Joseph, 44–45
Bonaparte, Napoleon, 5, 39, 41, 44, 119
Brión, Pedro Luis, 128, 136, 152
Bruno, Pedro, 112–13
Buadas, José, 112–13

Caballo Blanco, 72, 85, 91, 97, 213n19. See also *Défenseur de la Patrie (Caballo Blanco)*
Caracas, 5, 48, *61*, 114–16, 136–37. See also Venezuela
Caremarí, 123–24
Carmelita, 96
Carmen, 125
Caroline, 61–62, 66, 113
Carpentier, Alejo, 183n37, 184n40, 213n19
Carrère, Juan, 77
Cartagena de Indias
 blockade and siege by Spain, 119–26, 133–36
 charter of, 52–54, *53*
 citizenship rights in, 9–10, 71–74, 201n46
 Constitution of 1812, 53–54
 economic reform and free trade policies, 41–51, *47*, 62, 73, 87, 99, 126
 and Haitian Revolution, 26–27
 junta, 50–52, 60
 maps, *3*, *42–43*
 maritime defense of, 44, 57, 63–65, 87–88
 political and economic reform in, 39
 privateering policy of, 13, 16, 41, 54, 57, 65–71, 93–98, 100–103
 relations with United States, 55–62
 role in revolutionary Atlantic, 5–6, 11–12
 slavery and slave trade in, 53, 95, 98–100, 103–7
 sovereignty of, 10–11, 13–14, 16, 86–88, 90, 92, 104
Carthagenera, 72, 90, 97, 113
Casterés, Bertrand, 55
Castillo, Manuel del, 117–18
Catharina, 69
Catherine Anna, 96
Catholicism, 54, 73, 77–78, 81, 127
Cejudo, Anastasio, 29, 33–35
Centinela, 113
centralism, 10, 60, 64, 115–16, 130, 156
Charriol, Pierre, 71
Chasseur, Le (El Nariño), 75
Christophe, Henry, 36
Ciencia, 96–97
Cienfuegos, José, 139
citizenship rights, 10, 17, 44, 51–54, 58–59, 71–76, 147–50, 201n46
Clement, Joseph, 90–91
Cole, Abraham, 24
Colombia, Republic of, 5, 10–11, 144, 151–52, 154–56. See also Bogotá (Santa Fe)
Congreso, 146
Congreso de la Nueva Granada, 89
Conrad, Joseph, 175n15, 203n14
Criolla, 71, 142–44
criollos, 51–52
Cuba, 10, 29, 31–33, 64, 70, 93–102, 105–7, 209n37
Cuesta Manzanal & Hermano, 97
Cundinamarca, Free and Independent State of, 64
Cupido, 8, 94
Cyran, Jacques, 75

Défenseur de la Patrie (Caballo Blanco), 72, 85, 91, 97, 213n19
Descrubidor, 93–94

Index [231]

desperado, 38
Detruie, Jean, 21–22, 71
Díaz, Francisco, 18, 78
Dibü, Monsieur, 71
Dos Amigos, 96
Douglass, Frederick, 181n14, 226n32
Duchess of Manchester, 110
Durango, Nicolás, *89*

Eagle, 69
Ecuador, 5
Edward, 37–38
Equiano, Olaudah, 15–16, 18, 21
Estrella, 128
Expeditionary Army of Tierra Firme, 119, 121–25. See also Tierra Firme
Explosion in a Cathedral (Carpentier), 184n40

Fallena, John, 24
Favourite, 79–80
federalism, 57–60, 110, 117, 127–28, 130, 156
Ferdinand VII (king, Spain), 44–45, 117, 119
Fernández de Navarrete, Julián, 102
Fernandina, 146, 148. See also Florida Peninsula
Ferrer, Joaquín, 104
Filantrópico, 90, 96
Filibus Terre, 30–31
Florida Peninsula, 11, 24, 144–51
Floridas, Republic of the, 145–47
Four Brothers, 89
France
  and colonial struggles in Caribbean, 2–6, 12, 15–16, 27, 33–35, 39, 70, 146
  and Haitian independence, 111–12, 154–56
  and privateering, 25–30, 66, 71–72

Francisco (*Bellona* seaman), 106–7
Free Colored Battalion (Panama), 107. See also Panama
free people of color
  and Florida Peninsula, 147–50
  political influence of, 5–6, 35–36, 150
  as privateers, 9, 71, 103, 105
  rights and status of, 17, 32, 41, 44, 49–52, 71–73, 109, 146–48
free trade, 41, 45–49, 47, 62, 73, 87, 99, 126
French Antilles, 4, 10, 27, 33–35, 39, 71, 120, 146, 157
French Revolution, 2–6, 12, 25–26, 28–30. See also France

Gainer, John, 24
Gallatin, Albert, 58
Gara, Jean, 71
García de Toledo, José María, xii, 47–51, 53, 64, 121, 126
Gareché Brothers, 19–20
Gaspard (captain), 37
Gay, Timothy, 136
General Bolívar, 90–91
George Washington, 65–66
Georgia, 144–45, 147–50. See also United States
Governor Brook, 24
Governor McKean, 91–92
Granada, New Kingdom of, 5, 40
Grand Diable, 81
Great Britain
  and anti-colonial struggles, 114, 119, 122–23, 146, 155
  and maritime warfare, 5, 15–16, 62, 68–70
  and trade relations, 36–38, 55
Great Devil, 80–81
Guadeloupe, 4–5, 8, 25–26, 29, 35

Gual, Pedro, xi, 7, 66–68, 87, 145–47, 155
guardacostas, 63
Guerra y Posada, José María, 73
Gulf of Mexico, 10–11, 120, 131, 134, 137–40
Gutiérrez de Piñeres, Gabriel, 51–52, 62
Guzmán, Jorge, 33

Haiti
   and anti-colonial struggle, 10, 35–36, 108–14, 120, 124–31, 136–37, 144, 154–55
   political entities of, 36–37
   and privateering crews, 6, 8, 37–38, 57–58, 71, 105–6
   Republic of, 36–37, 109–10, 113–14, 118
   and Republic of Colombia, 11, 154–57
   Revolution (1791–1804), 2, 4, 12, 17, 21, 26–33, 35–39, 99–100, 111–12
   and shipping, 55, 62, 69, 111–12, 140–42
   slavery in, 4, 8, 18–21, 24–26, 31–33, 38–39, 143
   and United States, 147–50, 226n32
Hamilton, 55
Haynes (captain), 79–80
Heredia, Pedro de, 40
Hetty, 46, 59
Hidalgo, Pedro, 106
Hilario (Haitian sailor), 7–8, 87, 106, 112
History of the Revolution of the Republic of Colombia (Restrepo), 156
Hugues, Victor, 26, 184n40, 213n19

Ignacio the Younger, xi, 7–8, 12, 18, 80–81, 86–87, 106–7, 112, 157

immigration, 9, 27–34, 44–46, 52–54, 71–74, 103–4, 109–10, 194n41
intelligence operations, 90–91
irregular warfare, 4–5, 16, 25, 81, 90–91, 97, 100, 128, 154

Jamaica, 45–48, 55, 62, 69–70, 95–96, 99, 105–6, 124–27
Joaquín, José, 73
Juan Esteban, 106
juntas, 45, 48, 50–52, 60, 114–15
Júpiter, 128

Kean, Gustavus, 24
King, Tom, 19
Kingston, 69–70, 125–27. *See also* Jamaica
Kingston Packet, 38, 68

Labarrière, Antoine, 30–31
Lady Madison, 62, 68–69, 112
La Maison, Pedro, 71
legal systems, 86–91
Législateur, 105
Leleux, Pierre Antoine, 109, 114–15
Les Cayes
   merchant shipping and privateers in, 55, 62, 69, 111–12, 140–42
   as political refuge, 10, 110, 112–14, 120, 124–31, 136–37, 155
   See also Haiti
letters of marque
   and Cartagena privateering policy, 57–58, 65–68, 67, 70, 72, 87–91, 95–97, 100
   definition and record keeping, 2, 12
   and maritime defense, 57–58, 154
   and political allegiance, 85, 128, 146
   and revenue, 65–66, 131, 139, 171n2
Little, George, 65–66

López Tagle, Juan Elías, 124
Louisiana, 55, 105–6, 139–40, 150. *See also* United States
Louis XVI (king, France), 28
Lynd, John, 91

Machin, Charles, 90
Manguar, Agustín, 104
maps, *3, 42–43, 61*
Margariteña, 138
Marie, Pierre, 71
maritime flags
   and nationality and commissions, 10, 84–85, 88, 92, 94–95, 154
   tactical use by privateers, 66, 69–70, 81, 84–86, 104, 113, 136–37
maritime trades
   employment in, 15–22, 63, 76, 105, 140, 197n18
   internationalization of, 113, 182n26
maroons (runaway slaves), 9, 18–19, 21. *See also* slavery
Martin, John, 24
Martinique, 8, 18, 20
masterless Caribbean, 9, 19, 73, 143, 146, 156, 176n23
matrícula de mar, 63
McGregor, Gregor, 145–46
Mendinueta, Pedro de, 35
merchants
   and Cartagena trade, 41, 44–49, 55, 63–64, 90, 126
   and Cuban shipping, 92, 96–98, 100–102
   as privateering victims, 2, 90, 92, 134
   relations with seamen, 76, 79–81
   support for independence movements, 44, 55–57, 59, 130
   and United States, 139
Merrill, Mark, 24
Mesnier Brothers, 19–20

Mexico, 6, 131, 137, 139–40
Mikella, Archbeld, 135
Miranda, Francisco de, 114
Miranda, José, 75
Mitchell, William, 135–36, 151
Monroe, James, 66, 150
Montes, Francisco Antonio de, 47–48, 50
Moreau de Saint-Méry, M. L. E., 111
Morgiana, 147
Morillo y Morillo, Pablo, xi, 119–23, 125–26, 129–33, 137–38, 151
Mulita, 55
multilingualism, 9, 18
multinationalism, 7, 18, 22–24, 128, 144, 194n41
mutiny, 50, 76, 78, 132, 140–43, 182n26, 223n36

Napoleon Bonaparte, 5, 39, 41, 44, 119
navigation, 16
Negro Seamen Acts, 150
Neptuno, 82
New Granada, United Provinces of
   Act of Federation (1811), 60
   map, *61*
   maritime defense of, 63–64
   privateering policy of, 65–71, 88
   and Spanish American independence, 5–6, 13, 115–17, 119, 122, 126–27, 131, 151
New Orleans, 4–6, 55, 59, 105, 123–24, 135, 138, 140–42. *See also* United States
newspapers and printing, 19–20, 28, 32, 37–38, 54, 149, 194n39
Nuestra Señora del Nevis, 84, 96, 213n19

Old Providence Island, 151, *153*
Once de Noviembre, 96
Onyx, 91

Páez, José Antonio, 150–51
Palacio Fajardo, Manuel, xi, 56–58, 66
Panama, 5, 64, 78, 80, 86, 88, 107, 112
Patriota, 146
Pemerlé, Jean Baptiste, 73
Peña, José, 141–42, 222n29
peninsulares, 51, 64
Pérez, Juan Francisco, 72, 113
Perl-Rosenthal, Nathan, 201n46
Pétion, Alexandre, xi, 10, 86, 109–10, 114, 120, 127–30, 136, 154–55
Philips, Peter, 24
piracy
  and accusations of privateers, 66, 69–70, 76, 78, 82
  and arrests of seamen, 80, 86, 106–7, 112
  definition of, 1–2, 13–14, 72, 88–90, 103, 152, 154
  and Gulf of Mexico, 139–40
piraterías, 139. *See also* piracy
Plancha, 128
plantation economy, 16–17, 25, 95, 98
political ideology, 3, 10, 75–80
Pombo, José Ignacio de, xii, 38–39, 46, 58–59, 73, 98–100
Popa de Cartagena, 97, 113
Portshire, 69
President, 96
printing and censorship, 54
prizes and prize money
  and anti-colonial struggle, 6, 66, 95–97
  and Cuban shipping, 98, 100–101
  sharing and adjudicating of, 2, 65, 79, 83, 88, 90
Prospero, 85
Providencia, 69–70

Ramírez, Alejandro, 139
Ramos, Andrés, 102

Ranché, André, 72–73, 91–92, 213n19
Raquel, 62
Rediker, Marcus, 12
religion, 54, 73, 77–78, 81, 127
renegades, 37
republicanism, 13, 145
Republicano, 128
Restrepo, José Manuel, 123, 156
Revenge, 55
Reyna, Juan, 127
Rodríguez Torices, Manuel, 62, 94
Romero, Francisco, 112–13
Romero, Mauricio José, 52
Romero, Pedro, xii, 50–52, 127
Rosa, 24, 77
Rosita, 112–13, 129
Rover, 69
Ruiz de Apodaca, Juan José, 82–83, 101, 129–30

Saint-Domingue
  and French rule, 4, 36, 99, 111
  slavery in, 4, 8, 18–21, 24–26, 31–33, 38–39, 143
  See also Haiti
San Andrés, 139
Sanarrusia, Francisco, 122
San Francisco de Paula, 68, 96
San José de la Unión, 85
San Sebastián, 96
Santa Fe (Bogotá). *See* Bogotá (Santa Fe)
Santa Isabel, 138
Santa Marta, 63–65, 90–91, 112, 115–17, 121, 129
Santa Rosalia, 105
Sappho, 72, 85
Saratoga, 62
schooners, 7, 25, 62–63. *See also* ships
Scott, Julius S., 9
seamanship, 8–9, 16–19

Index

seamen
  anti-authoritarian attitudes of, 10, 79–80
  and connection to land, 75–92
  cultural traditions of, 80–81
  diversity of, 7, 18, 23, 54, 73, 81
  mobility of, 8, 12, 16–17, 82–83
  political loyalty of, 9, 16–18, 32, 75–78, 81–82, 85–86, 95, 201n46
  and slavery, 16–17, 20, 150, 181n14
  working conditions and risks of, 9, 14, 16–17, 75–79, 82, 97, 106–7, 143–44
ships, 7, 25, 62–63, 183–84n37, 213n19. *See also names of individual ships*
Sisson, S., 65–66, 68
slavery
  abolition of, 17, 25–26, 53, 99–100, 109, 130
  in Cartagena, 32–35, 53, 95, 98–100, 103–7
  escape from, 9, 17–19, 21, 181n14
  and European colonial policy, 4, 99–100, 109
  and free status of seamen, 14–22, 106
  in Haiti, 4, 8, 18–21, 24–26, 31–33, 38–39, 143
  and plantation economy, 17, 31, 100
  and privateering, 4, 6, 8–9, 73, 105–6
  slave trade, 19–23, 31–35, 53, 95, 98–100, 103–7, 138, 147–48
  and United States, 144–47, 150
smuggling, 30, 45–46, 63, 141, 147–48
Snap Dragon, 62
South America, 5–6, 64, 119–21, 132, 146, 154, 157. *See also* Tierra Firme
Southampton, 37
sovereignty
  of Cartagena, 10–11, 13–14, 16, 86–88, 90, 92, 104
  of Haiti, 37, 155
  of Spanish colonial rule, 44–45, 128–29, 148–51
Spain
  Cartagena blockade and siege, 119–25, 128
  defense of Caribbean territories, 11, 29, 40, 45, 102–3, 108–10, 138, 146–48
  and French territories, 29–30
  privateer attacks on shipping of, 6, 13–14, 16, 33–39, 49, 63, 93–98, 138–39
  and sovereignty of colonial rule, 44–45, 128–29, 148–51
Spanish Inquisition, 54
Spanish Peninsular War, 12
State of Cartagena de Indias. *See* Cartagena de Indias
Suárez, Antonio, 97, 137
Swift, 140
Syerr, John, 77

Tardif, J. P., 21
taxes, 45, 102, 209n37
Tierra Firme
  Haitian support for independence struggles in, 108–11, 114, 118, 129–30
  revolutionary influences on, 28–30, 33–35, 39, 41, 45
  role in maritime history, 128–29, 151–54, 156–57
  Spanish rule in, 64, 119–26
  territories of, 3, 5–6
  and United States influence on, 56–62
Trinidad, 96
26 October 1812, 77, 84
Two Brothers, 62

United Provinces of New Granada.
  See New Granada, United
  Provinces of
United States
  American Revolution, 2, 12, 25, 55,
    58–59, 126
  Articles of Confederation and
    Perpetual Union, 59
  Baltimore, 6, 46, 57–60, 66–68,
    138–41
  Constitution, 59, 61
  Florida Peninsula, 146, 148–50
  Louisiana, 55, 105–6, 139–40, 150
  neutrality laws and foreign policy,
    4–5, 16, 68, 139–40, 155, 226n32
  New Orleans, 4–6, 55, 59, 105,
    123–24, 135, 138, 140–42
  and relations with Cartagena, 45–48,
    55–62, 68, 119, 123, 139–41,
    196n14
  and slave trade, 105–6, 144–50
  War of 1812, 12, 22, 38, 62, 148

Variable, 85
Venezuela, 5, 48, *61*, 114–18, 136–37, 151
Vigre, José, 83–84, 137

War of 1812, 12, 22, 38, 62, 148
Washington, George, 61
Whelan, John, 24
work contracts, 9, 79, 82, 97

Yolet, Pierre, 71–72
Yturen, Manuel, 34

www.ingramcontent.com/pod-product-compliance
Lightning Source LLC
Chambersburg PA
CBHW051219300426
44116CB00006B/633